FIX-IT and FORGET-IT®
BIG BOOK OF
KETO RECIPES

275 HEALTHY SLOW COOKER & INSTANT POT FAVORITES

HOPE COMERFORD

Good Books
New York, New York

Good Books books may be purchased in bulk at special discounts for sales promotion, corporate gifts, fund-raising, or educational purposes. Special editions can also be created to specifications. For details, contact the Special Sales Department, Good Books, 307 West 36th Street, 11th Floor, New York, NY 10018 or info@skyhorsepublishing.com.

Good Books is an imprint of Skyhorse Publishing, Inc.®, a Delaware corporation.

Visit our website at www.goodbooks.com.

10 9 8 7 6 5 4 3 2 1

Library of Congress Cataloging-in-Publication Data is available on file.

Cover design by Abigail Gehring
Cover photos by Meredith Special Interest Media

Print ISBN: 978-1-68099-530-5
Ebook ISBN: 978-1-68099-541-1

Printed in China

Table of Contents

Welcome to *Fix-It and Forget-It Big Book of Keto Recipes*

Following a keto diet has never been easier with this *big* book full of 500 keto-friendly recipes. I've taken the guesswork out of "What should I eat?" for you and compiled hundreds of recipes that follow keto guidelines. Most of the recipes are for your slow cooker or Instant Pot (look for the little orange icons below the recipe titles), but you'll also find recipes to make on the stove-top, in your oven, on the grill, or in the microwave or freezer! Remember that your Instant Pot also has a slow cooker function, so any slow cooker recipes in this book can also be made in your Instant Pot. Whether you're new to the keto diet or a keto veteran, you're sure to find lots of new ideas and recipes to enjoy. So dig in, find lots of new favorites, and enjoy the delicious, flavorful, healthy keto recipes in this brand-new cookbook.

What Is a Keto Diet?

A keto diet involves eating foods high in fat and low in carbs. By lowering the level of carbs you are eating and increasing the amount of fat you're eating to replace the carbs, your body goes into a metabolic state known as ketosis. You will also find this is a no-sugar diet. There are several natural (plant-based) sweeteners recommended for those following a keto diet, and you will see those throughout the book in various recipes.

It is also said that by following a keto diet, your blood sugar and insulin levels decrease dramatically. Many believe there are some major health benefits to achieve by following this diet, including weight loss.

As always, it is recommended that you consult your physician before beginning any diet to make sure it is the right choice for you. If you choose to follow this diet, we hope you have great success and that this book helps you along your journey.

Guide to Nutrition Info

You'll find basic nutrition info below each recipe. Please keep in mind that it is approximate and does not take into account any optional ingredients.

The numbers reflect the following units of measurement:

- Calories = kilocalories
- Fat = grams
- Sodium = milligrams
- Carbs = grams
- Sugar = grams
- Protein = grams

Choosing a Slow Cooker

Not all slow cookers are created equal . . . or work equally as well for everyone!

Those of us who use slow cookers frequently know we have our own preferences when it comes to which slow cooker we choose to use. For instance, I love my programmable slow cooker, but there are many programmable slow cookers I've tried that I've strongly disliked. Why? Because some go by increments of 15 or 30 minutes and some go by 4, 6, 8, or 10 hours. I dislike those restrictions, but I have family and friends who don't mind them at all! I am also pretty brand loyal when it comes to my manual slow cookers because I've had great success with those and have had unsuccessful moments with slow cookers of other brands. So, which slow cooker(s) is/are best for your household?

It really depends on how many people you're feeding and if you're gone for long periods of time. Here are my recommendations:

For 2–3 person household	3–5 quart slow cooker
For 4–5 person household	5–6 quart slow cooker
For a 6+ person household	6½–7 quart slow cooker

Large slow cooker advantages/disadvantages:

Advantages:

- You can fit a loaf pan or a baking dish into a 6- or 7-quart, depending on the shape of your cooker. That allows you to make bread or cakes, or even smaller quantities of main dishes. (Take your favorite baking dish and loaf pan along when you shop for a cooker to make sure they'll fit inside.)
- You can feed large groups of people, or make larger quantities of food, allowing for leftovers, or meals, to freeze.

Disadvantages:

- They take up more storage room.
- They don't fit as neatly into a dishwasher.
- If your crock isn't ⅔–¾ full, you may burn your food.

Small slow cooker advantages/disadvantages:

Advantages:
- They're great for lots of appetizers, for serving hot drinks, for baking cakes straight in the crock, and for dorm rooms or apartments.
- Great option for making recipes of smaller quantities.

Disadvantages:
- Food in smaller quantities tends to cook more quickly than larger amounts. So keep an eye on it.
- Chances are, you won't have many leftovers. So, if you like to have leftovers, a smaller slow cooker may not be a good option for you.

My recommendation:

Have at least two slow cookers; one around 3 to 4 quarts and one 6 quarts or larger. A third would be a huge bonus (and a great advantage to your cooking repertoire!). The advantage of having at least a couple is you can make a larger variety of recipes. Also, you can make at least two or three dishes at once for a whole meal.

Manual vs. Programmable

If you are gone for only six to eight hours a day, a manual slow cooker might be just fine for you. If you are gone for more than eight hours during the day, I would highly recommend purchasing a programmable slow cooker that will switch to warm when the cook time you set is up. It will allow you to cook a wider variety of recipes.

The two I use most frequently are my 4-quart manual slow cooker and my 6½-quart programmable slow cooker. I like that I can make smaller portions in my 4-quart slow cooker on days I don't need or want leftovers, but I also love how my 6½-quart slow cooker can accommodate whole chickens, turkey breasts, hams, or big batches of soups. I use them both often.

Get to Know Your Slow Cooker

Plan a little time to get acquainted with your slow cooker. Each slow cooker has its own personality—just like your oven (and your car). Plus, many new slow cookers cook hotter and faster than earlier models. I think that with all of the concern for food safety, the slow cooker manufacturers have amped up their settings so that "High," "Low," and "Warm" are all higher temperatures than in the older models. That means they cook hotter—and therefore, faster—than the first slow cookers. The beauty of these little machines is that they're supposed to cook low and slow. We count on that when we flip the switch in the morning before we leave the house for ten hours or so. So, because none of us knows what kind of temperament our slow cooker has until we try it out, nor how hot it cooks—don't assume anything. Save yourself a disappointment and make the first recipe in your new slow cooker on a day when you're at home. Cook it for the shortest amount of time the recipe calls for. Then, check the food to see if it's done. Or if you start smelling food that seems to be finished, turn off the cooker and rescue your food.

Also, all slow cookers seem to have a "hot spot," which is of great importance to know, especially when baking with your slow cooker. This spot may tend to burn food in that area if you're not careful. If you're baking directly in your slow cooker, I recommend covering the "hot spot" with some foil.

Take Notes

Don't be afraid to make notes in your cookbook. It's yours! Chances are, it will eventually get passed down to someone in your family and they will love and appreciate all of your musings. Take note of which slow cooker you used and exactly how long it took to cook the recipe. The next time you make it, you won't need to try to remember. Apply what you learned to the next recipes you make in your cooker. If another recipe says it needs to cook 7–9 hours, and you've discovered your slow cooker cooks on the faster side, cook that recipe for 6–6½ hours and then check it. You can always cook a recipe longer—but you can't reverse things if it's overdone.

Get Creative

If you know your morning is going to be hectic, prepare everything the night before, take it out so the crock warms up to room temperature when you first get up in the morning, then plug it in and turn it on as you're leaving the house.

If you want to make something that has a short cook time and you're going to be gone longer than that, cook it the night before and refrigerate it for the next day. Warm it up when you get home. Or, cook those recipes on the weekend when you know you'll be home and eat them later in the week.

Slow Cooking Tips and Tricks and Other Things You May Not Know

- Slow cookers tend to work best when they're ⅔ to ¾ of the way full. You may need to increase the cooking time if you've exceeded that amount, or reduce it if you've put in less than that. If you're going to exceed that limit, it would be best to reduce the recipe, or split it between two slow cookers. (Remember how I suggested owning at least two or three slow cookers?)

- Keep your veggies on the bottom. That puts them in more direct contact with the heat. The fuller your slow cooker, the longer it will take its contents to cook. Also, the more densely packed the cooker's contents are, the longer they will take to cook. And finally, the larger the chunks of meat or vegetables, the more time they will need to cook.

- Keep the lid on! Every time you take a peek, you lose 20 minutes of cooking time. Please take this into consideration each time you lift the lid! I know, some of you can't help yourself and are going to lift anyway. Just don't forget to tack on 20 minutes to your cook time for each time you peeked!

- Sometimes it's beneficial to remove the lid. If you'd like your dish to thicken a bit, take the lid off during the last half hour to hour of cooking time.

- If you have a big slow cooker (7- to 8-quart), you can cook a small batch in it by putting the recipe ingredients into an oven-safe baking dish or baking pan and then placing that into the cooker's crock. First, put a trivet or some metal jar rings on the bottom of the crock, and then set your dish or pan on top of them. Or a loaf pan may "hook onto" the top ridges of the crock belonging to a large oval cooker and hang there straight and securely, "baking" a cake or quick bread. Cover the cooker and flip it on.

- The outside of your slow cooker will be hot! Please remember to keep it out of reach of children and keep that in mind for yourself as well!

- Get yourself a quick-read meat thermometer and use it! This helps remove the question of whether or not your meat is fully cooked, and helps prevent you from overcooking your meat as well.
  Internal Cooking Temperatures:
  - Beef—125–130°F (rare); 140–145°F (medium); 160°F (well-done)
  - Pork—140–145°F (rare); 145–150°F (medium); 160°F (well-done)
  - Turkey and Chicken—165°F
  - Frozen meat: The basic rule of thumb is, don't put frozen meat into the slow cooker. The meat does not reach the proper internal temperature in time. This especially applies to thick cuts of meat! Proceed with caution!

- Add fresh herbs 10 minutes before the end of the cooking time to maximize their flavor.

- If your recipe calls for cooked pasta, add it 10 minutes before the end of the cooking time if the cooker is on High; 30 minutes before the end of the cooking time if it's on Low. Then the pasta won't get mushy.
- If your recipe calls for sour cream or cream, stir it in 5 minutes before the end of the cooking time. You want it to heat but not boil or simmer.

  Approximate Slow Cooker Temperatures (Remember, each slow cooker is different):
  - High—212°F–300°F
  - Low—170°F–200°F
  - Simmer—185°F
  - Warm—165°F

What Is an Instant Pot?

In short, an Instant Pot is a digital pressure cooker that also has multiple other functions. Not only can it be used as a pressure cooker, but depending on which model Instant Pot you have, you can set it to do things like sauté, cook rice, multigrains, porridge, soup/stew, beans/chili, porridge, meat, poultry, cake, and eggs, to make yogurt, to steam or slow-cook, or even set it manually. Because the Instant Pot has so many functions, it takes away the need for multiple appliances on your counter and many pots and pans.

Getting Started with Your Instant Pot

The very first thing most Instant Pot owners do is called the water test. It helps you get to know your Instant Pot a bit, familiarizes you with it, and might even take a bit of your apprehension away (because if you're anything like me, you may be scared to death to use it!).

Step 1: Plug in your Instant Pot. This may seem obvious to some, but when we're nervous about using a new appliance, sometimes we forget things like this.

Step 2: Make sure the inner pot is inserted in the cooker. You should NEVER attempt to cook anything in your device without the inner pot, or you will ruin your Instant Pot. Food should never come into contact with the actual housing unit.

Step 3: The inner pot has lines for each cup (how convenient, right?!). Fill the inner pot with water until it reaches the 3-cup line.

Step 4: Check the sealing ring to be sure it's secure and in place. You should not be able to move it around. If it's not in place properly, you may experience issues with the pot letting out a lot of steam while cooking, or not coming to pressure.

Step 5: Seal the lid. There is an arrow on the lid between "open" and "close." There is also an arrow on the top of the base of the Instant Pot between a picture of a locked lock and an unlocked lock. Line those arrows up, then turn the lid toward the picture of the lock (left). You will hear a noise that will indicate the lid is locked. If you do not hear a noise, it's not locked. Try it again.

Step 6: ALWAYS check to see if the steam valve on top of the lid is turned to "sealing." If it's not on "sealing" and is on "venting," it will not be able to come to pressure.

Step 7: Press the "Steam" button and use the +/- arrow to set it to 2 minutes. Once it's at the desired time, you don't need to press anything else. In a few seconds, the Instant Pot will begin all on its own. For those of us with digital slow cookers, we have a tendency to look for the "start" button, but there isn't one on the Instant Pot.

Step 8: Now you wait for the "magic" to happen! The "cooking" will begin once the device comes to pressure. This can take anywhere from 5–30 minutes, in my experience. You will see the countdown happen (from the time you set it to). After that, the Instant Pot will beep, which means your meal is done!

Step 9: Your Instant Pot will now automatically switch to "warm" and begin a count of how many minutes it's been on warm. The next part is where you either wait for the NPR, or Natural Pressure Release (meaning the pressure releases all on its own), or you do what's called a QR, or Quick Release (meaning, you manually release the pressure). Which method you choose depends on what you're cooking, but in this case, you can choose either since it's just water. For NPR, you will wait for the lever to move all the way back over to "venting" and watch the pinion (float valve) next to the lever. It will be flush with the lid when at full pressure and will drop when the pressure is completely released. If you choose QR, be very careful not to have your hands over the vent as the steam is very hot and you can burn yourself.

The Three Most Important Buttons You Need to Know About
You will find the majority of recipes will use the following three buttons:

Manual/Pressure Cook: Some older models tend to say "Manual" and the newer models seem to say "Pressure Cook." They mean the same thing. From here, you use the +/- button to change the cook time. After several seconds, the Instant Pot will begin its process. The exact name of this button will vary on your model of Instant Pot.

Sauté: Many recipes will have you sauté vegetables, or brown meat before beginning the pressure-cooking process. For this setting, you will not use the lid of the Instant Pot.

Keep Warm/Cancel: This may just be the most important button on the Instant Pot.

When you forget to use the +/- buttons to change the time for a recipe, or you press a wrong button, you can hit "Keep Warm/Cancel" and it will turn your Instant Pot off for you.

What All the Buttons Do

With so many buttons, it's hard to remember what each one does or means. You can use this as a quick guide in a pinch.

Soup/Broth. This button cooks at high pressure for 30 minutes. It can be adjusted using the +/- buttons to cook more for 40 minutes, or less for 20 minutes.

Meat/Stew. This button cooks at high pressure for 35 minutes. It can be adjusted using the +/- buttons to cook more for 45 minutes, or less for 20 minutes.

Bean/Chili. This button cooks at high pressure for 30 minutes. It can be adjusted using the +/- buttons to cook more for 40 minutes, or less for 25 minutes.

Poultry. This button cooks at high pressure for 15 minutes. It can be adjusted using the +/- buttons to cook more 30 minutes, or less for 5 minutes.

Rice. This button cooks at low pressure and is the only fully automatic program. It is for cooking white rice and will automatically adjust the cooking time depending on the amount of water and rice in the cooking pot.

Multigrain. This button cooks at high pressure for 40 minutes. It can be adjusted using the +/- buttons to cook more for 45 minutes of warm water soaking time and 60 minutes pressure-cooking time, or less for 20 minutes.

Porridge. This button cooks at high pressure for 20 minutes. It can be adjusted using the +/- buttons to cook more for 30 minutes, or less for 15 minutes.

Steam. This button cooks at high pressure for 10 minutes. It can be adjusted using the +/- buttons to cook more for 15 minutes, or less for 3 minutes. Always use a rack or steamer basket with this function because it heats at full power continuously while it's coming to pressure and you do not want food in direct contact with the bottom of the pressure cooking pot or it will burn. Once it reaches pressure, the steam button regulates pressure by cycling on and off, similar to the other pressure buttons.

Less | Normal | More. Adjust between the *Less | Normal | More* settings by pressing the same cooking function button repeatedly until you get to the desired setting. (Older versions use the *Adjust* button.)

+/- Buttons. Adjust the cook time up [+] or down [-]. (On newer models, you can also press and hold [-] or [+] for 3 seconds to turn sound OFF or ON.)

Cake. This button cooks at high pressure for 30 minutes. It can be adjusted using the

+/- buttons to cook more for 40 minutes, or less for 25 minutes.

Egg. This button cooks at high pressure for 5 minutes. It can be adjusted using the +/- buttons to cook more for 6 minutes, or less for 4 minutes.

Instant Pot Tips and Tricks and Other Things You May Not Know

- Never attempt to cook directly in the Instant Pot without the Inner Pot!
- Once you set the time, you can walk away. It will show the time you set it to, then will change to the word "on" while the pressure builds. Once the Instant Pot has come to pressure, you will once again see the time you set it for. It will count down from there.
- Always make sure your sealing ring is securely in place. If it shows signs of wear or tear, it needs to be replaced.
- Have a sealing ring for savory recipes and a separate sealing ring for sweet recipes. Many people report of their desserts tasting like a roast (or another savory food) if they try to use the same sealing ring for all recipes.
- The stainless steel rack (trivet) your Instant Pot comes with can used to keep food from being completely submerged in liquid, like baked potatoes or ground beef. It can also be used to set another pot on, for pot-in-pot cooking.
- If you use warm or hot liquid instead of cold liquid, you may need to adjust the cooking time, or your food may not come out done.
- Always double-check to see that the valve on the lid is set to "sealing" and not "venting" when you first lock the lid. This will ensure your Instant Pot comes to pressure.
- Use Natural Pressure Release for tougher cuts of meat, recipes with high starch (like rice or grains), and recipes with a high volume of liquid. This means you let the Instant Pot naturally release pressure. The little bobbin will fall once pressure is released completely.
- Use Quick Release for more delicate cuts of meat and vegetables—like seafood, chicken breasts, and steaming vegetables. This means you manually turn the vent (being careful not to put your hand over the vent!) to release the pressure. The little bobbin will fall once pressure is released completely.
- Make sure there is a clear pathway for the steam to release. The last thing you want is to ruin the bottom of your cupboards with all that steam.
- You MUST use liquid in your Instant Pot. The MINIMUM amount of liquid you should have in your inner pot is ½ cup; however, most recipes work best with at least 1 cup.

- Do NOT overfill your Instant Pot! It should only be ½ full for rice or beans (food that expands greatly when cooked) or ⅔ of the way full for most everything else. Do not fill it to the max filled line.
- In this book, the Cooking Time DOES NOT take into account the amount of time it will take your Instant Pot to come to pressure, or the amount of time it will take the Instant Pot to release pressure. Be aware of this when choosing a recipe to make.
- If your Instant Pot is not coming to pressure, it's usually because the sealing ring is not on properly, or the vent is not set to "sealing."
- The more liquid, or the colder the ingredients, the longer it will take for the Instant Pot to come to pressure.
- Always make sure that the Instant Pot is dry before inserting the inner pot, and make sure the inner pot is dry before inserting it into the Instant Pot.
- Doubling a recipe does not change the cook time, but it will take longer to come up to pressure.
- You do not always need to double the liquid when doubling a recipe. Depending on what you're making, more liquid may make your food too watery. Use your best judgment.

Slow Cooker	Instant Pot
Warm	Less or Low
Low	Normal or Medium
High	More or High

Breakfast & Brunch

Fresh Veggie and Herb Omelet

Hope Comerford
Clinton Township, MI

Makes 8 servings
Prep. Time: 20 minutes
Cooking Time: 4–6 hours
Ideal slow-cooker size: 6-qt.

12 eggs

1 cup unsweetened almond milk or whole milk

½ tsp. kosher salt

¼ tsp. pepper

3 cloves garlic, minced

1 tsp. fresh chopped basil

6 dashes Frank's RedHot Original Cayenne Pepper Sauce

2 cups broccoli florets

1 yellow bell pepper, diced

1 red bell pepper, diced

1 medium onion, diced

1 cup crumbled feta cheese

1 cup diced cherry tomatoes

½ cup fresh chopped parsley

1. Spray crock with nonstick spray.

2. In a bowl, mix together the eggs, milk, salt, pepper, garlic, basil, and hot sauce.

3. Place the broccoli, yellow pepper, red pepper, and onion in crock. Gently mix with a spoon.

4. Pour egg mixture over the top.

5. Cover and cook on Low for 4–6 hours, or until center is set.

6. Sprinkle feta over the top, then cook an additional 30 minutes.

7. To serve, sprinkle the omelet with the chopped tomatoes and fresh parsley.

- Calories 198
- Fat 12
- Sodium 456
- Carbs 9
- Sugar 4
- Protein 14

Vegetable Omelet

Phyllis Good
Lancaster, PA

Makes 4–6 servings
Prep. Time: 20 minutes
Cooking Time: 2 hours
Ideal slow-cooker size: 6-qt.

5 eggs

⅓ cup whole milk

¼ tsp. salt

pinch black pepper

⅓ cup chopped onion

1 clove garlic, minced

1 cup small broccoli florets

1 cup thinly sliced zucchini

½ cup thinly sliced red bell pepper

½ cup your favorite grated cheese

1. Beat eggs with milk, salt, and pepper.

2. Add onion, garlic, broccoli, zucchini, and bell pepper. Stir.

3. Pour mixture into lightly greased baking dish that will fit in your slow cooker. Set dish on a small trivet or jar rings in slow cooker.

4. Cover and cook on High for 2 hours, until eggs are set and vegetables are softened.

5. Sprinkle with cheese and allow to melt before serving. Carefully, wearing oven mitts, remove hot dish from hot slow cooker. Slice and serve.

- Calories 117
- Fat 6
- Sodium 272
- Carbs 5
- Sugar 2
- Protein 8

Mushroom Oven Omelet

Elaine Patton
West Middletown, PA

Makes 4 servings
Prep. Time: 20 minutes
Baking Time: 20 minutes

½ lb. fresh mushrooms, cleaned and sliced

2 Tbsp. butter

2 Tbsp. almond flour

6 eggs

⅓ cup whole milk

⅛ tsp. pepper

¼ cup chopped onions, *optional*

¼ cup chopped green pepper, *optional*

1½ cups shredded cheddar cheese, *divided*

½ cup chopped cooked bacon

1. In a small skillet, sauté mushrooms in butter until tender. Drain. Set aside.

2. In a bowl, combine almond flour, eggs, milk, and pepper until smooth. Add chopped vegetables if you wish.

3. Stir in 1 cup cheese, bacon, and mushrooms.

4. Pour into a greased 8-inch-square baking dish.

5. Baked uncovered at 375°F for 18–20 minutes, or until eggs are completely set.

6. Sprinkle with remaining cheese, return to warm oven for 1 minute, and then serve.

- Calories 453
- Fat 34
- Sodium 773
- Carbs 8
- Sugar 3
- Protein 28

Cheddar-Ham Oven Omelet

Jolene Schrock
Millersburg, OH

Makes 9–12 servings
Prep. Time: 10 minutes
Baking Time: 40–45 minutes
Standing Time: 10 minutes

16 eggs

2 cups whole milk

8 oz. shredded cheddar cheese

¾ cup cubed fully cooked ham

6 green onions, chopped

sliced mushrooms and green peppers, *optional*

1. In a large bowl, beat eggs and milk until well blended. Stir in cheese, ham, and onions. Add optional ingredients if you wish.

2. Pour the egg mixture into a greased 9×13-inch baking dish.

3. Bake, uncovered, at 350°F for 40–45 minutes, or until a knife inserted near the center comes out clean. Let stand 10 minutes before cutting and serving.

- Calories 222
- Fat 15
- Sodium 374
- Carbs 4
- Sugar 3
- Protein 17

Omelet Roll

Anita Troyer
Fairview, MI

Makes 6 servings
Prep. Time: 15–20 minutes
Baking Time: 20 minutes

6 eggs

1 cup whole milk

½ cup almond flour

1 cup shredded cheddar cheese

1 cup browned sausage

Optional filling ingredients:

sliced mushrooms

sliced onions

cubed cooked ham

crispy bacon pieces

1. Blend eggs, milk, and almond flour in a blender until frothy. Pour into a well-greased 9×13-inch baking pan. Bake at 450°F approximately 20 minutes until fully cooked in the center.

2. As soon as you remove pan from oven, gently turn the pan upside down on a baking sheet. The eggs should drop onto the baking sheet in one piece.

3. Sprinkle cheese and sausage onto eggs. Add any optional filling ingredients that you wish. Starting at the narrow end of the omelet, roll it up jelly-roll fashion.

4. You can serve the eggs immediately or refrigerate and reheat when you are ready to serve the omelet.

5. Slice and serve with salt and pepper, prepared mustard, and/or salsa, if you wish.

- Calories 348
- Fat 27
- Sodium 522
- Carbs 5
- Sugar 3
- Protein 21

Mexican Omelet

Irma H. Schoen
Windsor, CT

Makes 1 serving
Prep. Time: 3 minutes
Cooking Time: 2–3 minutes

2 large eggs

2 Tbsp. water

1 Tbsp. butter

¼ cup no-sugar-added salsa, room temperature

1. Beat eggs with a fork in a small mixing bowl.

2. Stir in water.

3. Heat butter in a nonstick (or regular) frying pan.

4. Add eggs and cook to desired doneness.

5. Drain salsa a bit to remove some of the liquid. Then spoon over half of the egg.

6. Fold egg over salsa and slide onto dinner plate.

- Calories 263
- Fat 21
- Sodium 599
- Carbs 5
- Sugar 3
- Protein 14

Italian Frittata

Hope Comerford
Clinton Township, MI

Makes 6 servings
Prep. Time: 10 minutes
Cooking Time: 3–4 hours
Ideal slow-cooker size: 5- or 6-qt.

10 eggs

1 Tbsp. chopped fresh basil

1 Tbsp. chopped fresh mint

1 Tbsp. chopped fresh sage

1 Tbsp. chopped fresh oregano

½ tsp. sea salt

⅛ tsp. pepper

1 Tbsp. grated Parmesan cheese

¼ cup diced prosciutto

½ cup chopped onion

1. Spray your crock with nonstick spray.

2. In a bowl, mix together the eggs, basil, mint, sage, oregano, sea salt, pepper, and Parmesan. Pour this mixture into the crock.

3. Sprinkle the prosciutto and onion evenly over the egg mixture in the crock.

4. Cover and cook on Low for 3–4 hours.

- Calories 137
- Fat 9
- Sodium 327
- Carbs 2
- Sugar 1
- Protein 9

Spinach Fritatta

Shirley Unternahrer
Wayland, IA

Makes 4-6 servings
Prep. Time: 15 minutes
Cooking Time: 1½-2 hours
Ideal slow-cooker size: 5-qt.

4 eggs

½ tsp. kosher salt

½ tsp. dried basil

freshly ground pepper, to taste

3 cups chopped fresh spinach, stems removed

½ cup chopped tomato, liquid drained off

⅓ cup freshly grated Parmesan cheese

1. Whisk eggs well in mixing bowl. Whisk in salt, basil, and pepper.

2. Gently stir in spinach, tomato, and Parmesan.

3. Pour into lightly greased slow cooker.

4. Cover and cook on High for 1½–2 hours, until middle is set. Serve hot.

- Calories 68
- Fat 4
- Sodium 299
- Carbs 2
- Sugar 1
- Protein 6

Crustless Quiche

Mary Jones
Marengo, OH

Makes 9-12 servings
Prep. Time: 15 minutes
Baking Time: 45 minutes
Standing Time: 5 minutes

1 stick (8 Tbsp.) butter

½ cup almond flour

6 eggs

1 cup milk

1 tsp. Low-Carb Baking Powder (recipe on pg. 305)

½ tsp. garlic salt

1 lb. Monterey Jack cheese, shredded

3 oz. cream cheese, softened

2 cups cottage cheese

1. Melt butter in small saucepan.

2. Add almond flour and cook, stirring, until smooth.

3. Remove from heat.

4. In a mixing bowl, beat eggs and add milk, baking powder, garlic salt, Monterey Jack cheese, cream cheese, cottage cheese, and flour mixture.

5. Beat again.

6. Pour into greased 9×13-inch baking pan.

7. Bake at 350°F for 40–45 minutes or until set in the middle. Allow to stand 5 minutes before cutting and serving.

- Calories 333
- Fat 27
- Sodium 495
- Carbs 6
- Sugar 2
- Protein 173

Spinach Mushroom Frittata

J. B. Miller
Indianapolis, IN

Makes 6 servings
Prep. Time: 20 minutes
Cooking/Baking Time: 25–30 minutes

3 cloves garlic, minced

1 cup onion, chopped

2 tsp. olive oil, *divided*

½ lb. fresh mushrooms, sliced

½ tsp. dried thyme

10-oz. bag fresh spinach

10 eggs

1 tsp. dried dill, or 1 Tbsp. fresh dill

¼ tsp. black pepper

¼ cup feta cheese

1. Preheat oven to 350°F.

2. In a large 10- or 12-inch nonstick skillet, sauté garlic and onion in 1 tsp. olive oil for about 5 minutes.

3. Add mushrooms and thyme. Cook an additional 5 minutes. Remove skillet from stove.

4. Place spinach in a separate saucepan. Add 1 Tbsp. water. Cover and cook until just wilted.

5. Drain spinach and let cool in a colander.

6. Squeeze out any liquid. Chop leaves.

7. In a good-sized bowl, beat together eggs, dill, and pepper.

8. Stir in spinach, mushroom mixture, and feta cheese.

9. Clean nonstick skillet. Pour the rest of the olive oil into the pan. Return skillet to stove over medium heat.

10. When skillet is hot, swirl the oil around in the pan to coat all sides, then pour in egg mixture. Place in oven, uncovered.

11. Check frittata in 10 minutes. Check every 5 minutes thereafter until center of frittata is slightly firm. Do not overcook.

12. When frittata is done, place a large serving platter over skillet. Flip skillet over so frittata falls onto the plate.

13. Cut into six servings and serve.

- Calories 186
- Fat 11
- Sodium 220
- Carbs 8
- Sugar 0
- Protein 14

Tomato Herb Mini Frittatas

Nancy Leaman
Bird-in-Hand, PA

Makes 8 servings (4–5 cups)
Prep. Time: 10 minutes
Baking Time: 30 minutes

12 large eggs

1 cup half-and-half or whole milk

½ tsp. sea salt

½ tsp. pepper

2 Tbsp. chopped fresh basil

2 Tbsp. chopped fresh parsley

1 tsp. chopped fresh oregano

1 pt. grape tomatoes, halved

1½ cups shredded Italian 3-cheese blend, *divided*

1. Process eggs, half-and-half, salt, and pepper in a blender.

2. Mix together basil, parsley, and oregano in a small bowl.

3. Place 8 lightly greased 4-inch ramekins on 2 baking sheets.

4. Layer tomatoes, 1 cup cheese, and herb mixture into the ramekins, dividing these ingredients equally.

5. Pour the egg mixture over top and sprinkle with the remaining ½ cup cheese, again dividing among the ramekins.

6. Bake at 450°F for 7 minutes, placing 1 baking sheet on the middle oven rack and the other on the lower oven rack. Switch baking sheets and bake 7 to 8 more minutes, or until set.

7. Remove the top baking sheet from oven. Transfer bottom sheet to middle rack and bake 1–2 minutes or until lightly brown.

- Calories 210
- Fat 13
- Sodium 527
- Carbs 6
- Sugar 3
- Protein 17

Tomato Pesto Frittata

Rebekah Zehr
Lowville, NY

Makes 4-6 servings
Prep. Time: 10 minutes
Cooking Time: 15 minutes

3-5 green onions, chopped

2 Tbsp. olive oil

2-3 fresh tomatoes, chopped

6 eggs

1 Tbsp. half-and-half

salt and pepper, to taste

¼ cup slivered fresh basil, *divided*

3 oz. feta cheese, crumbled

2 Tbsp. coarsely chopped pine nuts

1. In a large ovenproof skillet, sauté green onions in olive oil for 2-3 minutes.

2. Add tomatoes and cook until heated through, about 3–5 minutes. Turn off heat but leave vegetables in skillet.

3. Whisk together eggs, half-and-half, salt, and pepper in a bowl. Stir in 2 Tbsp. of slivered basil.

4. Pour egg mixture evenly over tomato-scallion mixture. Do not mix.

5. Turn heat on to medium-low to cook eggs. Do not scramble but gently tilt skillet and lift edges of cooked egg with a spatula. This will let the uncooked egg run to the bottom of the pan. Cook for about 5 minutes, or until eggs begin to set.

6. Turn off heat and sprinkle top with feta, pine nuts, and rest of basil.

7. Place under broiler until nuts begin to brown, about 3–5 minutes.

8. Remove from oven and cut into pie shaped wedges.

- Calories 197
- Fat 16
- Sodium 291

- Carbs 5
- Sugar 3
- Protein 8

Crustless Spinach Quiche

Barbara Hoover
Landisville, PA

Barbara Jean Fabel
Wausau, WI

Makes 8 servings
Prep. Time: 10 minutes
Cooking Time: 4–6 hours
Ideal slow-cooker size: 3-qt.

2 10-oz. pkgs. frozen chopped spinach, thawed and
    squeezed dry

2 cups cottage cheese

½ stick (4 Tbsp.) butter, cut into pieces

1½ cups sharp cheese, cubed

3 eggs, beaten

¼ cup almond flour

1 tsp. salt

1. Combine ingredients thoroughly.

2. Pour into a greased slow cooker. Cover.

3. Cook on Low 4–6 hours.

Note: Recipe may be doubled for a 5-qt. slow cooker.
—Barbara Jean Fabel

- Calories 261
- Fat 18
- Sodium 718
- Carbs 10
- Sugar 3
- Protein 17

Crustless Chicken and Spinach Quiche

Phyllis Good
Lancaster, PA

Makes 6 servings
Prep. Time: 20 minutes
Cooking Time: 1½–2 hours
Standing Time: 20–30 minutes
Ideal slow-cooker size: 5-qt.

1 cup chopped, cooked chicken

1 cup shredded Swiss cheese

½ cup cooked, chopped spinach, drained
    (about ⅓ of a 10-oz. frozen pkg., thawed)

¼ cup chopped onion

2 eggs

¾ cup mayonnaise

¾ cup whole milk

⅛ tsp. pepper

1. In a good-sized bowl, mix together chicken, cheese, spinach, and onion.

2. Grease the inside of your crock with nonstick cooking spray. Spread the contents of the bowl around the inside of the crock.

3. In the same bowl, stir together eggs, mayonnaise, milk, and pepper until smooth.

4. Pour over chicken-spinach mixture.

5. Cover. Cook on High 1½–2 hours, or until knife inserted into center of quiche comes out clean.

6. Uncover quickly, swooping lid away from yourself so no water drips on quiche from the inside of the lid.

- Calories 339
- Fat 23
- Sodium 478
- Carbs 8
- Sugar 3
- Protein 26

Turkish Crustless Quiche

Tina Campbell
Lancaster, PA

Makes 8–10 servings
Prep. Time: 10 minutes
Baking Time: 35–40 minutes

1 lb. feta cheese, crumbled

1½ cups plain yogurt

3 eggs

1 lb. zucchini, grated

4 cloves garlic, minced

4-oz. can green chiles, drained

2–4 Tbsp. minced fresh dill, or to taste

2–4 Tbsp. minced fresh parsley, or to taste

2–4 Tbsp. minced fresh mint, or to taste

½ cup pine nuts

salt and pepper, to taste

1. Combine feta, yogurt, and eggs in a food processor or blender and process until well blended.

2. In a mixing bowl, combine zucchini, garlic, chiles, dill, parsley, mint, pine nuts, salt, and pepper.

3. Pour egg mixture into other ingredients. Mix with a spoon.

4. Pour into greased 9×13-inch baking dish, or 10-inch pie dish.

5. Bake at 350°F for 35–40 minutes, or until center is firm.

- Calories 260
- Fat 20
- Sodium 673
- Carbs 9
- Sugar 3
- Protein 14

Easy Quiche

Becky Bontrager Horst
Goshen, IN

Makes 6 servings (1 slice per serving)
Prep. Time: 15 minutes
Baking Time: 55 minutes

¼ cup chopped onion

¼ cup chopped mushroom, *optional*

1 tsp. olive oil

3 oz. 75%-less-fat cheddar cheese, shredded

2 Tbsp. chopped ham, cooked chopped bacon pieces, or browned sausage

4 eggs

¼ tsp. salt

1½ cups whole milk

½ cup almond flour

1 Tbsp. butter

1. Sauté onion and mushroom in oil. Combine cheese, meat, and vegetables in greased 9-inch pie pan.

2. Combine remaining ingredients in medium bowl. Pour over meat and vegetables mixture.

3. Bake at 350°F for 45 minutes. This quiche will make its own crust.

- Calories 130
- Fat 5
- Sodium 301
- Carbs 10
- Sugar 2
- Protein 11

Bacon & Cheese Crustless Quiche

Deb Herr
Mountaintop, PA

Makes 6-8 servings
Prep. Time: 15 minutes
Baking Time: 40-45 minutes
Standing Time: 10 minutes

8 slices bacon, cut into squares

½ lb. cheddar, or Monterey Jack, cheese, cut into strips

2 Tbsp. almond flour

4 large eggs

1½ cups whole milk

1. Place bacon squares in skillet and fry until crisp. Remove from drippings and place on paper towels to drain.

2. Meanwhile, in a medium-sized mixing bowl, toss cheese with almond flour.

3. In another large mixing bowl, beat eggs slightly. Add milk, bacon, and floured cheese. Mix well.

4. Spray a 9-inch pie pan with nonstick cooking spray. Pour egg mixture into pan.

5. Place filled pan in the middle of the oven. Bake at 350°F for 40–45 minutes, or until a toothpick inserted in center comes out clean.

6. Cool 10 minutes before cutting into wedges and serving.

- Calories 145
- Fat 10
- Sodium 286
- Carbs 3
- Sugar 2
- Protein 10

California Egg Bake

Leona M. Slabaugh
Apple Creek, OH

Makes 2 servings
Prep. Time: 10-15 minutes
Baking Time: 25-30 minutes

3 eggs

¼ cup sour cream

⅛ tsp. salt

1 medium tomato, chopped

1 green onion, sliced

¼ cup shredded cheddar cheese

1. In a small bowl, beat eggs, sour cream, and salt.

2. Stir in tomato, onion, and cheese.

3. Pour into greased 2-cup baking dish.

4. Bake at 350°F for 25–30 minutes, or until a knife inserted in center comes out clean.

- Calories 225
- Fat 17
- Sodium 330
- Carbs 5
- Sugar 3
- Protein 14

Mexican Egg Casserole

Jan McDowell
New Holland, PA

Makes 3–4 servings
Prep. Time: 10 minutes
Cooking Time: 45 minutes
Standing Time: 20 minutes

1 small can chopped green chiles, drained

¼ cup chopped onion

1 cup shredded cheese of your choice

1 cup Monterey Jack cheese, shredded

4 eggs, beaten frothy

1. Spray an 8×8-inch baking dish with nonstick cooking spray.

2. Spread chiles and onion in bottom of dish.

3. Cover with cheeses.

4. Pour eggs over top.

5. Bake for 45 minutes at 325°F.

6. Let stand 20 minutes before cutting into squares.

- Calories 419
- Fat 32
- Sodium 729
- Carbs 6
- Sugar 2
- Protein 25

Southwestern Egg Casserole

Eileen Eash
Lafayette, CO

Makes 12 servings (approximately 3×3-inch square per serving)
Prep. Time: 20–30 minutes
Baking Time: 35–45 minutes
Standing Time: 5–10 minutes

10 eggs

½ cup almond flour

1 tsp. Low-Carb Baking Powder (see recipe on pg. 305)

⅛ tsp. salt

⅛ tsp. pepper

1½ cups shredded sharp cheddar cheese

2 cups cottage cheese

4 Tbsp. butter

2 4-oz. cans chopped green chiles

1. Beat eggs in a large mixing bowl.

2. In a smaller bowl, combine flour, baking powder, salt, and pepper. Stir into eggs. Batter will be lumpy.

3. Add cheeses, butter, and chiles to batter.

4. Pour into greased 9×13-inch baking dish.

5. Bake at 350°F for 35–45 minutes, or until knife inserted near center comes out clean.

6. Let stand 5–10 minutes before cutting.

- Calories 224
- Fat 17
- Sodium 410
- Carbs 3
- Sugar 2
- Protein 15

Sausage, Eggs, and Bread Dish

Betty B. Dennison
Grove City, PA

Jan Pembleton
Arlington, TX

Makes 6 servings
Prep. Time: 10–15 minutes
Chilling Time: 1 hour
Baking Time: 1 hour

1 lb. bulk sausage

6 eggs

1½ cups whole milk

4 cups stale keto bread, cubed

4 oz. shredded cheddar cheese

1. Brown sausage in a skillet and drain. Set aside.

2. In a large mixing bowl, beat eggs and then add milk.

3. Fold in cubes of stale bread, cheese, and sausage.

4. Pour into a greased 8×8-inch baking dish.

5. Refrigerate for 1 hour.

6. Bake at 325°F for 1 hour. Cut into squares to serve.

- Calories 443
- Fat 34
- Sodium 860
- Carbs 7
- Sugar 4
- Protein 27

Breakfast Sausage Ring

Joanne E. Martin
Stevens, PA

Makes 8 servings
Prep. Time: 15 minutes
Cooking Time: 40–45 minutes
Standing Time: 10 minutes

2 lbs. bulk pork sausage

2 eggs, beaten

1½ cups almond meal

¼ cup chopped parsley, *optional*

salt and pepper, to taste, *optional*

1. Lightly grease a 9-inch oven-safe ring mold.

2. In a large mixing bowl, mix all ingredients well. Then pack into the mold.

3. Bake at 350°F for 20 minutes.

4. Remove from the oven and pour off any accumulated fat. Return to oven to bake for 20 minutes more.

5. Remove from oven and allow to stand for 10 minutes.

Serving suggestion: Turn onto a platter and fill the center with scrambled eggs.

- Calories 506
- Fat 43
- Sodium 948
- Carbs 6
- Sugar 2
- Protein 27

Easy Breakfast Casserole

Barbara Walker
Sturgis, SD

Makes 8 servings
Prep. Time: 20 minutes
Chilling Time: overnight
Cooking Time: 1 hour

stale keto bread slices to cover bottom of 9×13-inch
    baking pan

1½–2 lbs. bacon, fried until crispy and broken up

2 cups shredded cheese of your choice

12 eggs

1 cup whole milk

1. Cover the bottom of a greased 9×13-inch baking pan with slices of bread cut to fit.

2. Sprinkle the bacon and cheese over bread.

3. Use a blender and blend the eggs and milk. Pour over the top.

4. Refrigerate overnight.

5. Bake 1 hour at 350°F.

- Calories 872
- Fat 65
- Sodium 2500
- Carbs 8
- Sugar 2
- Protein 60

Breakfast Delight

Agnes Dick
Vanderhoof, BC

Makes 4 servings
Prep. Time: 20–25 minutes
Cooking Time: 15 minutes

¼–½ lb. bacon, sliced sausage, or cubed, sliced, or
    chopped cooked ham

4 eggs

salt and pepper, to taste

¼ lb. sliced or grated cheese of your choice

1. Fry bacon or brown sausage or ham in a nonstick skillet. Remove and keep warm.

2. Break eggs into a mixing bowl. Stir in seasonings. Beat with a fork, then pour into hot skillet.

3. Lay meat on top of eggs. Lay cheese on top of meat.

4. Fold one third of egg/meat/cheese mixture into the center of the pan. Fold the opposite side over into the center of the pan to form a "blanket." Roll or flip the whole "blanket" over and cook until done.

- Calories 400
- Fat 30
- Sodium 1590
- Carbs 2
- Sugar 0
- Protein 29

Huevas en Rabo de Mestiza

Marlene Fonken
Upland, CA

Makes 1 serving
Prep. Time: 3 minutes
Cooking Time: 5–7 minutes

1 cup Tomato/Chili Poaching Sauce (see recipe on pg. 328)

1 egg

1 oz. Monterey Jack or cheddar cheese, shredded

1. Heat sauce in a small saucepan.

2. Break egg in middle of heated sauce.

3. Top with cheese.

4. Cover and cook approximately 3–5 minutes, or until egg is set and cheese is melted.

- Calories 267
- Fat 19
- Sodium 512
- Carbs 10
- Sugar 5
- Protein 16

Egg and Broccoli Casserole

Joette Droz
Kalona, IA

Makes 6 servings
Prep. Time: 15 minutes
Cooking Time: 2½–3 hours
Ideal slow-cooker size: 4-qt.

24-oz. carton small-curd cottage cheese

10-oz. pkg. frozen chopped broccoli, thawed and drained

2 cups (8 oz.) shredded cheddar cheese

6 eggs, beaten

⅓ cup almond flour

¼ cup melted butter

3 Tbsp. finely chopped onion

½ tsp. salt

1. Combine ingredients. Pour into greased slow cooker.

2. Cover and cook on High 1 hour. Stir. Reduce heat to Low. Cover and cook 2½–3 hours, or until temperature reaches 160°F and eggs are set.

- Calories 455
- Fat 33
- Sodium 908
- Carbs 10
- Sugar 4
- Protein 30

Breakfast Bake

Kristi See
Weskan, KS

Makes 10 servings
Prep. Time: 15 minutes
Cooking Time: 3–4 hours
Ideal slow-cooker size: 4- to 5-qt.

12 eggs

1½–2 cups grated cheese of your choice

1 cup diced cooked ham

1 cup whole milk

1 tsp. salt

½ tsp. pepper

1. Beat eggs. Pour into slow cooker.

2. Mix in remaining ingredients.

3. Cover and cook on Low 3-4 hours.

- Calories 223
- Fat 15
- Sodium 654
- Carbs 3
- Sugar 2
- Protein 19

Spinach Soufflé

Kaye Taylor
Florissant, MO

Makes 8 servings (½ cup portions)
Prep. Time: 5–10 minutes
Baking Time: 60–75 minutes

4 Tbsp. almond flour

2 oz. Colby cheese, grated

2 oz. cheddar cheese, grated

2 Tbsp. olive oil

8 Tbsp. (1 stick) butter, melted

1-lb. carton small-curd cottage cheese

3 eggs

⅛ tsp. pepper

10-oz. pkg. chopped spinach, thawed and squeezed dry

1. Blend together almond flour, cheeses, olive oil, and butter in a large mixing bowl.

2. Stir in remaining ingredients.

3. Pour into a greased 2-qt. baking casserole.

4. Bake uncovered at 325°F for 60–75 minutes, or until knife inserted in center comes out clean.

- Calories 301
- Fat 26
- Sodium 354
- Carbs 5
- Sugar 2
- Protein 14

Shirred Eggs

Margaret W. High
Lancaster, PA

Makes 4 servings
Prep. Time: 20 minutes
Cooking Time: 2 hours
Ideal slow-cooker size: 4- or 5-qt.

4 eggs, room temperature

1 Tbsp. butter

salt and pepper, to taste

1. Have ready a shallow baking dish that fits into your slow cooker without touching the sides. Butter it.

2. Break eggs into buttered dish, being careful not to break the yolks. Salt and pepper.

3. Place dish on jar lid or ring or trivet in slow cooker.

4. Cover and cook on High until whites are set and yolks are as firm as you like them, about 2 hours.

5. Wearing oven gloves to protect your knuckles, remove hot dish from cooker. Gently cut eggs apart into 4 servings, and serve immediately.

Variations: Sprinkle with grated cheese in Step 2. Place a few fresh spinach leaves on top in Step 2. The spinach will wilt by the end of cooking.

- Calories 97
- Fat 8
- Sodium 71
- Carbs 0
- Sugar 0
- Protein 6

Shirred Jumbo Eggs

Willard E. Roth
Elkhart, IN

Makes 4 servings
Prep. Time: 15 minutes
Baking Time: 10–15 minutes

1 small onion, chopped

1 clove garlic, minced

2 tsp. olive oil

4 jumbo eggs

freshly ground pepper

4 Tbsp. whole milk

4 Tbsp. fresh Parmesan or Asiago cheese, grated

1. In a small skillet, sauté onion and garlic in the oil. Divide vegetables among four glass or stoneware baking cups.

2. Break an egg atop onion in each cup. Season with ground pepper.

3. Add 1 Tbsp. milk to each cup.

4. Top each with 1 Tbsp. freshly grated cheese.

5. Place cups on baking sheet. Place in preheated 350°F oven for 10–15 minutes (the longer the time in the oven, the harder the egg).

- Calories 167
- Fat 12
- Sodium 204
- Carbs 4
- Sugar 2
- Protein 12

Elegant Scrambled Eggs

John D. Allen
Rye, CO

Makes 6–8 servings
Prep. Time: 15 minutes
Cooking Time: 10 minutes

12 eggs

½ tsp. salt

⅛ tsp. pepper

2 Tbsp. butter

2 Tbsp. whipping cream

1. Combine the first three ingredients in a large bowl. Beat until well mixed.

2. Melt butter in a skillet over medium heat, making sure the bottom is covered. Add eggs.

3. Stir constantly until eggs firm up but are not dry. Remove from heat.

4. Stir in the cream. Serve immediately.

- Calories 145
- Fat 11
- Sodium 227
- Carbs 1
- Sugar 0
- Protein 10

Eggs à la Shrimp

Willard E. Roth
Elkhart, IN

Makes 6 servings
Prep. Time: 15 minutes
Cooking Time: 15 minutes

1 Tbsp. olive oil

3 green onions with tops, sliced, or 1 small onion, chopped fine

¼ cup finely chopped celery with leaves

4 oz. shrimp, frozen or canned

3 Tbsp. plus ¼ cup chicken bone broth, *divided*

8 large eggs

¼ tsp. salt

¼ tsp. pepper

fresh parsley

1. Preheat electric skillet to 375°F, or cast-iron skillet to medium high.

2. Heat oil in skillet. Sauté onions until limp.

3. Add celery and sauté until softened.

4. Add shrimp and 3 Tbsp. chicken bone broth. Cover and steam over low heat for 3 minutes.

5. In a medium-sized mixing bowl, toss eggs with ¼ cup remaining chicken bone broth. Pour into skillet.

6. Stir in salt and pepper.

7. Turn skillet to 300°F, or medium low. Stir gently as mixture cooks. Cook just until mixture sets, according to your liking.

8. Serve on warm platter surrounded with fresh parsley.

- Calories 113
- Fat 9
- Sodium 308
- Carbs 1
- Sugar 0.5
- Protein 11

Breakfast in a Bag

Donna Lantgen
Golden, CO

Makes 1 serving
Prep. Time: 1–2 minutes
Cooking Time: 12 minutes

2 eggs

Optional ingredients:

¼ cup cooked sausage

1 slice cooked bacon, crumbled

¼ cup cooked and cubed ham

thin onion slices

several Tbsp. chopped red or green bell pepper

several Tbsp. sliced black olives

¼ cup sliced mushrooms

¼ cup grated cheese of your choice

¼ cup chopped fresh tomato

1. Place a 4-qt. saucepan, ⅔ full of water, over high heat. Bring to a boil.

2. Meanwhile, place 2 raw eggs in a sturdy plastic bag. Holding it shut, mash the eggs a bit.

3. Add optional ingredients of your choice. Press the air out of the bag. Zip close, or tie shut with a twist tie.

4. Place bag in boiling water and cook for 12 minutes.

5. Remove from water and slide eggs right out of the bag.

- Calories 143
- Fat 10
- Sodium 142
- Carbs 1
- Sugar 0
- Protein 13

Eggs California

Vonda Ebersole
Mount Pleasant Mills, PA

Judy Gonzales
Fishers, IN

Esther Gingerich
Parnell, IA

Makes 10 servings
Prep. Time: 20 minutes
Baking Time: 40–45 minutes

10 eggs

2 cups cottage cheese

½ cup almond flour

1 tsp. Low-Carb Baking Powder (see recipe on pg. 305)

½ tsp. salt

½ cup melted butter

1 lb. grated cheddar, Swiss, or Monterey Jack cheese

1 or 2 4-oz. cans chopped green chiles, depending upon your taste preference

1. In a mixing bowl, beat together eggs, cottage cheese, almond flour, baking powder, salt, and butter.

2. Stir in cheese and green chilies.

3. Pour into a greased 9x13-inch baking dish.

4. Bake at 350°F for 40–45 minutes, or until set.

- Calories 263
- Fat 22
- Sodium 511
- Carbs 3
- Sugar 1
- Protein 14

Greek Eggs

Rosanne Hankins
Stevensville, MD

Makes 4 servings
Prep. Time: 15 minutes
Cooking Time: 20 minutes

2 cloves garlic, sliced

¼ cup sliced white onion

1 Tbsp. olive oil

10-oz. pkg. frozen chopped spinach, thawed and squeezed as dry as possible

8 eggs, beaten

½–1 tsp. dried oregano, according to your taste preference

4 oz. feta cheese

1. In a large skillet, sauté garlic and onion in oil for 3–4 minutes.

2. Stir in spinach.

3. Pour eggs and oregano into hot skillet.

4. Cook, turning 2–3 times, until eggs are lightly cooked, about 5 minutes.

5. Turn off heat, crumble cheese over top of spinach-egg mixture. Cover and let set for 2 minutes, or until cheese melts into eggs.

- Calories 275
- Fat 19
- Sodium 528
- Carbs 7
- Sugar 0
- Protein 20

Swiss Chard Scramble

Elaine Good
Lititz, PA

Makes 3 servings
Prep. Time: 15 minutes
Cooking Time: 15 minutes

1 Tbsp. olive oil

1 small sweet onion, chopped

2 cloves garlic, chopped or pressed

4-6 Swiss chard leaves, chopped

¼ cup chopped fresh basil, oregano, or parsley

6 eggs, beaten

½ cup grated Parmesan, Romano, or Asiago cheese

¼ tsp. salt

coarsely ground pepper, to taste

1. Heat oil in large skillet.

2. Add onion and garlic and sauté for 5 minutes.

3. Add chard and basil, oregano, or parsley. Sauté until wilted, about 2 minutes.

4. Add eggs, cheese, salt, and pepper.

5. Cook, stirring, until eggs are set.

- Calories 248
- Fat 18
- Sodium 544
- Carbs 5
- Sugar 1
- Protein 17

Baked Creamed Eggs

Marilyn Widrick
Adams, NY

Makes 8 servings
Prep. Time: 15 minutes
Baking Time: 20–30 minutes

8 eggs, hard-boiled and cut in half lengthwise

4 Tbsp. (½ stick) butter

¼ cup almond flour

1 tsp. konjac flour

2 cups whole milk

⅜ tsp. salt

⅛ tsp. pepper

⅛ tsp. garlic powder

¼ tsp. dry mustard

1 cup grated sharp cheddar cheese

½ cup grated Parmesan cheese

1. Place eggs cut side down in a 9×13-inch greased baking dish.

2. In a saucepan, melt the butter. Add the almond flour and konjac flour. Cook, stirring, for 2–3 minutes until bubbly and tan.

3. Add the milk gradually, whisking. Stir and cook over low heat until mixture thickens. Turn off heat.

4. Season with salt, pepper, garlic powder, and dry mustard.

5. Add the cheddar cheese and stir until melted.

6. Pour the sauce over the eggs and sprinkle top with the Parmesan cheese.

7. Bake for 20–30 minutes at 350°F until bubbling and top is golden brown.

- Calories 142
- Fat 21
- Sodium 453
- Carbs 5
- Sugar 4
- Protein 14

Poached Eggs

Hope Comerford
Clinton Township, MI

Makes 4 servings
Prep. Time: 5 minutes
Cooking Time: 2–5 minutes
Setting: Steam
Pressure: High
Release: Manual

1 cup water

4 large eggs

1. Place the trivet in the bottom of the inner pot of the Instant Pot and pour in the water.

2. You will need small silicone egg poacher cups that will fit in your Instant Pot to hold the eggs. Spray each silicone cup with nonstick cooking spray.

3. Crack each egg and pour it into the prepared cup.

4. Very carefully place the silicone cups into the Inner Pot so they do not spill.

5. Secure the lid by locking it into place and turn the vent to the sealing position.

6. Push the Steam button and adjust the time— 2 minutes for a very runny egg all the way to 5 minutes for a slightly runny egg.

7. When the timer beeps, release the pressure manually and remove the lid, being very careful not to let the condensation in the lid drip into your eggs.

8. Very carefully remove the silicone cups from the inner pot.

9. Carefully remove the poached eggs from each silicone cup and serve immediately.

- Calories 72
- Fat 5
- Sodium 73
- Carbs 0
- Sugar 0
- Protein 6

Scrambled Egg Muffins

Julia Horst
Gordonville, PA

Mary Kay Nolt
Newmanstown, PA

Makes 12 servings
Prep. Time: 20 minutes
Baking Time: 20-30 minutes

½ lb. bulk sausage

12 eggs

½ cup chopped onion

¼ cup chopped green pepper

½ tsp. salt

¼ tsp. pepper

¼ tsp. garlic powder

½ cup shredded cheddar cheese

1. In a skillet, brown sausage. Drain.

2. In a bowl, beat the eggs.

3. Add onion, green pepper, salt, pepper, and garlic powder to the eggs and blend well. Stir in sausage.

4. Spoon by ⅓-cupfuls into greased muffin cups. Sprinkle with shredded cheese.

5. Bake at 350°F for 20–30 minutes, or until knife inserted near centers comes out clean.

- Calories 149
- Fat 11
- Sodium 321
- Carbs 2
- Sugar 1
- Protein 10

Eggs Florentine

Mary Ann Wasick
West Allis, WI

Makes 2 servings
Prep. Time: 10 minutes
Cooking Time: 5-7 minutes

1 Tbsp. butter

2 cups fresh spinach, torn, with heavy stems removed

3 large eggs

½ cup whole milk

sliced cheese of your choice

1. Melt butter in a nonstick skillet.

2. Maintaining a low heat, add spinach and cover for 2–3 minutes. Stir once or twice.

3. Meanwhile, whisk eggs and milk together in a small bowl.

4. Pour over spinach in skillet.

5. Cook over low heat until eggs are almost set. Then add slices of cheese to cover eggs.

6. Turn off heat, and cover skillet for a minute, or until cheese melts into eggs.

Serving suggestion: Serve, offering salt, pepper, and cubed fresh tomatoes, if you wish.

- Calories 202
- Fat 15
- Sodium 157
- Carbs 5
- Sugar 0
- Protein 12

Old-Timey French Toast

Jennifer Kellogg
Whately, MA

Makes 4–6 servings
Prep. Time: 5 minutes
Cooking Time: 5–8 minutes

1 cup milk

2 eggs

½ tsp. liquid stevia

1 tsp. grated nutmeg, *divided*

4 Tbsp. (½ stick) butter

16-oz. loaf of sliced keto bread

1. In a large mixing bowl, whisk together the milk, eggs, liquid stevia, and half of the nutmeg.

2. Melt butter in the bottom of the skillet over medium-high heat.

3. Dip individual slices of bread into milk mixture and place in hot skillet. Cook until golden brown.

4. Sprinkle each slice with remaining nutmeg. Flip over to brown the other side.

5. Serve immediately.

- Calories 342
- Fat 16
- Sodium 518
- Carbs 39
- Sugar 8
- Protein 10

Baked French Toast with Cream Cheese

Blanche Nyce
Hatfield, PA

Makes 10 servings
Prep. Time: 15–20 minutes
Chilling Time: 8 hours, or overnight
Baking Time: 40–45 minutes

1-lb. loaf keto bread, *divided*

8-oz. pkg. cream cheese

2 cups berries of your choice—strawberries, blueberries, or raspberries

10 eggs

½ cup half-and-half

¼ cup keto-friendly pancake syrup

4 Tbsp. (½ stick) butter, melted

1. Cube bread and layer half in well-greased 9×13-inch baking pan.

2. Cut cream cheese into small pieces and scatter across bread.

3. Sprinkle with berries.

4. Cover berries with remaining half of bread.

5. In a mixing bowl, beat together eggs, half-and-half, syrup, and melted butter.

6. Pour over contents of baking pan.

7. Press down until bread is submerged as much as possible.

8. Cover and refrigerate for 8 hours, or overnight.

9. Bake uncovered at 375°F for 40–45 minutes, or until lightly browned and puffy.

- Calories 346
- Fat 21
- Sodium 453
- Carbs 32
- Sugar 8
- Protein 12

Blueberry French Toast

Stacie Skelly
Millersville, PA

Makes 12 servings
Prep. Time: 30 minutes
Chilling Time: 6–8 hours, or overnight
Baking Time: 1 hour

12 slices day-old keto bread

8 oz. cream cheese

1 cup frozen blueberries

12 eggs

2 cups whole milk

⅓ cup xylitol

Sauce:
¼ cup Splenda Sugar Blend

1 Tbsp. ground flaxseed mixed with 4 Tbsp. water

1 cup water

1 cup blueberries

1. Grease 9×13-inch baking pan.

2. Cube bread and spread in pan.

3. Cube cream cheese. Distribute evenly over bread.

4. Sprinkle blueberries on top.

5. In a mixing bowl, blend eggs, milk, and xylitol.

6. Pour over baking-pan contents.

7. Cover. Refrigerate 6–8 hours, or overnight.

8. Remove from refrigerator 30 minutes before baking.

9. Bake, covered, at 350°F for 30 minutes.

10. Uncover. Bake 30 more minutes.

11. Meanwhile, mix together the sauce ingredients. When the French Toast is ready, serve with the sauce.

- Calories 177
- Fat 8
- Sodium 270
- Carbs 26
- Sugar 6
- Protein 10

Healthy Banana Pancakes

Hope Comerford
Clinton Township, MI

Makes 3–4 servings
Prep. Time: 5 minutes
Cook Time: 10 minutes

1 Tbsp. butter

2 bananas, very ripe

4 eggs

½ tsp. cinnamon, *optional*

1. Melt the butter in a medium-sized pan over medium heat.

2. Mash the bananas and mix in the eggs and cinnamon, if using.

3. Cook about 4 pancakes per batch, cooking each side for about 1–2 minutes, covering the pan while cooking.

- Calories 150
- Fat 8
- Sodium 72
- Carbs 14
- Sugar 2
- Protein 7

Keto Coconut Flour Pancakes

Hope Comerford
Clinton Township, MI

Makes 3–4 servings
Prep. Time: 5 minutes
Cooking Time: 10 minutes

¼ cup butter or coconut oil, melted

4 eggs

¼ cup coconut milk

1 tsp. vanilla extract

½ tsp. cinnamon

¼ tsp. salt

¼ cup coconut flour

½ tsp. Low-Carb Baking Powder (see recipe on pg. 305)

1. Melt the butter or coconut oil in a medium-sized pan.

2. Mix together the eggs, coconut milk, vanilla, cinnamon, and salt until smooth and well-mixed. Whisk in the coconut flour and baking powder until the batter is smooth.

3. Use about ¼ cup of batter for each pancake, cooking about 1–2 minutes on each side. (Use a super-thin spatula as these pancakes are delicate.)

Tip: You may need to add more butter to the pan between batches to keep the pancakes from sticking.

- Calories 242
- Fat 21
- Sodium 209
- Carbs 6
- Sugar 1
- Protein 8

Protein Pancakes

Hope Comerford
Clinton Township, MI

Makes 3–4 servings
Prep. Time: 5 minutes
Cooking Time: 10 minutes

4 Tbsp. (½ stick) butter

3 eggs

1 cup unsweetened almond milk

1 tsp. vanilla extract

¼ tsp. salt

1½ cups almond flour

1. Melt the butter in a medium-sized pan over medium heat.

2. Whisk together the eggs, almond milk, vanilla, and salt. Whisk in the almond flour until smooth.

3. Pour about ¼ cup of batter for each pancake into the pan (about 4 at a time). Cook for 2–3 minutes on each side.

Tips: You can add more almond milk if you like your pancakes on the thinner side. You may need to add a bit more butter to your pan between batches to prevent sticking.

- Calories 408
- Fat 37
- Sodium 236
- Carbs 10
- Sugar 2
- Protein 14

Green Smoothie

Hope Comerford
Clinton Township, MI

Makes 1 serving
Prep. Time: 5 minutes

¾ cup unsweetened almond milk

½ cup plain Greek yogurt

10 drops liquid stevia

½ banana

¼ cup strawberries

1 cup spinach leaves

¼ cup ice

1. Place all ingredients into the blender and blend until smooth.

- Calories 210
- Fat 8
- Sodium 205
- Carbs 24
- Sugar 14
- Protein 13

Slow-Cooker Yogurt

Becky Fixel
Grosse Pointe Farms, MI

Makes 12–14 servings
Prep. Time: 2 minutes
Cooking Time: 12–14 hours
Ideal slow-cooker size: 6-qt.

1 gallon whole milk

5.3 oz. Greek yogurt with cultures

1. Empty the gallon of whole milk into your slow cooker and put it on High heat for 2–4 hours. Length of time depends on your model, but the milk needs to heat to just below boiling point, about 180–200°F.

2. Turn off your slow cooker and let your milk cool down to 110–115°F. Again, this will take 2–4 hours. Set your starter Greek yogurt out so it can reach room temperature during this step.

3. In a small bowl, add about 1 cup of the warm milk and the Greek yogurt and mix together. Pour the mixture into the milk in the slow cooker and mix it in by stirring back and forth. Replace the lid of your slow cooker and wrap the whole thing in a towel. Let sit for 12–14 hours.

4. After 12 hours check on your glorious yogurt!

5. Line a colander with cheesecloth and place in bowl. Scoop your yogurt inside and let it sit for at least 4 hours. This will help separate the extra whey from the yogurt and thicken your final yogurt.

- Calories 180
- Fat 10
- Sodium 124
- Carbs 14
- Sugar 14
- Protein 8

Instant Pot Yogurt

Cynthia Hockman-Chupp
Canby, OR

Makes 16 servings
Prep. Time: 10 minutes
Cooking Time: 8 hours+
Setting: Yogurt

1 gallon whole milk

¼ cup plain yogurt with active cultures

1. Pour milk into the inner pot of the Instant Pot.

2. Lock lid, move vent to sealing, and press the Yogurt button. Press Adjust till it reads "boil."

3. When boil cycle is complete (about 1 hour), check the temperature. It should be at 185°F. If it's not, use the sauté function to warm to 185°F.

4. After it reaches 185°F, unplug Instant Pot, remove inner pot, and cool. You can place on cooling rack and let it slowly cool. If in a hurry, submerge the base of the pot in cool water. Cool milk to 110°F.

5. When mixture reaches 110°F, stir in the ¼ cup of yogurt. Lock the lid in place and move vent to sealing.

6. Press Yogurt. Use the Adjust button until the screen says 8:00. This will now incubate for 8 hours.

7. After 8 hours (when the cycle is finished), chill yogurt, or go immediately to straining in step 8.

8. After chilling, or following the 8 hours, strain the yogurt using a nut milk bag. This will give it the consistency of Greek yogurt.

- Calories 150
- Fat 8
- Sodium 105
- Carbs 12
- Sugar 12
- Protein 8

Turkey Sausage

Becky Frey
Lebanon, PA

Makes 6 servings
Prep. Time: 10 minutes
Broiling Time: 10–15 minutes

¾ lb. ground turkey

¼ tsp. pepper

¼ tsp. dried basil

¼ tsp. dried sage

¼ tsp. dried oregano

1 egg white

⅛ tsp. allspice

⅛ tsp. nutmeg

⅛ tsp. garlic powder

⅛ tsp. chili powder

⅛ tsp. Frank's RedHot Original Cayenne Pepper Sauce, *optional*

2 Tbsp. water

1. Mix all ingredients together in a large bowl.

2. Shape into 6 patties. Place on baking sheet.

3. Broil 2–3 inches from heat, 5–7 minutes.

4. Flip burgers over. Broil 5–7 more minutes.

Serving suggestion: Serve on a bed of lettuce or on keto-friendly buns or bread.

- Calories 106
- Fat 7
- Sodium 40
- Carbs 0
- Sugar 0
- Protein 10

KETO TIP
When you're in ketosis, your body needs more sodium. Sprinkle your food with additional Himalayan sea salt to help balance your electrolytes.

Appetizers

Guacamole

Kara Maddox
Lincoln, NE

Judy Houser
Hershey, PA

Makes about 1¼–2 cups
Prep. Time: 10 minutes

2 avocados

½ cup chopped red onion

½ cup cubed tomatoes

salt and pepper, to taste

1 tsp. lime juice

1. Cut the avocados in half, remove the stone, and peel. Then mash the avocados in a medium-sized mixing bowl with a fork.

2. Stir in remaining ingredients gently.

Serving suggestion: Serve with fresh cut-up vegetables.

- Calories 62
- Fat 5
- Sodium 52
- Carbs 4
- Sugar 1
- Protein 1

Turbo Guacamole

Cliff Snyder
Waterloo, ON

Makes ¾ cup
Prep. Time: 5 minutes

1 avocado

1 Tbsp. sour cream

1 Tbsp. mayonnaise

¼ tsp. salt

¼ tsp. pepper (I always use freshly ground)

¼ tsp. lemon juice

¼ tsp. balsamic vinegar, *optional*

dash Frank's RedHot Original Cayenne Pepper Sauce, *optional*

dash Worcestershire sauce, *optional*

1. Cut avocado in half. Remove pit. Peel off the skin.

2. Place peeled avocado in a mixing bowl. Add all other ingredients. Mix, using a fork to squish the avocado. Don't try to puree the guacamole— ideally some small chunks of avocado should remain intact.

Serving suggestion: Serve with fresh cut-up vegetables.

- Calories 85
- Fat 8
- Sodium 243
- Carbs 3
- Sugar 1
- Protein 1

Fruit Salsa

Maryann Markano
Wilmington, DE

Makes 4 servings (⅓ cup per serving)
Prep. Time: 15 minutes
Marinating Time: 20 minutes

¾ cup chopped strawberries

⅓ cup chopped blueberries

2 Tbsp. chopped sweet green bell pepper

2 Tbsp. chopped sweet yellow bell pepper

1 Tbsp. chopped onion

2 tsp. cider vinegar

1 tsp. minced jalapeño pepper

1. Combine all ingredients in small bowl.

2. Let stand 20 minutes to allow flavors to blend.

- Calories 19
- Fat 0
- Sodium 1
- Carbs 5
- Sugar 3
- Protein 0.5

Slow-Cooked Salsa

Andy Wagner
Quarryville, PA

Makes 2 cups
Prep. Time: 15 minutes
Cooking Time: 1½–3 hours
Standing Time: 2 hours
Ideal slow-cooker size: 3-qt.

10 plum tomatoes

2 cloves garlic

1 small onion, cut into wedges

1–2 jalapeño peppers

½ cup chopped fresh cilantro

½ tsp. sea salt, *optional*

1. Core tomatoes. Cut a small slit in two tomatoes. Insert a garlic clove into each slit.

2. Place all tomatoes and onion in a 3-qt. slow cooker.

3. Cut stems off jalapeños. (Remove seeds if you want a milder salsa.) Place jalapeños in the slow cooker.

4. Cover and cook on High for 2½–3 hours or until vegetables are softened. Some may brown slightly. Cool at least 2 hours with the lid off.

5. In a blender, combine the tomato mixture, cilantro, and salt if you wish. Cover and process until blended.

6. Refrigerate leftovers.

Tip: Wear disposable gloves when cutting hot peppers; the oils can burn your skin. Avoid touching your face when you've been working with hot peppers.

Serving suggestion: Garnish with cilantro and jalapeño. Serve with bell pepper strips.

- Calories 17
- Fat 0
- Sodium 101
- Carbs 4
- Sugar 2
- Protein 1

Fresh Salsa

Barbara Kuhns
Millersburg, OH

Makes 3 cups (½ cup per serving)
Prep. Time: 20 minutes

3 tomatoes

½ cup chopped green bell peppers

¼ cup chopped onion

1 tsp. garlic powder

1 tsp. cumin

½ tsp. ground red pepper

2 tsp. vinegar

1 tsp. olive oil

2 tsp. lemon juice

1. Chop tomatoes.

2. Add remaining ingredients and mix well.

3. Serve.

- Calories 23
- Fat 1
- Sodium 4
- Carbs 3
- Sugar 2
- Protein 1

Fresh Chunky Cherry Tomato Salsa

J. B. Miller
Indianapolis, IN

Makes 8 servings (⅓ cup per serving)
Prep. Time: 15 minutes
Marinating Time: 2 hours

½ cucumber, seeded and cut into small dice

2 cups cherry tomatoes, quartered

1 clove garlic, finely chopped

1 lemon

2 Tbsp. chili oil

¼ tsp. dried pepper flakes

2 Tbsp. fresh dill

pepper, to taste

1. Prepare cucumber and tomatoes in mixing bowl. Add finely chopped garlic.

2. Grate lemon rind finely and add to tomatoes along with juice of lemon.

3. Add chili oil, pepper flakes, and dill. Stir and let marinate at room temperature for at least 2 hours. Sprinkle with pepper.

- Calories 40
- Fat 3
- Sodium 3
- Carbs 2
- Sugar 1
- Protein 0.5

Salsa

Wilma J. Haberkamp
Fairbank, IA

Makes 6–7 pints (or 48 or more 4-Tbsp.–sized servings)
Prep. Time: 45–50 minutes
Cooking Time: 3 hours
Ideal slow-cooker size: 6- or 7-qt.

13 tomatoes, peeled and seeded

1 tsp. salt

4 tsp. white vinegar

2 6½-oz. cans tomato paste

⅔ cup Frank's RedHot Original Cayenne Pepper Sauce

1 large yellow onion, chopped

1 large red onion, chopped

1 green bell pepper, seeded and chopped

1 red bell pepper, seeded and chopped

1 yellow bell pepper, seeded and chopped

1–2 hot peppers, seeded

3 banana peppers, seeded and chopped

1. Combine all ingredients in large bowl and mix well. Ladle into 6-qt. or larger slow cooker.

2. Cook on High 1 hour, and then reduce to Low for 2 hours.

3. Pour into sterilized jars and follow directions from your canner for sealing and preserving.

- Calories 10
- Fat 0
- Sodium 50
- Carbs 2
- Sugar 1
- Protein 0.5

Salsa Dip

Beverly High
Bradford, PA

Makes 3½ cups
Prep. Time: 10 minutes

8-oz. pkg. cream cheese, softened

½ cup sour cream

1 cup no-sugar-added salsa

¾ cup grated mozzarella cheese

1. In a medium-sized mixing bowl, beat cream cheese until soft and creamy. Fold in sour cream.

2. Spread mixture in a 9-inch pie plate.

3. Spoon salsa over top.

4. Sprinkle with mozzarella cheese.

5. Cover and refrigerate until serving.

- Calories 52
- Fat 5
- Sodium 128
- Carbs 2
- Sugar 1
- Protein 2

Veggie Dip

Mary Ann Bowman
East Earl, PA

Arlene Snyder
Millerstown, PA

Makes 2 cups
Prep. Time: 5 minutes
Chilling Time: 1+ hours

1 cup sour cream

1 cup mayonnaise

1 tsp. seasoned salt

1 tsp. minced onion

1 tsp. chives

1. Mix all ingredients together until well blended.

2. Cover and chill for an hour or more to allow flavors to blend.

Serving suggestion: Serve with fresh vegetables.

- Calories 235
- Fat 25
- Sodium 373
- Carbs 1
- Sugar 1
- Protein 1

Veggie Dip

Janelle Nolt
Richland, PA

Makes about 2 cups
Prep. Time: 10 minutes

2 8-oz. pkgs. cream cheese, softened

½ cup mayonnaise

⅓ cup Parmesan cheese

10 slices bacon, fried and crumbled

minced onion, to taste

1. In a large mixing bowl, blend cream cheese and mayonnaise together until smooth.

2. Stir in remaining ingredients.

Serving suggestion: Serve with veggie sticks.

- Calories 261
- Fat 25
- Sodium 467
- Carbs 2
- Sugar 1
- Protein 7

Vegetable Dip

Beth Shank
Wellman, IA

Makes 3 cups
Prep. Time: 10 minutes
Chilling Time: 8 hours, or overnight

2 cups mayonnaise

1 Tbsp. dill weed

3 Tbsp. dried parsley

1 cup sour cream

3 Tbsp. dried onion

dash salt, *optional*

1. Place all ingredients in a medium-sized mixing bowl and stir together well.

2. Cover and refrigerate for 8 hours or overnight to allow flavors to blend.

Serving suggestion: Serve with cut-up fresh vegetables.

- Calories 141
- Fat 15
- Sodium 119
- Carbs 0
- Sugar 0
- Protein 0

Salmon Dip for Vegetables

Dede Peterson
Rapid City, SD

Makes 6 servings
Prep. Time: 20 minutes

15-oz. can salmon, no salt added, flaked and drained

½ cup sour cream

¼ cup diced celery

2 Tbsp. chopped green onion

2 Tbsp. diced sweet bell pepper

1 Tbsp. lemon juice

2 tsp. chopped fresh dill

1. Mix all ingredients.

2. Cover and chill until ready to serve.

Serving suggestion: Serve with assorted raw vegetables such as bell peppers, zucchini, carrots, cucumbers, cauliflower, jicama, broccoli, radishes, etc.

- Calories 224
- Fat 14
- Sodium 12
- Carbs 2
- Sugar 1
- Protein 22

French Onion Dip

Hope Comerford
Clinton Township, MI

Makes 6 servings
Prep. Time: 10 minutes
Cooking Time: 8 hours
Ideal slow-cooker size: 2-qt.

2 large sweet yellow onions, finely chopped

4 Tbsp. olive oil

1½ cups plain Greek yogurt

2 cloves garlic, minced

2 tsp. liquid aminos

¼ tsp. salt

½ tsp. black pepper

pinch cayenne

1. Place onions and olive oil in the crock and stir so onions are coated in the olive oil.

2. Cover and cook on Low for 8 hours, or until the onions are a deep caramel-brown color.

3. Strain the onions.

4. In a bowl, combine the yogurt, garlic, liquid aminos, salt, pepper, cayenne, and onions.

Serving suggestion: Serve with crispy baked green beans.

- Calories 130
- Fat 9
- Sodium 12
- Carbs 6
- Sugar 4
- Protein 6

Cheese Dip

Lena Hoover
Ephrata, PA

Makes 3 cups
Prep. Time: 15 minutes

8-oz. pkg. cream cheese, softened

8-oz. tub cheddar cheese spread

scant ½ cup mayonnaise

⅓ cup chopped walnuts

vegetable sticks, for serving

1. Mix first 3 ingredients together in a medium-sized bowl.

2. Spoon dip into serving dish and cover with chopped walnuts.

3. Cover and chill. Serve with fresh vegetable sticks.

- Calories 220
- Fat 21
- Sodium 241
- Carbs 2
- Sugar 1
- Protein 6

Taco Dip with Fresh Tomatoes

Linda Hartzler
Minonk, IL

Kathryn Yoder
Minot, ND

Makes 4 cups
Prep. Time: 15–20 minutes

2 8-oz. pkgs. cream cheese, softened

16 oz. sour cream

1 envelope dry keto-friendly taco seasoning mix

1 cup shredded sharp cheddar cheese

1½ cups chopped tomatoes

1. Mix cream cheese, sour cream, and taco seasoning together.

2. Spread into a 9-inch pie plate or dish.

3. Top with shredded cheese and then with tomatoes just before eating.

- Calories 192
- Fat 18
- Sodium 244
- Carbs 5
- Sugar 3
- Protein 4

Taco Dip

Janice Muller
Derwood, MD

Makes about 8 cups
Prep. Time: 25 minutes
Cooking Time: 10 minutes

16-oz. pkg. cheddar cheese spread

2 8-oz. pkgs. cream cheese, softened

16-oz. jar no-sugar-added chunky salsa

1 envelope keto-friendly dry taco seasoning mix

1 lb. ground beef, browned and drained of drippings

1. Place cheeses in a large saucepan. Stir over low heat until melted.

2. Combine salsa, taco seasoning, and browned beef in a bowl. Stir into cheese mixture.

3. Cook over low heat 10 minutes, stirring frequently.

- Calories 151
- Fat 12
- Sodium 216
- Carbs 2
- Sugar 1
- Protein 8

Creamy Jalapeño Dip

Hope Comerford
Clinton Township, MI

Makes 10 servings
Prep. Time: 5 minutes
Cooking Time: 12 minutes
Setting: Manual
Pressure: High
Release: Manual

1 lb. boneless chicken breast

8 oz. cream cheese

3 jalapeños, seeded and sliced

½ cup water

8 oz. shredded cheddar cheese

¾ cup sour cream

1. Place the chicken, cream cheese, jalapeños, and water in the inner pot of the Instant Pot.

2. Secure the lid so it's locked and turn the vent to sealing.

3. Press Manual and set the Instant Pot for 12 minutes on high pressure.

4. When cooking time is up, turn off Instant Pot, do a quick release of the remaining pressure, then remove lid.

5. Shred the chicken between 2 forks, either in the pot or on a cutting board, then place back in the inner pot.

6. Stir in the shredded cheese and sour cream. Enjoy!

- Calories 238
- Fat 13
- Sodium 273
- Carbs 7
- Sugar 5
- Protein 24

Kickin' Dip

Rose Hankins
Stevensville, MD

Makes 3–4 cups (12–16 servings)
Prep. Time: 15 minutes
Cooking Time: 3–4 hours
Ideal slow-cooker size: 4-qt.

4 cups (16 oz.) shredded cheddar cheese

14-oz. can diced tomatoes, drained, with juice reserved

7-oz. can chopped green chiles, drained

1 cup chopped onions

1 Tbsp. cumin

1 tsp. chili powder

1 tsp. hot pepper sauce

1. Mix all ingredients in slow cooker.

2. Cover. Cook on Low 3–4 hours.

3. Stir before serving. If dip is stiffer than you like, stir in some of reserved tomato juice.

- Calories 130
- Fat 10
- Sodium 289
- Carbs 4
- Sugar 1
- Protein 7

White Queso Dip

Janie Steele
Moore, OK

Makes 10–12 servings
Prep. Time: 10–15 minutes
Cooking Time: 1 hour
Ideal slow-cooker size: 2-qt.

2 8-oz. pkgs. cream cheese, softened

1 cup sour cream

½ tsp. Frank's RedHot Original Cayenne Pepper Sauce

10-oz. can Ro*Tel tomatoes, your choice of hot or mild

1 tsp. cumin

4-oz. can green chiles, chopped

8-oz: pkg. grated Monterey Jack cheese, or grated Mexican cheese mix

1. Combine cream cheese, sour cream, and hot sauce in a bowl with a mixer until smooth.

2. Drain half the liquid off the tomatoes and discard.

3. Add tomatoes with half their juice, cumin, chilies, and grated cheese to creamy mixture. Stir to combine.

4. Pour mixture into slow cooker.

5. Turn to High until cheese melts, about 1 hour. Stir about every 15 minutes.

6. Turn to Low to keep dip warm while serving.

Serving suggestion: Serve with baked, crispy cauliflower.

- Calories 242
- Fat 22
- Sodium 341
- Carbs 5
- Sugar 3
- Protein 8

Hot Artichoke and Spinach Dip

Jennifer Archer
Kalona, IA

Makes 2½ cups
Prep. Time: 10–15 minutes
Baking Time: 20–25 minutes

6-oz. jar artichoke hearts, drained

9–11-oz. pkg. frozen creamed spinach, thawed

¼ cup mayonnaise

¼ cup sour cream

½ cup grated Parmesan cheese

1 clove garlic, minced, *optional*

1. Chop artichoke hearts and place in small bowl. Stir in spinach.

2. Fold in mayonnaise and sour cream.

3. Mix in Parmesan cheese, and garlic if you wish.

4. Spoon into a small baking dish. Bake at 350°F for 20–25 minutes, or until bubbly.

- Calories 116
- Fat 10
- Sodium 313
- Carbs 5
- Sugar 5
- Protein 2

Artichoke Chiles Dip

Irene J. Dewar
Pickering, ON

Makes 2½ cups
Prep. Time: 5 minutes
Cooking Time: 3–4 minutes

8-oz. jar of artichoke hearts, drained and chopped

4-oz. can chopped green chiles, drained

½ cup mayonnaise

½ cup grated Parmesan cheese

1. Combine all ingredients in a medium-sized mixing bowl. Place in microwave-safe dish.

2. Microwave for 3–4 minutes on High, until hot and bubbly.

Serving suggestion: Serve with cut-up fresh vegetables.

- Calories 138
- Fat 13
- Sodium 265
- Carbs 3
- Sugar 3
- Protein 1

Spinach and Artichoke Dip

Michele Ruvola
Vestal, NY

Makes 10–12 servings
Prep. Time: 5 minutes
Cooking Time: 4 minutes
Setting: Manual
Pressure: High
Release: Manual

8 oz. cream cheese

10-oz. box frozen spinach

½ cup chicken bone broth

14-oz. can artichoke hearts, drained

½ cup sour cream

½ cup mayonnaise

3 cloves garlic, minced

1 tsp. onion powder

16 oz. shredded Parmesan cheese

8 oz. shredded mozzarella cheese

1. Put all ingredients in the inner pot of the Instant Pot, except the Parmesan cheese and the mozzarella cheese.

2. Secure the lid and set vent to sealing. Place on Manual high pressure for 4 minutes.

3. Do a quick release of steam.

4. Immediately stir in the cheeses.

- Calories 288
- Fat 18
- Sodium 1007
- Carbs 15
- Sugar 3
- Protein 19

Garlicky Spinach Artichoke Dip

Hope Comerford
Clinton Township, MI

Makes 6–8 servings
Prep. Time: 10 minutes
Cooking Time: 4 hours
Ideal slow-cooker size: 3-qt.

9 oz. frozen chopped spinach, thawed, drained

14-oz. can quartered artichoke hearts, drained

½ cup plain Greek yogurt

4 oz. cream cheese, room temperature

8 cloves garlic, minced

1 cup shredded mozzarella cheese

½ cup shredded Parmesan cheese

¼ tsp. black pepper

½ tsp. kosher salt

1. Spray crock with nonstick spray.

2. Place all ingredients into crock and stir to combine well.

3. Cover and cook on Low for 4 hours.

Serving suggestion: Serve with strips of bell peppers.

- Calories 122
- Fat 7
- Sodium 394
- Carbs 7
- Sugar 2
- Protein 9

Creamy Spinach Dip

Jessica Stoner
Arlington, OH

Makes 10–12 servings
Prep. Time: 10–15 minutes
Cooking Time: 5 minutes
Setting: Bean/Chili
Pressure: High
Release: Manual

8 oz. cream cheese

1 cup sour cream

½ cup finely chopped onion

½ cup vegetable broth

5 cloves garlic, minced

½ tsp. salt

¼ tsp. black pepper

10-oz. box frozen spinach

12 oz. shredded Monterey Jack cheese

12 oz. shredded Parmesan cheese

1. Add cream cheese, sour cream, onion, vegetable broth, garlic, salt, pepper, and spinach to the inner pot of the Instant Pot.

2. Secure lid, make sure vent is set to sealing, and set to the Bean/Chili setting on high pressure for 5 minutes.

3. When done, do a manual release.

4. Add the cheeses and mix well until creamy and well combined.

- Calories 274
- Fat 18
- Sodium 918
- Carbs 10
- Sugar 3
- Protein 19

Bacon Spinach Dip

Amy Bauer
New Ulm, MN

Makes 8–10 servings
Prep. Time: 15 minutes
Cooking Time: 1–2 hours
Ideal slow-cooker size: 3-qt.

½ lb. bacon, diced

1 lb. cheddar cheese, shredded

8-oz. pkg. cream cheese, room temperature

10-oz. pkg. frozen chopped spinach, thawed, drained

14½-oz. can Ro✳Tel tomatoes and green chiles, undrained

1. Fry bacon in skillet until crisp. Remove bacon and set aside on a paper towel. Transfer bacon drippings to slow cooker.

2. Add rest of ingredients (except bacon pieces) to crock and stir.

3. Cover and cook on Low 2 hours, or until cheese is melted.

4. Just before serving, stir in the bacon pieces.

Serving suggestion: Serve with carrot and celery sticks.

- Calories 384
- Fat 31
- Sodium 947
- Carbs 6
- Sugar 2
- Protein 21

Bacon Cheddar Dip

Arlene Snyder
Millerstown, PA

Makes 15 servings
Prep. Time: 10–15 minutes
Cooking Time: 1½–2 hours
Ideal slow-cooker size: 4-qt.

2 8-oz. pkgs. cream cheese, softened

2 cups sour cream

1 lb. bacon, fried and crumbled

4 cups shredded cheddar cheese, *divided*

White corn chips

1. In a mixing bowl, beat cream cheese and sour cream until smooth.

2. Fold in bacon and 3 cups cheddar cheese.

3. Place mixture in slow cooker and sprinkle with remaining cheese.

4. Cover and cook on Low 1½–2 hours, or until heated through.

5. Serve with white corn chips.

Tips:
1. *Save a few bacon crumbs to sprinkle on top.*
2. *For a spicier version, stir in some fresh herbs, or some chopped chiles, in Step 2.*

- Calories 420
- Fat 36
- Sodium 808
- Carbs 4
- Sugar 2
- Protein 20

Ham Dip

John D. Allen
Rye, CO

Makes 4 cups (8–10 servings)
Prep. Time: 15 minutes
Chilling Time: 8 hours, or overnight

8 oz. finely chopped cooked ham

1½ cups mayonnaise

1⅓ cups sour cream

2 Tbsp. chopped onion

2 Tbsp. chopped fresh parsley

2 tsp. dill seed

2 tsp. Beau Monde seasoning

1. Combine all ingredients thoroughly.

2. Refrigerate for 8 hours, or overnight.

Serving suggestion: Serve with crackers, chips, or cocktail rye bread.

- Calories 316
- Fat 32
- Sodium 567
- Carbs 2
- Sugar 1
- Protein 6

Buffalo Chicken Dip

Amy Troyer
Garden Gove, IA

Makes 4–5 servings
Prep. Time: 10 minutes
Cooking Time: 2–3 hours
Ideal slow-cooker size: 2-qt.

8-oz. pkg. cream cheese

1 cup keto-friendly blue cheese or ranch dressing

½ cup Frank's RedHot Original Cayenne Pepper Sauce

1 cup mozzarella cheese, or your favorite cheese

2 cups cooked and shredded chicken

1. Combine all ingredients in slow cooker.

2. Cover and cook on Low for 2–3 hours.

Serving suggestion: Serve with cauliflower or bell pepper slices for dipping.

- Calories 563
- Fat 49
- Sodium 1238
- Carbs 5
- Sugar 4
- Protein 25

Crab Dip

Susan J. Heil
Strasburg, PA

Makes about 2 cups
Prep. Time: 10 minutes
Baking Time: 15–20 minutes

8-oz. pkg. cream cheese, softened

2 Tbsp. whole milk

¼ cup minced onion

1 Tbsp. Worcestershire sauce

14-oz. can crabmeat, drained and picked through for shells

1. Beat cream cheese and milk together in a medium-sized mixing bowl until smooth.

2. Stir in onion and Worcestershire sauce until well blended.

3. Fold in crabmeat.

4. Place dip in an ovenproof serving dish.

5. Bake at 350°F for 15–20 minutes, or until bubbly.

- Calories 140
- Fat 10
- Sodium 339
- Carbs 3
- Sugar 2
- Protein 10

Dilly Crab Dip

Joyce M. Shackelford
Green Bay, WI

Makes 1½ cups
Prep. Time: 30 minutes
Chilling Time: 2–8 hours

½ cup mayonnaise

½ cup sour cream

1 cup flaked crabmeat, *divided*

1 tsp. dried dill weed

2 tsp. finely chopped onion or green onion

½ tsp. finely shredded lime peel

1 tsp. lime juice

dash Frank's RedHot Original Cayenne Pepper Sauce

dash ground red pepper, *optional*

salt and pepper, to taste

1. Stir together mayonnaise, sour cream, ⅔ cup crabmeat, dill weed, onion, lime peel, lime juice, hot pepper sauce, and red pepper. Season with salt and pepper, to taste.

2. Refrigerate for 2 hours, or overnight.

3. Just before serving, sprinkle with reserved crabmeat.

Serving suggestion: Serve with warm or chilled artichoke.

- Calories 185
- Fat 17
- Sodium 295
- Carbs 1
- Sugar 1
- Protein 7

Smoked Salmon Dip

Lois Ostrander
Lebanon, PA

Makes 2 cups
Prep. Time: 10 minutes
Chilling Time: 2–3 hours

2 6-oz. cans smoked salmon

8-oz. pkg. cream cheese, softened

⅓ cup ground walnuts or parsley, *optional*

1. Mix salmon and cream cheese in a medium-sized mixing bowl, using a fork.

2. Chill for an hour or so until mixture becomes stiff enough to handle.

3. Shape into a ball. Return to mixing bowl and fridge. Let stand for another hour or so to blend flavors.

4. Just before serving, roll in ground nuts or finely chopped parsley, if you wish.

- Calories 149
- Fat 12
- Sodium 939
- Carbs 2
- Sugar 1
- Protein 10

Shrimp Dip

Joyce M. Shackelford
Green Bay, WI

Makes 1½ cups (9 2-Tbsp.servings)
Prep. Time: 15 minutes
Chilling Time: 1 hour

3-oz. pkg. Neufchâtel cream cheese, softened

1 cup sour cream

2 tsp. lemon juice

1 oz. keto-friendly Italian Dressing Mix (see recipe on pg. 326)

2 Tbsp. green pepper, finely chopped

½ cup shrimp, finely chopped

1. Blend all ingredients together.

2. Chill at least 1 hour.

- Calories 76
- Fat 6
- Sodium 440
- Carbs 4
- Sugar 1
- Protein 3

Cheesy New Orleans Shrimp Dip

Kelly Amos
Pittsboro, NC

Makes 3–4 cups (24 servings)
Prep. Time: 20–30 minutes
Cooking Time: 1 hour
Ideal slow-cooker size: 2-qt.

1 slice bacon

3 medium-sized onions, chopped

1 clove garlic, minced

4 jumbo shrimp, peeled and deveined

1 medium-sized tomato, peeled and chopped

3 cups Monterey Jack cheese, shredded

4 drops Frank's RedHot Original Cayenne Pepper Sauce

⅛ tsp. cayenne pepper

dash black pepper

1. Cook bacon until crisp. Drain on paper towel. Cut fine.

2. Sauté onions and garlic in bacon drippings. Drain on paper towel.

3. Coarsely chop shrimp.

4. Combine all ingredients in slow cooker.

5. Cover. Cook on Low 1 hour, or until cheese is melted. Thin with milk if too thick.

- Calories 63
- Fat 5
- Sodium 120
- Carbs 1
- Sugar 1
- Protein 4

Seafood Dip

Joan Rosenberger
Stephens City, VA

Makes 24 servings (2 Tbsp. each)
Prep. Time: 5–10 minutes
Cooking Time: 3 hours
Ideal slow-cooker size: 3½-qt.

10-oz. pkg. cream cheese

6-oz. can lump crabmeat

2 Tbsp. onion, finely chopped

4–5 drops Frank's RedHot Original Cayenne Pepper Sauce

½ cup walnuts, finely chopped

1 tsp. paprika

1. Blend all ingredients except nuts and paprika until well mixed.

2. Spread in slow cooker. Sprinkle with nuts and paprika.

3. Cook on Low 3 hours.

Serving suggestion: Stuff this dip inside celery sticks or serve alongside celery and bell pepper slices.

- Calories 55
- Fat 5
- Sodium 45
- Carbs 1
- Sugar 1
- Protein 2

Zesty Pizza Dip

Hope Comerford
Clinton Township, MI

Makes 14 servings
Prep. Time: 15 minutes
Cooking Time: 5–6 hours
Ideal slow-cooker size: 3½- or 4-qt.

1 lb. bulk turkey sausage

⅔ cup chopped onion

4 cloves garlic, minced

2 15-oz. cans low-sodium tomato sauce

14½-oz. can diced tomatoes

6-oz. can low-sodium tomato paste

1 Tbsp. dried oregano

1 Tbsp. dried basil

¾ tsp. crushed red pepper

7 drops liquid stevia

½ cup sliced black olives

1. In a large skillet, brown the turkey sausage, onion, and garlic. Drain the grease.

2. In the crock, combine all the remaining ingredients except the olives.

3. Cover and cook on Low for 5–6 hours. Just before serving, stir in the olives.

Serving suggestion: Serve with a rainbow of bell pepper slices to dip with. Garnish with microgreens or chopped parsley.

- Calories 115
- Fat 5
- Sodium 758
- Carbs 10
- Sugar 5
- Protein 7

Dill, Feta, and Garlic Cream Cheese Spread

Kathleen Rogge
Alexandria, IN

Makes about 3 cups
Prep. Time: 15 minutes
Chilling Time: 4 or more hours

2 8-oz. pkgs. cream cheese, softened

8-oz. pkg. feta cheese, crumbled

3 cloves garlic, peeled and minced

2 Tbsp. chopped fresh dill, or 2 tsp. dried dill

1. In a medium bowl, thoroughly blend ingredients with electric mixer.

2. Cover and chill for at least 4 hours.

3. Serve in a dish alongside firm, raw veggies.

- Calories 163
- Fat 15
- Sodium 252
- Carbs 3
- Sugar 1
- Protein 4

Roasted Pepper and Artichoke Spread

Sherril Bieberly
Sauna, KS

Makes 3 cups (about 12 servings)
Prep. Time: 10 minutes
Cooking Time: 1 hour
Ideal slow-cooker size: 1- to 1½-qt.

1 cup grated Parmesan cheese

½ cup mayonnaise

8-oz. pkg. cream cheese, softened

1 clove garlic, minced

14-oz. can artichoke hearts, drained and chopped finely

⅓ cup finely chopped roasted red bell peppers (from 7¼-oz. jar)

1. Combine Parmesan cheese, mayonnaise, cream cheese, and garlic in food processor. Process until smooth. Place mixture in slow cooker.

2. Add artichoke hearts and roasted peppers. Stir well.

3. Cover. Cook on Low 1 hour. Stir again.

Serving suggestion: Serve as a spread for fresh, cut-up vegetables.

- Calories 162
- Fat 15
- Sodium 242
- Carbs 3
- Sugar 1
- Protein 3

Warm Broccoli Cheese Spread

Mary Ann Bowman
East Earl, PA

Makes 3½ cups
Prep. Time: 10 minutes
Baking Time: 25 minutes

8-oz. pkg. cream cheese, cubed, at room temperature

8 oz. sour cream

1 oz. dry keto-friendly Italian Dressing Mix (see recipe on pg. 326)

10-oz. pkg. frozen chopped broccoli, thawed, drained, and patted dry

2 cups shredded cheddar cheese, *divided*

1. In a large mixing bowl, stir together cream cheese, sour cream, and salad dressing mix until blended.

2. Fold in broccoli and 1½ cups cheese.

3. Spoon into shallow 1-qt. baking dish coated with non-stick cooking spray.

4. Bake uncovered for 20 minutes at 350°F. Remove from oven and sprinkle with remaining cheese.

5. Bake 5 minutes longer, or until cheese is melted.

- Calories 161
- Fat 14
- Sodium 188
- Carbs 4
- Sugar 2
- Protein 6

Olive Spread

Susan Kasting
Jenks, OK

Makes 3 cups
Prep. Time: 10–15 minutes

2 8-oz. pkgs. cream cheese, softened

16-oz. can black olives, finely chopped

½ cup green olives, finely chopped

1-2 cloves garlic, minced

2 Tbsp. lemon juice

¾ cup chopped parsley, *optional*

1. In a large mixing bowl, blend all ingredients together. Push into ball shape in the bowl, cover, and refrigerate.

2. When firm, shape with your hands into two balls.

3. If you wish, roll in chopped parsley.

4. Wrap and refrigerate until ready to use.

Serving suggestion: Serve with cut-up fresh vegetables.

- Calories 190
- Fat 19
- Sodium 543
- Carbs 5
- Sugar 2
- Protein 3

Cheese and Olive Spread

Suzanne Yoder
Gap, PA

Makes 2 cups (1 Tbsp. per serving)
Prep. Time: 15 minutes
Chilling Time: 1 hour

8-oz. pkg. shredded mild cheddar cheese

8 oz. Neufchâtel cream cheese, softened

½ cup mayonnaise

¼ cup stuffed green olives, chopped

¼ cup chopped green onions

2 Tbsp. lemon juice

¼ tsp. ground red pepper, or to taste

1. Mix together all ingredients.

2. Refrigerate at least an hour.

- Calories 51
- Fat 17
- Sodium 267
- Carbs 2
- Sugar 1
- Protein 6

Tuna Cheese Spread

Elizabeth Yutzy
Wauseon, OH

Makes 15 servings (about 1½ Tbsp. per serving)
Prep. Time: 10 minutes
Chilling Time: 1 hour or more

4 Tbsp. (½ stick) butter, softened

8-oz. pkg. cream cheese

6-oz. can tuna, drained

1 onion, minced

½ tsp. Worcestershire sauce

⅛ tsp. dried thyme

⅛ tsp. dried basil

⅛ tsp. dried marjoram

pinch dried parsley

1. Cream together butter and cream cheese. Add tuna and all other ingredients and mix well.

2. Chill at least an hour.

- Calories 110
- Fat 9
- Sodium 97
- Carbs 1
- Sugar 1
- Protein 4

Crab Spread

Jeanette Oberholtzer
Manheim, PA

Makes 8 servings
Prep. Time: 20 minutes
Cooking Time: 4 hours
Ideal slow-cooker size: 1- to 3-qt.

½ cup mayonnaise

8 oz. cream cheese, softened

2 Tbsp. water

3–4 drops liquid stevia

1 onion, minced

1 lb. lump crabmeat, picked over to remove cartilage and shell bits

1. Mix mayonnaise, cheese, water, and stevia in medium-sized bowl until blended.

2. Stir in onion, mixing well. Gently stir in crabmeat.

3. Place in slow cooker, cover, and cook on Low for 4 hours.

4. Dip will hold for 2 hours. Stir occasionally.

- Calories 237
- Fat 20
- Sodium 437
- Carbs 3
- Sugar 2
- Protein 11

Italiano Spread

Nanci Keatley
Salem, OR

Makes 24 servings
Prep. Time: 20–30 minutes
Cooking Time: 2–3 hours
Ideal slow-cooker size: 2-qt.

2 8-oz. pkgs. cream cheese, softened

½ cup prepared pesto

3 medium fresh tomatoes, chopped

½ cup fresh basil, chopped

1 cup mozzarella cheese, shredded

½ cup Parmesan cheese, shredded

1. Spread cream cheese on bottom of slow cooker.

2. Spread pesto over cream cheese.

3. Add layer of chopped tomatoes over cream cheese and pesto.

4. Sprinkle with chopped basil.

5. Sprinkle cheeses on top of basil.

6. Cook on Low 2–3 hours, or until cheese is melted.

- Calories 110
- Fat 10
- Sodium 168
- Carbs 2
- Sugar 1
- Protein 3

Pesto Tomato Spread

Hope Comerford
Clinton Township, MI

Makes 24 servings
Prep. Time: 20 minutes
Cooking Time: 2–3 hours
Ideal slow-cooker size: 2-qt.

2 8-oz. pkgs. cream cheese, room temperature

⅔ cup prepared pesto

3 medium tomatoes, sliced

½ cup sliced Kalamata olives

½ cup chopped fresh basil

1 cup shredded Italian cheese blend

½ cup grated Parmesan cheese

2 tsp. Italian seasoning

1. Place cream cheese in bottom of lightly greased slow cooker. Push gently to make an even layer.

2. Layer rest of ingredients on top in order given, finished with the Italian seasoning sprinkled over the top.

3. Cover and cook on Low for 2–3 hours until cheese is melted and spread is hot throughout.

Serving suggestion: Serve stuffed into celery sticks, or dipped with bell pepper slices.

- Calories 236
- Fat 22
- Sodium 407
- Carbs 5
- Sugar 3
- Protein 6

Herby Cheese Ball

Jenelle Miller
Marion, SD

Makes 2½–3 cups
Prep. Time: 10 minutes
Chilling Time: 2–3 hours

2 8-oz. pkgs. cream cheese, softened

3½ cups shredded sharp cheddar cheese, softened

1-oz. pkg. dry keto-friendly ranch dressing mix

1 cup finely chopped pecans

1. Using a heavy-duty mixer and a large bowl, beat together first 3 ingredients until thoroughly blended. Push mixture together in bowl, cover, and refrigerate.

2. After chilling for 2–3 hours to firm up the cheese, form into 2 balls with your hands.

3. Roll balls in pecans to coat all surfaces.

4. Wrap in plastic wrap. Refrigerate until ready to use.

5. Serve with crispy bell pepper slices.

- Calories 68
- Fat 6
- Sodium 86
- Carbs 1
- Sugar 0
- Protein 2

Zesty Cheese Ball

Mary Ann Bowman
East Earl, PA

Makes 3½ cups
Prep. Time: 10 minutes
Chilling Time: 2–3 hours

4 oz. sharp cheese, grated and softened

3 8-oz. pkgs. cream cheese, softened

2 tsp. Worcestershire sauce

¼ tsp. onion salt

¾–1 cup finely chopped pecans

1. Mix first 4 ingredients together in a large mixing bowl. When thoroughly blended, push ingredients together, cover, and refrigerate.

2. After mixture has firmed up, about 2–3 hours, shape into one or two balls with your hands.

3. Roll ball(s) in pecans. Wrap well and refrigerate until ready to use.

- Calories 75
- Fat 7
- Sodium 72
- Carbs 1
- Sugar 0
- Protein 2

Jalapeño Poppers

Amanda Gross
Souderton, PA

Makes 10 servings
Prep. Time: 10 minutes
Cooking Time: 2–3 hours
Ideal slow-cooker size: 5½-qt.

10 medium jalapeños

4 oz. cream cheese, room temperature

¼ cup sour cream, room temperature

9 slices bacon, cooked and crumbled

¼ tsp. garlic salt

⅓ cup water

1. Cut off the tops and remove seeds and membranes to hollow out jalapeños.

2. In a bowl, mix together cream cheese, sour cream, bacon, and garlic salt.

3. Gently stuff cheese mixture into peppers.

4. Put water in the bottom of the slow cooker. Place peppers on top.

5. Cover and cook on High 2–3 hours, until peppers look slightly wrinkly and wilted.

Tip: Wear gloves to prepare the jalapeños if you are sensitive to the burning oils in hot peppers.

- Calories 45
- Fat 3
- Sodium 151
- Carbs 2
- Sugar 1
- Protein 4

Stuffed Jalapeños

Barbara Walker
Sturgis, SD

Makes 12 servings
Prep. Time: 20 minutes
Baking Time: 45 minutes

12 fresh jalapeño peppers, halved lengthwise and seeded

8-oz. pkg. cream cheese, softened

12 slices bacon

1. Preheat oven to 400°F.

2. Stuff each pepper half with cream cheese.

3. Wrap half a slice of bacon around each stuffed pepper.

4. Place in single layer on baking sheet.

5. Bake for 45 minutes, or until bacon is done.

Tip: Use rubber gloves to halve and seed peppers. Keep hands away from your face; the liquid and seeds from the peppers can burn your eyes.

- Calories 113
- Fat 10
- Sodium 244
- Carbs 2
- Sugar 1
- Protein 4

Chicken Lettuce Wraps

Hope Comerford
Clinton Township, MI

Makes about 12 wraps
Prep. Time: 15 minutes
Cooking Time: 2¼–3¼ hours
Ideal slow-cooker size: 5- or 7-qt.

2 lbs. ground chicken, browned

4 cloves garlic, minced

½ cup minced sweet yellow onion

4 Tbsp. liquid aminos

1 Tbsp. natural crunchy peanut butter (make sure it's no-sugar-added)

1 tsp. rice wine vinegar

1 tsp. sesame oil

¼ tsp. kosher salt

¼ tsp. red pepper flakes

¼ tsp. black pepper

3 green onions, sliced

8-oz. can sliced water chestnuts, drained, rinsed, chopped

12 good-sized pieces of iceberg lettuce, rinsed and patted dry

1. In the crock, combine the ground chicken, garlic, yellow onion, liquid aminos, peanut butter, vinegar, sesame oil, salt, red pepper flakes, and black pepper.

2. Cover and cook on Low for 2–3 hours.

3. Add in the green onions and water chestnuts. Cover and cook for an additional 10–15 minutes.

4. Serve a good spoonful on each piece of iceberg lettuce.

Serving Suggestion: Garnish with diced red bell pepper and diced green onion.

- Calories 143
- Fat 7
- Sodium 312
- Carbs 6
- Sugar 1
- Protein 15

Mini Eggplant Pizzas

Maryann Markano
Wilmington, DE

Makes 4 servings
Prep. Time: 20 minutes
Baking Time: 11–13 minutes

1 eggplant, 3-inch diameter

½ tsp. dried oregano

¼ tsp. dried basil

½ tsp. garlic powder

1 Tbsp. olive oil

⅛ tsp. black pepper

1 large ripe tomato, cut into 4 slices

¼ cup low-sodium, no-sugar-added pizza sauce

½ cup shredded mozzarella cheese

1. Preheat oven to 425°F.

2. Peel eggplant and cut into 4½-inch-thick slices.

3. Combine spices and set aside.

4. Brush both sides of eggplant slices with oil and season with pepper.

5. Arrange on baking sheet and bake until browned, about 8 minutes. Turn once during baking to brown both sides.

6. Place a tomato slice on each eggplant slice and sprinkle with spice mixture. Drizzle each slice with 1 Tbsp. pizza sauce.

7. Top with cheese and bake until cheese melts, about 3–5 minutes. Serve hot.

- Calories 104
- Fat 8
- Sodium 229
- Carbs 5
- Sugar 3
- Protein 4

Tomato-Zucchini Ratatouille

Barb Yoder
Angola, IN

SLOW COOKER

Makes about 3½ cups (about 13 servings)
Prep. Time: 20–30 minutes
Cooking Time: 7–8 hours
Ideal slow-cooker size: 4-qt.

1½ cups chopped onion

6-oz. can tomato paste

1 Tbsp. olive oil

2 cloves garlic, minced (1 tsp.)

1½ tsp. crushed dried basil

½ tsp. dried thyme

15-oz. can chopped low-sodium tomatoes, with juice drained but reserved

1 large zucchini, halved lengthwise and sliced thin

salt and pepper, to taste, *optional*

keto bread slices

1. Mix all ingredients in slow cooker, except bread.

2. Cover. Cook on Low 7–8 hours.

3. If mixture is stiffer than you wish, stir in some reserved tomato juice.

4. Serve hot or cold over toasted keto bread slices.

- Calories 35
- Fat 1
- Sodium 155
- Carbs 6
- Sugar 3
- Protein 1

Meatballs

Carol Eveleth
Cheyenne, WY

Makes 16 meatballs
Prep. Time: 10 minutes
Cooking Time: 20 minutes
Setting: Manual and Sauté
Pressure: Low
Release: Natural

2 lbs. ground beef

1½ cups chopped onions

1½ cups almond meal

2 tsp. salt

½ tsp. black pepper

2½ Tbsp. Worcestershire sauce

3 eggs

8 oz. low-sodium tomato sauce

1 cup water

3½ Tbsp. vinegar

1¼ Tbsp. Truvia brown sugar blend

2½ Tbsp. mustard

1 Tbsp. liquid smoke

2 Tbsp. olive oil

1. Combine ingredients in a medium bowl and mix thoroughly by hand.

2. Form into approximately 20 two-inch meatballs.

3. Coat the bottom of the Instant Pot inner pot with oil.

4. If you wish to brown the meatballs, turn on the Sauté function and brown on both sides or brown in a separate nonstick pan first.

5. Layer the browned or raw meatballs in the inner pot, leaving ½ inch of space between them. Don't press down.

6. Secure the lid and make sure vent is set to sealing.

7. Set the Instant Pot to Manual and select low pressure.

8. Set the cook time to 10 minutes.

9. Once the timer goes off, manually release the pressure.

10. Remove the lid and serve the meatballs.

Serving suggestion: Serve with keto-friendly barbecue sauce, if desired (see page 327)..

- Calories 293
- Fat 25
- Sodium 404
- Carbs 6
- Sugar 3
- Protein 12

Artichokes

Susan Yoder Graber
Eureka, IL

Makes 4 servings
Prep. Time: 10 minutes
Cooking Time: 2–10 hours
Ideal slow-cooker size: 4-qt.

4 artichokes

1 tsp. sea salt

2 Tbsp. lemon juice

1. Wash and trim artichokes by cutting off the stems flush with the bottoms of the artichokes and by cutting ¾–1 inch off the tops. Stand upright in slow cooker.

2. Mix together salt and lemon juice and pour over artichokes. Pour in water to cover ¾ of artichokes.

3. Cover. Cook on Low 8–10 hours or on High 2–4 hours.

Serving suggestion: Serve with melted butter. Pull off individual leaves and dip bottom of each into butter. Strip the individual leaf of the meaty portion at the bottom of each leaf.

- Calories 62
- Fat 0
- Sodium 600
- Carbs 14
- Sugar 1
- Protein 4

Ham Roll-Ups

Hope Comerford
Clinton Township, MI

Makes 80 roll-ups
Prep. Time: 20 minutes
Chilling Time: 2 hours or more

8-oz. pkg. spreadable cream cheese

8 thinly sliced slices of deli boiled ham

dried dill

8-10 green onions, ends trimmed

1. Spread cream cheese to edges of each ham slice and sprinkle lightly with dill.

2. Lay a green onion (or two if they're very thin) at the end of each slice.

3. Beginning at short end, roll up tightly. Cut each roll crosswise into 10 slices, making sure to trim the end of each piece of ham so you don't have green onion pieces hanging out.

4. Refrigerate on covered trays or platters for 2 hours or more, until ready to serve.

- Calories 30
- Fat 2
- Sodium 73
- Carbs 0.5
- Sugar 0
- Protein 2

Shrimp Mousse on Cucumbers

J. B. Miller
Indianapolis, IN

Makes 36 slices
Prep. Time: 10 minutes

3 green onions

3-oz. pkg. cream cheese, at room temperature

1 lb. cooked baby shrimp

3 Tbsp. fresh lemon juice

10-inch-long seedless cucumber, or 2 smaller
   cucumbers

1. Trim the green onions and cut into small pieces. Place them in a food processor and pulse several times to chop.

2. Add the cream cheese and mix. Add the shrimp and lemon juice and puree until creamy and smooth.

3. Slice the cucumber about ¼-inch thick and place on serving platter.

4. Spoon 1 Tbsp. mousse on top of each cucumber slice, or place mousse in pastry bag and pipe onto cucumbers.

- Calories 18
- Fat 1
- Sodium 79
- Carbs 1
- Sugar 0
- Protein 2

Shrimp Stuffed Celery

Lois W. Benner
Lancaster, PA

Makes 25 servings (1 Tbsp. spread and 1 5-inch celery stick each)
Prep. Time: 20 minutes
Cooking Time: 5 minutes
Cooling Time: 20 minutes
Chilling Time: 1 hour or longer

1 lb. fresh unshelled shrimp

3 cups boiling water

1 tsp. salt

¼ cup vinegar

dash pepper

3 oz. cream cheese, softened

1 Tbsp. grated onion

½ tsp. Worcestershire sauce

⅓ cup mayonnaise

½ tsp. horseradish

dash garlic salt, *optional*

25 stalks celery, each 5 inches long

cherry tomatoes or olives, *optional*

1. Rinse shrimp thoroughly. Cook shrimp for 5 minutes in boiling water to which has been added salt, vinegar, and pepper. Drain water. Cool shrimp, take off shells, and shred in blender.

2. Combine cream cheese, onion, Worcestershire sauce, mayonnaise, horseradish, garlic salt, and shredded shrimp. Mix well and chill at least an hour.

3. Fill celery stalks with shrimp mixture and arrange in an attractive manner on a platter. Add either cherry tomatoes or olives for additional color.

- Calories 52
- Fat 4
- Sodium 243
- Carbs 2
- Sugar 1
- Protein 3

Taco Appetizer Platter

Rachel Spicher Hershberger
Sarasota, FL

Makes 15 servings (about 3½ oz. per serving)
Prep. Time: 20 minutes
Cooking Time: 10 minutes

1 lb. ground beef

½ cup water

7 tsp. keto-friendly Taco Seasoning (see recipe
 on pg. 327)

2 8-oz. pkgs. cream cheese, softened

¼ cup whole milk

4-oz. can chopped green chiles, drained

2 medium tomatoes, seeded and chopped

1 cup chopped green onions

lettuce, *optional*

½ cup keto-friendly barbecue sauce (see Phyllis's
 Homemade Barbecue Sauce on pg. 327)

1 cup shredded cheddar cheese

1. In a skillet, cook beef over medium heat until no longer pink. Drain. Add water and taco seasoning; simmer for 5 minutes.

2. In a bowl, combine the cream cheese and milk; spread on 14-inch serving platter or pizza pan. Top with meat mixture. Sprinkle with chiles, tomatoes, and onions. Add lettuce, if desired.

3. Drizzle with barbecue sauce. Sprinkle with cheddar cheese.

- Calories 253
- Fat 22
- Sodium 378
- Carbs 5
- Sugar 2
- Protein 8

Lacy Parmesan Crisps

Gwendolyn P. Chapman
Gwinn, MI

Makes 6 servings
Prep. Time: 10 minutes
Baking Time: 7–10 minutes

3-oz. piece Parmesan cheese, grated

1. Put oven rack in middle position and preheat oven to 375°F. Line nonstick baking sheet with greased tinfoil or Silpat.

2. Arrange mounds (approximately 1 Tbsp. rounded) of cheese 3 inches apart. Flatten each mound lightly to form a 3-inch round.

3. Bake until golden, 7–10 minutes.

4. Transfer with spatula to rack. Cool 5 minutes before serving or storing.

- Calories 56
- Fat 4
- Sodium 195
- Carbs 0
- Sugar 0
- Protein 5

Instant Pot Hard-Boiled Eggs

Colleen Heatwole
Burton, MI

Makes 6–8 servings
Prep. Time: 10 minutes
Cooking Time: 5 minutes
Setting: Manual
Pressure: High
Release: Manual

1 cup water

6–8 eggs

1. Pour the water into the inner pot. Place the eggs in a steamer basket or rack that came with pot.

2. Close the lid and secure to the locking position. Be sure the vent is turned to sealing. Set for 5 minutes on Manual at high pressure. (It takes about 5 minutes for pressure to build and then 5 minutes to cook.)

3. Let pressure naturally release for 5 minutes, then do quick pressure release.

4. Place hot eggs into cool water to halt cooking process. You can peel cooled eggs immediately or refrigerate unpeeled.

- Calories 72
- Fat 5
- Sodium 71
- Carbs 0
- Sugar 0
- Protein 6

Hard-Boiled Eggs

Phyllis Good
Lancaster, PA

Makes 6 eggs (serving size is 1 egg)
Prep. Time: 30 minutes
Cooking Time: 20 minutes

6 eggs

To hard-boil eggs:

1. Place eggs in a single layer in a lidded pan.

2. Fill the pan with cold water to just cover the eggs.

3. Bring to a full boil over high heat, covered.

4. As soon as the water begins the full boil, immediately turn the heat down to low for a simmer. Allow to barely simmer for exactly 18 minutes.

5. Pour off hot water. Run cold water and/or ice over the eggs to quickly cool them.

- Calories 72
- Fat 5
- Sodium 71
- Carbs 0
- Sugar 0
- Protein 6

Traditional Eggs

Jan Mast
Lancaster, PA

Makes 6 servings
Prep. Time: 20 minutes

6 large eggs, hard-boiled and peeled

¼ cup plain yogurt or mayonnaise

1 Tbsp. onion, minced

1 tsp. dried parsley

1 tsp. lemon juice

1 tsp. prepared mustard

¼ tsp. salt

¼ tsp. Worcestershire sauce

⅛ tsp. pepper

paprika

olive slices or pimento pieces, for garnish, *optional*

1. Cut eggs in half lengthwise. Gently remove yolk sections into a bowl.

2. Discard two yolks. Mash remaining yolk sections together with a fork. Stir in remaining ingredients except the garnish with yolk mixture until smooth.

3. Fill empty egg whites. The filling will make a little mound in the egg white. Garnish, if desired.

4. Refrigerate.

- Calories 141
- Fat 12
- Sodium 212
- Carbs 1
- Sugar 1
- Protein 6

Tex-Mex Eggs

Jan Mast
Lancaster, PA

Makes 6 servings
Prep. Time: 20 minutes

6 large eggs, hard-boiled and peeled

¼ cup plain yogurt or mayonnaise

1 Tbsp. finely diced onion

1 tsp. lemon juice

1 tsp. prepared mustard

1 tsp. keto-friendly Taco Seasoning (see recipe on pg. 327)

¼ tsp. salt

⅛ tsp. pepper

paprika

black olive slices, for garnish, *optional*

1. Cut eggs in half lengthwise. Gently remove yolk sections into a bowl.

2. Discard two yolks. Mash remaining yolk sections together with a fork. Stir in remaining ingredients with yolk mixture until smooth.

3. Fill empty egg whites. The filling will make a little mound in the egg white. Garnish with olives, if desired.

4. Refrigerate.

- Calories 143
- Fat 12
- Sodium 245
- Carbs 1
- Sugar 1
- Protein 7

Horseradish Eggs

Anna Marie Albany
Broomall, PA

Makes 6 servings
Prep. Time: 20 minutes

6 large eggs, hard-boiled and peeled

¼ cup mayonnaise

1 or 2 Tbsp. horseradish

½ tsp. dill weed

¼ tsp. ground mustard

⅛ tsp. salt

dash pepper

dash paprika

1. Cut eggs in half lengthwise. Gently remove yolk sections into a bowl.

2. Discard two yolks. Mash remaining yolk sections together with a fork. Stir in remaining ingredients with yolk mixture until smooth.

3. Fill empty egg whites. The filling will make a little mound in the egg white.

4. Refrigerate.

- Calories 141
- Fat 12
- Sodium 220
- Carbs 1
- Sugar 1
- Protein 6

Grandma's Zippy Deviled Eggs

Nan Decker
Albuquerque, NM

Makes 6–12 servings
Prep. Time: 15 minutes
Cooking Time: 25 minutes

6 hard-boiled eggs, peeled

¼ tsp. salt

¼ tsp. pepper

½ tsp. dry mustard

½ tsp. cider vinegar

about 3 Tbsp. mayonnaise

½ stuffed green olive on top of each egg, *optional*

1. Cut hard-boiled eggs in halves.

2. Slip out yolks. Mash yolks with fork in a small mixing bowl.

3. Mix yolks with salt, pepper, mustard, vinegar, and mayonnaise.

4. Refill egg whites with egg yolk mixture, heaping it up lightly.

5. Add olive halves to egg tops, if desired.

- Calories 125
- Fat 11
- Sodium 195
- Carbs 1
- Sugar 0.5
- Protein 6

Salmon-Stuffed Eggs

Ruth C. Hancock
Earlsboro, OK

Makes 12 servings
Prep. Time: 15 minutes

12 eggs, hard-boiled and peeled

6-oz. can salmon, no salt added, drained and flaked

½ cup mayonnaise

1 Tbsp. finely chopped fresh dill weed

⅛ tsp. black pepper

1. Cut eggs in half lengthwise and remove yolks to medium bowl. Set aside egg whites. Reserve half of the yolks for another use.

2. Add salmon, mayonnaise, dill, and pepper to yolks. Mix until well combined.

3. Spoon or pipe salmon mixture back into egg whites.

4. Serve, or cover and chill until ready to serve.

- Calories 160
- Fat 13
- Sodium 174
- Carbs 1
- Sugar 0.5
- Protein 10

Chili Peanuts

Hope Comerford
Clinton Township, MI

Makes 5 cups nuts
Prep. Time: 5 minutes
Cooking Time: 2–2¾ hours
Ideal slow-cooker size: 3-qt.

¼ cup melted butter

2 12-oz. cans unsalted peanuts

2 tsp. chili powder

½ tsp. cumin

½ tsp. paprika

½ tsp. sea salt

½ tsp. dried oregano

½ tsp. garlic powder

⅛ tsp. black pepper

⅛ tsp. cayenne pepper

1. Pour butter over nuts in slow cooker.

2. Mix together all of the spices and sprinkle over the nuts in the slow cooker. Toss together.

3. Cover. Cook on Low 2–2½ hours. Turn to High. Remove lid and cook 10–15 minutes.

- Calories 225
- Fat 19
- Sodium 42
- Carbs 7
- Sugar 1
- Protein 8

Curried Almonds

Barbara Aston
Ashdown, AR

Makes 4 cups
Prep. Time: 5 minutes
Cooking Time: 3½–4½ hours
Ideal slow-cooker size: 3-qt.

4 Tbsp. (½ stick) butter

1 Tbsp. curry powder

½ tsp. sea salt

⅛ tsp. turmeric

⅛ tsp. paprika

⅛ tsp. onion powder

⅛ tsp. garlic powder

1 drop liquid stevia

1 lb. blanched almonds

1. Combine butter with curry powder, sea salt, turmeric, paprika, onion powder, garlic powder, and liquid stevia.

2. Pour over almonds in slow cooker. Mix to coat well.

3. Cover. Cook on Low 2–3 hours. Turn to High. Uncover cooker and cook 1–1½ hours.

4. Serve warm or at room temperature.

- Calories 155
- Fat 14
- Sodium 44
- Carbs 4
- Sugar 1
- Protein 5

KETO TIP
If you're trying to lose weight, try intermittent fasting, which will help your body to burn fat faster. There are many ways to do this, but the simplest may be to skip breakfast occasionally. Check with your doctor first to make sure fasting is safe for you; everyone's body is different.

Cheddar-Ham Oven Omelet, page 14

Fresh Veggie and Herb Omelette, page 12

Crustless Spinach Quiche, page 20

Breakfast Bake, page 27

Cooked Salsa, page 43

French Onion Dip, page 48

Spinach and Artichoke Dip, page 52

Zesty Pizza Dip, page 59

Soups, Stews & Chilis

Soups

Broccoli-Cheese Soup

Hope Comerford
Clinton Township, MI

Makes 8 servings
Prep. Time: 20 minutes
Cooking Time: 5–6 hours
Ideal slow-cooker size: 4-qt.

2 16-oz. pkgs. frozen chopped broccoli

2¾ cups heavy cream

12-oz. can evaporated milk

½ cup chicken bone broth

¼ cup finely chopped onion

2 Tbsp. butter

1 Tbsp. Italian seasoning

¼ tsp. onion powder

¼ tsp. pepper

2 cups cheddar cheese

1. Combine all ingredients in the crock except the cheddar cheese, and stir to combine.

2. Cover. Cook on Low 5–6 hours.

3. Stir in the cheese and let cook another hour, stirring every 20 minutes or so.

- Calories 450
- Fat 40
- Sodium 289
- Carbs 12
- Sugar 7
- Protein 13

Broccoli Soup

Carolyn Snader
Ephrata, PA

Joyce Nolt
Richland, PA

Makes 4 servings
Prep. Time: 15–20 minutes
Cooking Time: 12 minutes

1 lb. (about 5 cups) chopped fresh, or frozen, broccoli

½ cup chopped onion

14½-oz. can chicken bone broth, or vegetable broth

12-oz. can evaporated milk

2 tsp. konjac flour

½ cup grated cheddar cheese

1. In a good-sized stockpot, cook broccoli and onion in chicken broth, 5–10 minutes.

2. Carefully puree half of mixture in blender.

3. Stir back into remaining broccoli in stockpot along with the evaporated milk.

4. Sprinkle the konjac flour into the soup and whisk until smooth.

5. Cover and simmer 2 minutes more.

6. Top each individual serving with 2 Tbsp. grated cheese.

Note: If desired thickness is not reached, you can add ½ tsp. more at a time of the konjac flour until it is the thickness you would like.

- Calories 232
- Fat 12
- Sodium 388
- Carbs 18
- Sugar 11
- Protein 15

Three-Cheese Broccoli Soup

Deb Kepiro
Strasburg, PA

Makes 4 servings
Prep. Time: 20 minutes
Cooking Time: 4–9 hours
Ideal slow-cooker size: 5-qt.

4 cups vegetable broth

2 cups whole milk

2 10-oz. bags frozen broccoli florets

½ cup very finely minced white onion

½ tsp. black pepper

½ tsp. kosher salt

½ tsp. nutmeg

3 cups shredded cheese, preferably 1 cup each of Jarlsberg, Gruyère, and cheddar, or cheeses of your choice

1. Mix broth, milk, broccoli, onion, pepper, salt and nutmeg together in slow cooker.

2. Cook on Low for 7–9 hours, or on High for 4–6 hours. The soup is done when the onions and broccoli are cooked as tender as you like them.

3. Twenty minutes or so before serving, stir in the cheese. The cheese will be stringy and will stick to the broccoli florets—that's okay!

- Calories 448
- Fat 31
- Sodium 1521
- Carbs 19
- Sugar 8
- Protein 26

Broccoli Rabe and Sausage Soup

Carlene Horne
Bedford, NH

Makes 5 servings
Prep. Time: 15 minutes
Cooking Time: 15 minutes

1 Tbsp. olive oil

1 onion, chopped

1 lb. lean fresh Italian turkey sausage, casing removed, sliced

5 cups chopped broccoli rabe, about 1 bunch

1 qt. chicken bone broth

1 cup water

1. Heat olive oil in a soup pot.

2. Add onion and sausage and sauté until tender.

3. Add broccoli rabe and sauté a few more minutes.

4. Pour broth and water into pan; bring to simmer.

Variation: Substitute Swiss chard or spinach for the broccoli rabe.

- Calories 258
- Fat 15
- Sodium 989
- Carbs 8
- Sugar 2
- Protein 23

Chicken Cheddar Broccoli Soup

Maria Shevlin
Sicklerville, NJ

Makes 4-6 servings
Prep. Time: 15 minutes
Cooking Time: 15 minutes
Setting: Manual and Sauté
Pressure: High
Release: Manual

1 lb. raw chicken breast, thinly chopped or sliced

1 lb. fresh broccoli, chopped

½ cup chopped onion

2 cloves garlic, minced

1 cup shredded zucchini

½ cup finely chopped celery

¼ cup finely chopped red bell pepper

3 cups chicken bone broth

½ tsp. salt

¼ tsp. black pepper

½ tsp. garlic powder

1 tsp. parsley flakes

pinch red pepper flakes

2 cups heavy cream

8 oz. freshly shredded cheddar cheese

2 Tbsp. Frank's RedHot Original Cayenne Pepper Sauce

1. Place chicken, broccoli, chopped onion, garlic, zucchini, celery, bell pepper, chicken broth, and seasonings in the pot and stir to mix.

2. Secure the lid and make sure vent is at sealing. Place on Manual at high pressure for 15 minutes.

3. Manually release the pressure when cook time us up, remove lid, and stir in heavy cream.

4. Place pot on sauté setting until it all comes to a low boil, approximately 5 minutes.

5. Stir in cheese and the hot sauce.

6. Turn off the pot as soon as you add the cheese and give it a stir.

7. Continue to stir until the cheese is melted.

Serving suggestion: Serve it up with slice or two of keto garlic bread or bread of your choice.

- Calories 489
- Fat 38
- Sodium 696
- Carbs 11
- Sugar 5
- Protein 29

Quickie French Onion Soup

Mary Puskar
Forest Hill, MD

Makes 6–8 servings
Prep. Time: 5–10 minutes
Cooking Time: 1 hour

4 Tbsp. (½ stick) butter

3–4 good-sized onions (enough to make 5 cups sliced onions)

6 cups beef bone broth

3 tsp. konjac flour

2 cups grated mozzarella cheese, *optional*

1. Melt butter in a large saucepan.

2. Meanwhile, slice onions.

3. Sauté onions in butter. After they become tender, continue cooking over low heat so that they brown and deepen in flavor, up to 30 minutes.

4. Stir in broth.

5. Sprinkle the konjac flour over the soup and whisk until smooth. Cover.

6. Heat to boiling and simmer 20 minutes.

7. Ladle into individual serving bowls.

8. Top each with grated cheese if you wish.

- Calories 176
- Fat 13
- Sodium 607
- Carbs 7
- Sugar 3
- Protein 10

Onion Soup

Lucille Amos
Greensboro, NC SLOW COOKER

Makes 10 servings
Prep. Time: 30 minutes
Cooking Time: 4–5 hours
Ideal slow-cooker size: 4- to 5-qt.

6 large onions

8 Tbsp. (1 stick) butter

8 cups beef bone broth

1½ tsp. liquid aminos

pepper, to taste

shredded mozzarella cheese and Parmesan cheese

1. In a large skillet or saucepan, sauté onions in butter until tender. Do not brown. Transfer to slow cooker.

2. Add broth, liquid aminos, and pepper.

3. Cover. Cook on Low 4–5 hours or until onions are very tender.

4. Top each serving with cheese.

- Calories 191
- Fat 14
- Sodium 633
- Carbs 7
- Sugar 3
- Protein 9

Tomato Basil Soup

Janet Melvin
Cincinnati, OH SLOW COOKER

Makes 12 servings
Prep. Time: 15 minutes
Cooking Time: 3½ hours
Ideal slow-cooker size: 4-qt.

½ cup very finely diced onion

2 cloves garlic, minced

2 cups low-sodium vegetable stock

2 28-oz. cans crushed tomatoes

¼ cup chopped fresh basil, plus more for garnish

1 Tbsp. salt

½ tsp. pepper

1 cup heavy cream at room temperature

1.   Combine onion, garlic, stock, tomatoes, basil, salt, and pepper in slow cooker.

2.   Cover and cook on High for 3 hours. May puree soup at this point if you wish for a totally smooth soup.

3.   Stir in heavy cream and cook an additional 30 minutes on Low.

4.   Garnish each serving with a few ribbons of fresh basil.

- Calories 115
- Fat 7
- Sodium 743
- Carbs 11
- Sugar 6
- Protein 2

Flavorful Tomato Soup

Shari Ladd
Hudson, MI

Makes 4 servings
Prep. Time: 10 minutes
Cooking Time: 20 minutes

2 Tbsp. chopped onion

1 Tbsp. extra-virgin olive oil

2 tsp. sugar

½ tsp. pepper

¼ tsp. dried basil

½ tsp. dried oregano

¼ tsp. dried thyme

1 qt. stewed tomatoes, no salt added, undrained

2 cups whole milk

1 tsp. konjac flour

1.   Sauté onion in oil in stockpot.

2.   Stir in seasonings.

3.   Stir in stewed tomatoes, stirring constantly. Bring to a boil and boil 1 minute.

4.   Add 2 cups milk. Stir well.

5.   Sprinkle in the konjac flour and whisk until smooth.

6.   Simmer 10 minutes but do not boil.

- Calories 200
- Fat 10
- Sodium 1952
- Carbs 22
- Sugar 11
- Protein 6

Tomato Basil Bisque

Betty Detweiler
Centreville, MI

Makes 6–8 servings
Prep. Time: 10 minutes
Cooking Time: 5–8 hours
Ideal slow-cooker size: 5-qt.

1-qt. can tomato juice

1-qt. can puréed tomatoes

2 14-oz. cans diced tomatoes with garlic, onion, and basil

1 Tbsp. dried basil

4 Tbsp. (½ stick) butter

2 Tbsp. minced onion

pepper, to taste

2 cups heavy cream

1. Combine juice, puréed tomatoes, diced tomatoes, basil, butter, onion, and pepper in slow cooker.

2. Cover. Cook on High for 5 hours or on Low for 8 hours.

3. Add heavy cream. Stir. Reheat on High if you wish, but do not allow to boil.

- Calories 256
- Fat 22
- Sodium 1243
- Carbs 12
- Sugar 6
- Protein 3

Tomato Mushroom Soup

D. Fern Ruth
Chalfont, PA

Makes 6 servings (¾ cup each)
Prep. Time: 15 minutes
Cooking Time: 30 minutes

2 cups sliced fresh mushrooms

⅓ cup chopped onion

2 cloves garlic, minced

4 Tbsp. (½ stick) butter

2½ cups chicken bone broth

14½-oz. can diced tomatoes, undrained

14½-oz. can no-salt-added diced tomatoes, undrained

4 Tbsp. chopped fresh basil leaves, or 1½ Tbsp. dried basil, plus more for garnish

15 drops liquid stevia

¼ tsp. pepper

1 tsp. konjac flour

1. In a large saucepan, sauté mushrooms, onion, and garlic in butter until tender.

2. Add chicken bone broth, tomatoes, basil, stevia, and pepper. Cook over medium heat 10–15 minutes, stirring occasionally.

3. Sprinkle the konjac flour over the soup and whisk until smooth. Continue to cook about 10 minutes more.

4. Remove from heat. Cool slightly. Then puree in tightly covered blender (¼ of the mixture at a time) until smooth.

5. Garnish with basil leaves and serve hot.

- Calories 145
- Fat 8
- Sodium 403
- Carbs 13
- Sugar 2
- Protein 6

Unstuffed Cabbage Soup

Colleen Heatwole
Burton, MI

Makes 4–6 servings
Prep. Time: 15 minutes
Cooking Time: 10 minutes
Setting: Sauté and Manual
Pressure: High
Release: Natural then Manual

2 Tbsp. coconut oil

1 lb. ground beef, turkey, or venison

1 medium onion, diced

2 cloves garlic, minced

1 small head cabbage, chopped, cored, cut into roughly
   2-inch pieces

6-oz. can tomato paste

1-qt. can diced tomatoes, with liquid

2 cups beef bone broth

1½ cups water

1–2 tsp. salt

½ tsp. black pepper

1 tsp. oregano

1 tsp. parsley

1. Melt coconut oil in the inner pot of the Instant Pot using Sauté function. Add ground meat. Stir frequently until meat loses color, about 2 minutes.

2. Add onion and garlic and continue to sauté for 2 more minutes, stirring frequently.

3. Add chopped cabbage.

4. On top of cabbage layer tomato paste, tomatoes with liquid, beef broth, water, and spices.

5. Secure the lid and set vent to sealing. Using Manual setting, select 10 minutes.

6. When time is up, let the pressure release naturally for 10 minutes, then do a quick release.

Serving suggestion: Serve over cauliflower rice in individual bowls.

- Calories 281
- Fat 6
- Sodium 898
- Carbs 33
- Sugar 6
- Protein 23

Cabbage Soup

**Margaret Jarrett
Anderson, IN**

Makes 8 servings
Prep. Time: 25 minutes
Cooking Time: 3½–4 hours
Ideal slow-cooker size: 4-qt.

½ head of cabbage, sliced thin

2 stalks celery, sliced thin

½ cup chopped cauliflower

¼ cup chopped celery

14-oz. can diced tomatoes

1 onion, chopped

2 cups chicken bone broth

2 cloves garlic, minced

1 qt. unsalted tomato juice (make sure it has no added sugar)

¼ tsp. pepper

water

1. Combine all ingredients except water in slow cooker. Add water to within 3 inches of top of slow cooker.

2. Cover. Cook on High 3½–4 hours, or until vegetables are tender.

- Calories 53
- Fat 1
- Sodium 498
- Carbs 9
- Sugar 5
- Protein 3

Cabbage and Green Bean Soup

**Ruth C. Hancock
Earlsboro, OK**

Makes 6 servings
Prep. Time: 15 minutes
Cooking Time: 3–4 hours
Ideal slow-cooker size: 5-qt.

1 qt. no-sugar-added tomato juice

1 medium head cabbage, chopped

1 bell pepper, chopped

1 cup finely chopped celery

15-oz. can French-style green beans

3 keto-friendly vegetarian bouillon cubes

1 Tbsp. soy sauce

2 Tbsp. onion flakes

1 Tbsp. dried parsley

1 tsp. garlic

1. Mix all ingredients together in 5-qt. slow cooker. Cover.

2. Cook on Low 3–4 hours, until vegetables are as tender as you like them.

- Calories 53
- Fat 1
- Sodium 1073
- Carbs 11
- Sugar 6
- Protein 3

Cauliflower Soup

Elaine Vigoda
Rochester, NY

Makes 8–10 servings
Prep. Time: 15 minutes
Cooking Time: 2⅔–3 hours
Ideal slow-cooker size: 6-qt.

2 lbs. frozen cauliflower

1 onion, diced

48 oz. vegetable broth

3 tsp. konjac flour

2 cups fresh cauliflower florets

½ cup sliced green onions

1 cup shredded Mexican cheese

¼ cup chopped fresh cilantro

1. Put frozen cauliflower and onions in slow cooker. Pour in broth.

2. Cook on High 2 hours, or until vegetables are soft.

3. Sprinkle in konjac flour and whisk until smooth. Cook for 10–20 minutes longer.

4. Purée soup with a hand blender or in a stand blender. Return to cooker.

5. Add fresh cauliflower. Cover and cook another 30–40 minutes on High until cauliflower florets are as tender as you like them.

6. Garnish each bowl with green onions, cheese, and cilantro.

- Calories 93
- Fat 5
- Sodium 586
- Carbs 9
- Sugar 4
- Protein 6

Slow-Cooker Loaded Cauliflower Soup

Hope Comerford
Clinton Township, MI

Makes 8–10 servings
Prep. Time: 15 minutes
Cooking Time: 6 hours
Ideal slow-cooker size: 5-qt.

1 qt. chicken bone broth

2 cups heavy cream

2 heads cauliflower, chopped

1 small onion, chopped

2 cloves garlic, minced

¼ tsp. pepper

1. Place all ingredients into crock. Stir until combined.

2. Cover and cook on Low for 6 hours.

3. With an immersion blender or a potato masher, mash any remaining chunks in your soup.

Serving suggestion: Top with shredded cheese, cooked chopped bacon, and chopped green onions.

- Calories 190
- Fat 18
- Sodium 173
- Carbs 4
- Sugar 3
- Protein 4

Mushroom Soup

Lauren Bailey
Mechanicsburg, PA

Makes 10 servings (¾ cup each)
Prep. Time: 20 minutes
Cooking Time: 30–35 minutes

2 Tbsp. olive oil

2 bay leaves

1 large onion, chopped

2 cloves garlic, minced (use more if you wish)

1½ cups beef bone broth

1 cup chicken bone broth

1 cup tomato juice, or fresh puree

2 cups cut-up tomatoes, fresh or canned

1½ lbs. fresh mushrooms, chopped

1¾ Tbsp. butter

1 tsp. dried thyme

salt and pepper, to taste

1½ tsp. konjac flour

1. In a medium-sized saucepan, heat olive oil. Add bay leaves and onion. Sauté until onion is golden. Stir in garlic and sauté one more minute.

2. Add broth and tomato juice. Add cut-up tomatoes.

3. In a larger pot, sauté mushrooms in 1¾ Tbsp. butter. Add thyme over high heat. Add tomato mixture, salt, and pepper. Lower heat and simmer for 20 minutes.

4. Sprinkle in the konjac flour and whisk until smooth. Simmer another 10 minutes. Remove bay leaves before serving.

- Calories 93
- Fat 5
- Sodium 245
- Carbs 10
- Sugar 2
- Protein 3

Chicken Mushroom Soup

Kelly Amos
Pittsboro, NC

Makes 4 servings
Prep. Time: 15–20 minutes
Cooking Time: 35 minutes

1 Tbsp. olive oil

1 lb. boneless skinless chicken, cut into bite-sized pieces

½ white onion, chopped

¼ cup chopped celery

1¾ cups sliced fresh white mushrooms

3 cups chicken bone broth

¼ tsp. dried thyme

pepper, to taste

1½ tsp. konjac flour

1 cup half-and-half

1. Put olive oil in stockpot and heat. Add the chicken and sauté until no longer pink.

2. Carefully add chopped onion and celery. Cook until tender.

3. Add mushrooms, chicken broth, thyme, and pepper.

4. Cover and heat through.

5. Sprinkle in the konjac flour and whisk until smooth.

6. Whisk in the half-and-half.

7. Cook over medium heat. Stir continually until thickened and bubbly.

- Calories 424
- Fat 16
- Sodium 912
- Carbs 22
- Sugar 6
- Protein 48

Zucchini Soup Base

Jana Beyer
Harrisonburg, VA

Makes 4 servings
Prep. Time: 15 minutes
Cooking Time: 2–3 hours
Ideal slow-cooker size: 4-qt.

Soup Base:

3 cups unpeeled diced zucchini

½ cup chopped onion

1 tsp. seasoned salt

½ cup water

1 tsp. keto-friendly powdered vegetarian bouillon

White Sauce:

8 Tbsp. (1 stick) butter

8 oz. cream cheese

2 cups whipping cream

½ tsp. salt

⅛ tsp. pepper

2 tsp. konjac flour

1. To make soup base, combine zucchini, onion, seasoned salt, water, and powdered bouillon in slow cooker. Cook on Low 2–3 hours until tender.

2. Put into blender and blend until very smooth.

3. Store in the freezer until needed.

4. To serve, thaw soup base.

5. Make white sauce: Melt butter in saucepan. Add cream cheese and whisk until smooth and bubbly.

6. Slowly, stirring continuously, add the whipping cream, salt, and pepper.

7. Whisk in the konjac flour until smooth. Continue cooking until thickened.

8. Add soup base to white sauce. Stir well. Heat and serve.

- Calories 840
- Fat 87
- Sodium 1082
- Carbs 12
- Sugar 9
- Protein 9

Zucchini Garden Chowder

Dawn Alderfer
Oley, PA

Makes 8–10 servings
Prep. Time: 5 minutes
Cooking Time: 3–4½ hours
Ideal slow-cooker size: 5-qt.

2 medium zucchini, chopped

3 Tbsp. minced fresh parsley

1 tsp. dried basil

1 tsp. salt

¼ tsp. pepper

1 drop liquid stevia

14½-oz. can diced tomatoes, undrained

10-oz. pkg. frozen green beans

3 cups vegetable broth

1 tsp. lemon juice

1½ tsp. konjac flour

12-oz. can evaporated milk

¼ cup grated Parmesan cheese

2 cups shredded cheddar cheese

1. Combine zucchini, parsley, basil, salt, pepper, stevia, tomatoes, and green beans in slow cooker.

2. Add vegetable broth and lemon juice. Cover and cook on Low 2–3 hours until zucchini is tender.

3. Sprinkle soup with konjac flour and whisk until smooth.

4. Cover and cook 30–60 minutes until thickened.

5. Add evaporated milk and cheeses. Stir and heat through.

- Calories 172
- Fat 11
- Sodium 678
- Carbs 10
- Sugar 5
- Protein 9

Creamy Asparagus Soup

Mary Riha
Antigo, WI

Makes 4 servings
Prep. Time: 15 minutes
Cooking Time: 35–40 minutes

2 Tbsp. sesame seeds

1 tsp. olive oil

1 medium onion, chopped

2 cups chopped cauliflower

1 lb. asparagus

4 cups chicken bone broth

1. In a good-sized stockpot, sauté sesame seeds in olive oil until brown.

2. Add onion and cauliflower. Cook, stirring, until cauliflower is slightly browned.

3. Break asparagus into pieces and add to cauliflower mixture, along with 2 cups chicken bone broth.

4. Bring to a boil. Cover, reduce heat, and simmer about 10–15 minutes.

5. Remove stockpot from stove. Blend soup mixture carefully and in batches until smooth.

6. Stir in remaining 2 cups chicken broth. Cover and heat through.

- Calories 96
- Fat 3
- Sodium 409
- Carbs 10
- Sugar 4
- Protein 9

Asparagus Soup

Wilma J. Haberkamp
Fairbank, IA

Makes 4–6 servings
Prep. Time: 30 minutes
Cooking Time: 30 minutes

3 cups chopped cauliflower

2 cups asparagus (cut into ½-inch pieces)

⅓ cup chopped onion

1 tsp. salt

1¾ cups vegetable broth

1½ cups whole milk

1½ tsp. konjac flour

1 cup grated good melting cheese of your choice

additional grated cheese, *optional*

1. In a large saucepan, combine cauliflower, asparagus, onion, salt, and vegetable broth.

2. Cook 20 minutes, or until vegetables are tender.

3. Slowly add milk to soup, stirring continually over medium heat.

4. Sprinkle soup with konjac flour and whisk until smooth. Cook about 10 more minutes.

5. Turn heat to low. Add 1 cup cheese. Stir until melted.

6. Pour into warmed soup bowls. Garnish with grated cheese, if you wish.

- Calories 147
- Fat 9
- Sodium 599
- Carbs 9
- Sugar 5
- Protein 10

Garden Vegetable Soup

Jan McDowell
New Holland, PA

Makes 6 servings
Prep. Time: 20 minutes
Cooking Time: 30 minutes

1 Tbsp. olive oil

1 chopped onion

1 tsp. chopped garlic

1 small zucchini, chopped

½ lb. fresh mushrooms, sliced or chopped

1 sweet bell pepper, chopped

24-oz. can tomatoes, no salt added, undrained

1 Tbsp. fresh basil

2 cups vegetable stock

dash hot sauce, *optional*

3 cups cauliflower rice, cooked

1. Heat olive oil in 4-qt. saucepan.

2. Sauté onion and garlic in oil until tender.

3. Add zucchini, mushrooms, bell pepper, tomatoes, basil, and vegetable stock. Add hot sauce if using.

4. Bring to a boil. Cover and simmer 10 minutes.

5. Serve over cauliflower rice in individual bowls.

- Calories 80
- Fat 3
- Sodium 176
- Carbs 13
- Sugar 6
- Protein 4

Easy Cream of Vegetable Soup

Norma Grieser
Sebring, FL

Makes 6 cups
Prep. Time: 20 minutes
Cooking Time: 20 minutes

¼ cup chopped celery

¼ cup chopped onion

1 Tbsp. olive oil

½ tsp. salt

pepper, to taste

1 bay leaf, or herb of your choice

3 cups whole milk

1½ tsp. konjac flour

2 cups fresh or frozen vegetables of your choice, cut up or sliced (spinach, asparagus, broccoli, cauliflower, tomatoes)

1. In a large stockpot, sauté celery and onion in oil.

2. Over low heat, stir in salt, pepper, herbs, and milk, stirring constantly.

3. Sprinkle in the konjac flour and whisk until smooth. Cook over medium heat until hot and bubbly.

4. Steam or microwave vegetables until crisp-tender.

5. Stir vegetables into thickened creamy sauce and heat through. Remove bay leaf, if used.

- Calories 142
- Fat 7
- Sodium 244
- Carbs 15
- Sugar 9
- Protein 6

Southwest Vegetable Soup

Joyce G. Zuercher
Hesston, KS

Makes 10 servings
Prep. Time: 30 minutes
Cooking Time: 45 minutes

1 Tbsp. olive oil

1 cup diced celery

¾ cup chopped onion

1 clove garlic, finely chopped

¼ cup chopped bell pepper

4 cups diced canned tomatoes, no salt added, undrained

2 cups tomato sauce, no salt added

2 cups chicken bone broth

2 cups diced broccoli

2 cups green beans

½ cup diced cauliflower

¾ cup chopped asparagus

hot peppers, dried and crushed or chopped, according to your taste preferences

1 tsp. chili seasoning

½ tsp. cumin

3 cups chopped, cooked chicken

pepper, to taste

1. In a large stockpot, cook celery, onion, garlic, and bell pepper in oil until transparent.

2. Add all other ingredients. Cover and simmer together at least 30 minutes, or until vegetables are done to your liking.

3. Adjust seasonings to your taste.

- Calories 98
- Fat 2
- Sodium 545
- Carbs 11
- Sugar 6
- Protein 9

Fresh Vegetable Soup

Sandra Chang
Derwood, MD

Makes 6 servings (¾ cup each)
Prep. Time: 25–30 minutes
Cooking Time: 60–70 minutes
Standing Time: 1 hour

3 Tbsp. olive oil

1 cup of each:

    diced celery

    diced onions

    chopped cabbage

    diced zucchini

    fresh or frozen cut-up green beans

2 cups canned whole tomatoes

4 cups beef bone broth

½ tsp. liquid stevia

salt, to taste

pepper, to taste

1. In 4-qt. saucepan, heat oil. Sauté celery, onions, cabbage, and zucchini in butter until vegetables are soft but not brown.

2. Add rest of ingredients.

3. Simmer gently for 30–45 minutes, or until vegetables are cooked but not mushy.

4. Take pan off heat. Allow soup to stand for one hour before serving.

5. Reheat just until heated through and serve.

- Calories 99
- Fat 7
- Sodium 700
- Carbs 6
- Sugar 3
- Protein 4

African Peanut Soup

Barbara Hershey
Lititz, PA

Makes 5–6 servings
Prep. Time: 20 minutes
Cooking Time: 50 minutes

2 Tbsp. coconut oil

1 onion, chopped

1 green bell pepper, diced small

1 red bell pepper, diced small

2 cloves garlic, minced

28-oz. can stewed tomatoes, puréed

4 cups vegetable stock

⅛ tsp. hot pepper flakes, or to taste

1 Tbsp. curry powder, *optional*

¼ cup natural no-sugar-added peanut butter

salt and pepper, to taste

2½–3 cups cauliflower rice, cooked

1. In a large pot, warm the coconut oil over medium heat.

2. Add onion, peppers, and garlic. Sauté until onion begins to brown.

3. Add tomatoes, stock, hot pepper flakes, and curry powder if you wish. Simmer uncovered over medium heat for 30 minutes.

4. Add peanut butter and stir. Cook, covered, for 20 minutes.

5. Season with salt and pepper, to taste.

6. Serve over cauliflower rice.

- Calories 243
- Fat 14
- Sodium 791
- Carbs 27
- Sugar 6
- Protein 7

Spicy African Chicken Peanut Soup

Rhoda Atzeff
Lancaster, PA

Makes 8 servings
Prep. Time: 15 minutes
Cooking Time: 40 minutes

1 tsp. coconut oil

1 cup chopped onion

1 large sweet green bell pepper, seeded and finely chopped

2 cloves garlic, minced or pressed

4 cups chicken bone broth

16-oz. can crushed tomatoes, no salt added, undrained

½ tsp. red pepper flakes

1 Tbsp. curry powder

⅛ tsp. black pepper

1 cup diced cooked chicken

¼ cup smooth natural no-sugar-added peanut butter

1. In a large stockpot, heat coconut oil over medium heat. Sauté onion, green peppers, and garlic until onions begin to brown.

2. Stir in broth, tomatoes, red pepper flakes, curry powder, pepper, and chicken.

3. Simmer uncovered over low heat for 30 minutes.

4. Whisk in peanut butter until soup is completely smooth. Heat through.

- Calories 122
- Fat 6
- Sodium 217
- Carbs 11
- Sugar 4
- Protein 8

Gazpacho

Maxine Hershberger
Dalton, OH

Makes 6 servings (about 5 oz. per serving)
Prep. Time: 30 minutes
Chilling Time: 4 hours or more

1 cup finely chopped tomato

½ cup chopped green pepper

½ cup chopped celery

½ cup chopped cucumber

¼ cup finely chopped onion

2 tsp. snipped parsley

1 tsp. snipped chives

1 small clove garlic, minced

2–3 Tbsp. tarragon wine vinegar

2 Tbsp. olive oil

½ tsp. salt

¼ tsp. black pepper

½ tsp. Worcestershire sauce

2 cups no-sugar-added tomato juice

1. Combine all ingredients in a glass bowl. Toss to mix well.

2. Cover and chill at least 4 hours before serving.

3. Serve as a salad or soup.

- Calories 71
- Fat 5
- Sodium 383
- Carbs 6
- Sugar 4
- Protein 1

Roasted Vegetable Gazpacho

J. B. Miller
Indianapolis, IN

Makes 6 servings
Prep. Time: 30 minutes
Baking Time: 20–25 minutes
Chilling Time: 4 hours

2 sweet red bell peppers, left whole

2 sweet yellow bell peppers, left whole

2 large red onions, quartered

2 Tbsp. extra-virgin olive oil

black pepper, to taste

1 lb. (about 4 cups) medium zucchini, cut in ½-inch-thick slices

2 lbs. (about 7 medium) vine-ripened tomatoes, cored, quartered, and seeds removed

3 cloves garlic

2 Tbsp. chopped fresh basil

1 Tbsp. chopped fresh oregano

1 cup cold water

2 Tbsp. lime juice, or more to taste

1. Preheat oven to 375°F.

2. Place peppers and onions in large mixing bowl. Toss with olive oil and black pepper.

3. Spoon peppers and onions into large shallow baking dishes or onto cookie sheets with sides. Allow seasoned olive oil to remain in mixing bowl. Place peppers and onions in oven.

4. Meanwhile, stir zucchini and tomatoes into large mixing bowl with remaining seasoned olive oil.

5. After peppers and onions have roasted 10–12 minutes, add zucchini and tomatoes to baking dishes.

6. Roast 10–12 minutes, or until peppers are soft and vegetables have browned along the edges and wrinkled. Total roasting time will be 20–25 minutes.

7. Remove baking dishes from oven. Lift out peppers and place in bowl. Cover with plastic wrap. Let cool 10 minutes. Then peel and seed peppers over a bowl, saving the juices.

8. Coarsely chop all vegetables.

9. Place chopped vegetables in food processor together with garlic, basil, oregano, and 1 cup cold water.

10. Blend at high speed until smooth. Strain through a fine mesh sieve.

11. Place mixture in covered container. Refrigerate 4 hours before serving.

12. Adjust seasoning with pepper, to taste.

13. Mix in lime juice just before serving.

- Calories 109
- Fat 5
- Sodium 18
- Carbs 15
- Sugar 9
- Protein 3

Chicken Vegetable Soup

Maria Shevlin
Sicklerville, NJ

Makes 6 servings
Prep. Time: 12–25 minutes
Cooking Time: 4 minutes
Setting: Manual
Pressure: High
Release: Manual

1-2 raw chicken breasts, cubed

½ medium onion, chopped

4 cloves garlic, minced

½ cup chopped broccoli

½ cup chopped cauliflower

4 stalks celery, chopped, leaves included

1 cup frozen green beans, bite sized

¼–½ cup chopped savoy cabbage

14½-oz. can petite diced tomatoes

3 cups chicken bone broth

1 tsp. salt

½ tsp. black pepper

1 tsp. garlic powder

¼ cup chopped fresh parsley

¼–½ tsp. red pepper flakes

1. Add all of the ingredients, in the order listed, to the inner pot of the Instant Pot.

2. Lock the lid in place, set the vent to sealing, and press Manual, and cook at high pressure for 4 minutes.

3. Release the pressure manually as soon as cooking time is finished.

- Calories 336
- Fat 3
- Sodium 170
- Carbs 18
- Sugar
- Protein 221

Chicken and Tomato Soup

Jean Harris Robinson
Pemberton, NJ

Makes 12 servings
Prep. Time: 25 minutes
Cooking Time: 5 hours
Ideal slow-cooker size: 5-qt.

2 lbs. boneless skinless chicken, cut into bite-sized pieces

2 Tbsp. olive oil

2-3 cloves garlic

1 large white onion, diced

5 small zucchini, diced

3 stalks celery, diced

2 14½-oz. cans diced tomatoes

8 cups chicken bone broth

½ cup chopped fresh basil leaves

½ cup chopped fresh cilantro leaves

2 Tbsp. balsamic vinegar or rice vinegar

salt and pepper, to taste

1. Combine chicken, olive oil, garlic, onion, zucchini, celery, tomatoes, and broth in slow cooker.

2. Cover. Cook on Low 5 hours or until vegetables are tender.

3. Add basil, cilantro, vinegar, and salt and pepper. Purée with hand blender or in stand blender.

- Calories 161
- Fat 4.5
- Sodium 508
- Carbs 7
- Sugar 5
- Protein 22

Chicken Soup with Lemon

Heidi Wood
Vacaville, CA

Makes 6 servings
Prep. Time: 30 minutes
Cooking Time: 20–30 minutes

⅓ cup olive oil

1 lb. boneless skinless chicken breast, cut into bite-sized pieces

2 large sweet onions, chopped

4 cloves garlic, minced

2 tsp. cumin

½ tsp. salt

½ tsp. freshly ground black pepper

¼ tsp. chili powder

8 cups chicken bone broth

1 medium zucchini, diced

2 Tbsp. tomato paste

4 Tbsp. lemon juice

1 cup chopped fresh cilantro

plain yogurt or sour cream, *optional*

1. Heat olive oil in a large pot over medium-high heat. Stir in the chicken, onions, and garlic, and cook until the onion is golden brown, about 5 minutes.

2. Stir in the cumin, salt, black pepper, and chili powder. Cook and stir until fragrant, about 2 minutes.

3. Add broth and zucchini to the mixture in the pot. Bring to a boil over high heat, then reduce the heat to medium-low.

4. Cover and simmer for 20–30 minutes.

5. Add tomato paste to soup pot and stir to combine thoroughly.

6. Just before serving, stir lemon juice into the pot of soup.

7. Ladle soup into bowls. Serve cilantro on the side to be added as a garnish. It is also good with a dollop of plain yogurt or sour cream for a slightly different taste.

- Calories 253
- Fat 14
- Sodium 766
- Carbs 7
- Sugar 3
- Protein 25

Chicken Soup with Onion, Cilantro, and Lime Salsa

Melanie Mohler
Ephrata, PA

Makes 6 servings
Prep. Time: 15 minutes
Cooking Time: 45 minutes

1 Tbsp. olive oil

1 lb. boneless skinless chicken breast, cut into bite-sized pieces

6 cups chicken bone broth

1 Tbsp. minced garlic puree

¼–½ tsp. dried thyme, according to your taste preference

3 Tbsp. konjac flour

3 Tbsp. sour cream

Salsa Ingredients:
⅓ cup fresh cilantro, washed and stemmed

½ onion, coarsely chopped

juice of ½ lime, or 1 Tbsp. bottled lime juice

1. Heat oil in a soup pot and then add in the chicken. Cook until lightly browned on each side.

2. Pour chicken broth, garlic puree, and thyme into pot.

3. Cover and simmer over medium-low heat, about 30 minutes.

4. Sprinkle in the konjac flour and whisk until smooth. Continue to simmer until thickened.

5. While soup is simmering, puree cilantro, onion, and lime juice in processor until smooth. Place in small bowl.

6. Place sour cream in another small bowl.

7. Serve salsa and sour cream with soup, to be spooned on top of each serving.

- Calories 171
- Fat 7
- Sodium 428
- Carbs 3
- Sugar 1
- Protein 23

Chicken Spinach Soup

Carna Reitz
Remington, VA

Makes 4-6 servings
Prep. Time: 5 minutes
Cooking Time: 20 minutes

6½ cups chicken bone broth, *divided*

2 cups cooked chicken

1-2 cups frozen chopped spinach

salt and pepper, to taste

3½ tsp. konjac flour

1. Place broth, chicken, spinach, and salt and pepper in a large stockpot. Bring to a boil.

2. Sprinkle in the konjac flour and whisk until smooth.

3. Continue stirring and cooking until soup thickens.

- Calories 122
- Fat 3
- Sodium 576
- Carbs 2
- Sugar 0
- Protein 22

Surprise Gumbo

Brenda J. Marshall
St. Marys, ON

Makes 8 servings (¾ cup each)
Prep. Time: 20-30 minutes
Cooking Time: 30-40 minutes

1¼ lbs. cooked chicken, cubed

2 medium-sized onions, cut in wedges

1 medium-sized green bell pepper, cut in narrow strips

28-oz. can whole tomatoes, undrained

¼ cup Worcestershire sauce

2 Tbsp. prepared mustard

2 Tbsp. minced garlic

1 tsp. dried thyme

1 tsp. dried rosemary

¼ tsp. pepper

½ lb. precooked shrimp

4 cups cooked cauliflower rice

1. In a large saucepan, combine chicken, onions, green pepper, tomatoes, Worcestershire sauce, mustard, garlic, thyme, rosemary, and pepper. Simmer for 25 minutes.

2. Add shrimp and cook 5 minutes more.

3. Serve over scoops of cooked cauliflower rice in individual serving bowls.

- Calories 196
- Fat 3
- Sodium 339
- Carbs 11
- Sugar 6
- Protein 31

Spicy Chicken Soup

J. B. Miller
Indianapolis, IN

Makes 8 servings
Prep. Time: 20 minutes
Cooking Time: 40 minutes

1 Tbsp. olive oil

1½ lbs. boneless, skinless, chicken breasts, cubed

1 bunch (about 6) green onions, thinly sliced

1 sweet red bell pepper, chopped

1 sweet yellow bell pepper, chopped

2 jalapeño peppers, seeded and finely chopped

4 cloves garlic

½ tsp. ground ginger

½ tsp. dried sage

½ tsp. freshly ground pepper

4 cups chicken bone broth

3 cups kale

1. Place oil in large skillet over medium heat. Add chicken and sauté just until no longer pink. Remove chicken from pan.

2. Sauté onions, peppers (including jalapeños), and garlic in same skillet.

3. Place chicken and sautéed vegetables in stockpot. Add seasonings. Mix thoroughly.

4. Add chicken broth. Cover and simmer 20 minutes.

5. Add kale. Simmer 5 more minutes.

- Calories 133
- Fat 4
- Sodium 239
- Carbs 5
- Sugar 1
- Protein 20

Chipotle Chicken Soup

Rebecca Weybright
Manheim, PA

Makes 6 servings
Prep. Time: 10 minutes
Cooking Time: 5 hours
Ideal slow-cooker size: 5-qt.

1 lb. boneless skinless chicken breast, cubed

1 onion, chopped

1 dried chipotle chile, soaked 10–15 minutes in cold water

4 cups water

1–2 tsp. salt

2 cups canned tomatoes with juice

1. Add chicken to slow cooker with onion, chile, and water.

2. Cover and cook on Low for 5 hours.

3. Add salt and tomatoes.

4. Puree soup, using an immersion blender.

Tip: If soup is not your desired thickness, you can whisk in a bit of konjac flour, ½ tsp. at a time, until desired thickness is reached.

- Calories 112
- Fat 2
- Sodium 576
- Carbs 4
- Sugar 3
- Protein 18

Chicken Taco Soup

Mary Puskar
Forest Hill, MD

Makes 8 servings (¾ cup each)
Prep. Time: 25 minutes
Cooking Time: 40 minutes

2 chicken breast halves

3 cups water

2 stalks celery

1 medium-sized onion

¾ cups grated zucchini

2 Tbsp. olive oil

1 Tbsp. chili powder

1 Tbsp. cumin

4½-oz. can green chiles

14-oz. chicken bone broth

14-oz. beef bone broth

14½-oz. can diced tomatoes, undrained

1 Tbsp. Worcestershire sauce

Monterey Jack cheese, grated, *optional*

1. In a large stockpot, cook chicken breasts in water until tender. Remove meat, reserving cooking water. When chicken is cool enough to handle, chop into bite-sized pieces. Set aside.

2. Chop celery and onion.

3. In the stockpot used for cooking chicken, sauté celery, onion, and grated zucchini in oil.

4. Combine all ingredients in stockpot, except the cooked chicken and cheese. Cover and simmer 15 minutes.

5. Add diced chicken. Heat through.

6. Top each serving with grated cheese, if desired.

- Calories 105
- Fat 5
- Sodium 358
- Carbs 7
- Sugar 2
- Protein 9

Egg Drop Chicken Soup

Kathryn Yoder
Minot, ND

Makes 6 servings
Prep. Time: 10 minutes
Cooking Time: 12–15 minutes

4½ cups chicken bone broth

4 oz. cooked chicken, shredded

1 tsp. finely chopped fresh parsley, or ½ tsp. dried parsley

1 tsp. soy sauce

2 egg whites, lightly beaten

4 tsp. sliced green onions

1. In a large saucepan, heat broth over medium heat.

2. Add shredded chicken, parsley, and soy sauce.

3. Bring to a boil, stirring occasionally. Continue boiling, 4–5 minutes.

4. Slowly dribble lightly beaten egg whites into boiling soup, stirring constantly, until the egg has cooked.

5. Serve with green onions as garnish.

- Calories 53
- Fat 1
- Sodium 380
- Carbs 0
- Sugar 0
- Protein 11

Taco Soup

Hope Comerford
Clinton Township, MI

SLOW COOKER

Makes 4–6 servings
Prep. Time: 20 minutes
Cooking Time: 8 hours
Ideal slow-cooker size: 4-qt.

2 lbs. ground turkey

1 large onion, chopped

2 tsp. chili powder

2 tsp. garlic powder

1 tsp. dried parsley

1 tsp. onion powder

½ tsp. cumin

½ tsp. paprika

½ tsp. dried dill

2 tsp. sea salt

½ tsp. dried oregano

¼ tsp. black pepper

⅛ tsp. cayenne pepper

2 14½-oz. cans diced tomatoes

4 cups beef bone broth

1. Brown turkey meat with the onion.

2. Place the browned meat into the crock and add all the remaining ingredients. Stir.

3. Cover and cook on Low for 8 hours.

Serving suggestion: Serve with sour cream, shredded cheese, and chunks of avocado.

- Calories 217
- Fat 1
- Sodium 1353
- Carbs 10
- Sugar 2
- Protein 40

Tuscany Peasant Soup

Alice Valine
Elma, NY

Makes 8 servings
Prep. Time: 20 minutes
Cooking Time: 25 minutes

1½ lbs. bulk turkey sausage

1 onion, chopped

2–3 cloves garlic, minced

2 14½-oz. cans diced tomatoes, no salt added, undrained

2 14-oz. cans chicken bone broth

2 tsp. no-salt Italian seasoning

3 medium zucchini, sliced

4 cups fresh spinach leaves, chopped, or baby spinach, un-chopped

shredded Parmesan, or Romano, cheese, *optional*

1. In Dutch oven or stockpot, cook sausage over medium heat until no longer pink. Drain off drippings.

2. Add onion and garlic. Sauté until tender.

3. Stir in tomatoes, broth, seasoning, and zucchini. Cook uncovered 10 minutes.

4. Add spinach and heat until just wilted.

5. Serve with cheese, if you wish.

- Calories 229
- Fat 12
- Sodium 953
- Carbs 10
- Sugar 3
- Protein 19

Turkey Sausage and Cabbage Soup

Bonita Stutzman
Harrisonburg, VA

Makes 8 servings
Prep. Time: 20 minutes
Cooking Time: 1 hour, or more

2 tsp. olive oil

1½ cups chopped onion

2 cloves garlic, finely chopped

¾ lb. turkey sausage, chopped in small pieces

6 cups green cabbage, shredded

3 lbs. canned tomatoes, no salt added, undrained

1½ qts. water

1 Tbsp. dried basil

2 tsp. dried oregano

¼ tsp. black pepper

1. Place olive oil in stockpot and heat on medium heat. Sauté onion and garlic until tender.

2. Add chopped sausage. Cook until lightly browned.

3. Stir in remaining ingredients.

4. Cover. Simmer until cabbage is very tender.

- Calories 150
- Fat 7
- Sodium 514
- Carbs 13
- Sugar 7
- Protein 10

Italian Sausage Soup

Esther Porter
Minneapolis, MN

Makes 8 servings (¾ cup each)
Prep. Time: 15–25 minutes
Cooking Time: 65–70 minutes

½ lb. lean turkey Italian sausage, casings removed

1 cup chopped onion

2 large cloves garlic, sliced

5 cups beef bone broth

2 cups chopped or canned tomatoes

8-oz. can no-salt-added tomato sauce

1½ cups sliced zucchini

1 medium-sized green bell pepper, diced

1 cup green beans, frozen or fresh

2 Tbsp. dried basil

2 Tbsp. dried oregano

salt, to taste

pepper, to taste

4 cups cooked cauliflower rice

freshly grated Parmesan cheese for topping, *optional*

1. Sauté sausage in heavy Dutch oven over medium heat until cooked through, about 10 minutes, breaking it up as it browns with a wooden spoon.

2. Using a slotted spoon, transfer sausage to a large bowl. Pour off all drippings from Dutch oven. Add onion and garlic to the Dutch oven and sauté until clear, about 5 minutes.

3. Return sausage to pan. Add beef broth, tomatoes, tomato sauce, zucchini, pepper, green beans, basil, and oregano. Simmer 30–40 minutes, or until vegetables are tender.

4. Season to taste with salt and pepper.

5. Ladle hot soup into bowls over cauliflower rice, divided evenly among the bowls, and sprinkle with Parmesan cheese, if using.

- Calories 122
- Fat 3
- Sodium 856
- Carbs 15
- Sugar 7
- Protein 10

Tuscan Soup

Jean Turner
Williams Lake, BC

Makes 4–6 servings
Prep. Time: 15 minutes
Cooking Time: 2½ hours
Ideal slow-cooker size: 4-qt.

1 lb. bulk Italian sausage

2 14-oz. cans chopped crushed tomatoes with herbs

1⅔ cups warm water

salt and pepper, to taste

2 cups Tuscan or curly kale, roughly shredded or chopped

4 Tbsp. extra-virgin olive oil

1. Brown Italian sausage over medium heat until no longer pink. Drain the grease.

2. Combine Italian sausage, tomatoes, warm water, salt, pepper, and kale in slow cooker.

3. Cook on High for 2½ hours.

4. Place soup into bowls and drizzle each bowl with a little olive oil.

- Calories 239
- Fat 16
- Sodium 869
- Carbs 12
- Sugar 7
- Protein 16

Spinach and Sausage Soup

Marilyn Widrick
Adams, NY

Makes 4–6 servings
Prep. Time: 20 minutes
Cooking Time: 5¼–5½ hours
Ideal slow-cooker size: 5-qt.

½ lb. bulk Italian sausage

1 Tbsp. olive oil

2 medium zucchini, chopped

1 small onion, diced

1 tsp. cumin

14½-oz. can diced tomatoes

1¾ cups chicken bone broth

2 cups water

¼ tsp. salt

⅛ tsp. pepper

5-oz. bag fresh spinach, chopped

1. Brown Italian sausage in a cooking pot until no longer pink. Drain grease.

2. Heat 1 Tbsp. olive oil in cooking pot. Add zucchini and onion. Cook 8–10 minutes over medium heat.

3. Place in slow cooker. Add cumin, diced tomatoes, broth, water, salt, and pepper.

4. Cover and cook on Low 5 hours.

5. Add spinach. Cook on Low an additional 15–25 minutes.

- Calories 116
- Fat 6
- Sodium 533
- Carbs 7
- Sugar 2
- Protein 9

Escarole and Sausage Soup

Karen Ceneviva
New Haven, CT

Makes 8 servings
Prep. Time: 10 minutes
Cooking Time: 1½ hours

1½ lb. bulk sausage

4 cups chicken bone broth

2 heads escarole, well washed and cut medium-fine (about 8 cups)

4 cloves garlic, sliced very thin

2 Tbsp. extra-virgin olive oil

3 basil leaves chopped fine, or 1 Tbsp. dried basil

1. Brown loose sausage in pan and drain grease.

2. Place sausage, broth, and escarole in large stockpot. Bring to a boil. Cover and simmer 30 minutes.

3. In another saucepan, gently sauté garlic in olive oil until transparent, but not browned.

4. Gently stir garlic and basil into the stockpot. Cover and let simmer 15 minutes. Stir occasionally with wooden spoon.

- Calories 313
- Fat 26
- Sodium 6497
- Carbs 2
- Sugar 0
- Protein 18

Napa Cabbage and Pork Soup

Shirley Unternahrer
Wayland, IA

Makes 8 servings
Prep. Time: 10 minutes
Cooking Time: 10 minutes
Standing Time: 15 minutes

1½ qts. water

½ lb. lean ground pork (not sausage)

2 Tbsp. fish sauce (found in Asian foods section)

2–3 drops liquid stevia

1 head (about 8 cups) Napa cabbage, or bok choy, cleaned and chopped into 1-inch strips

6 green onions, chopped

1. Bring water to boil in large stockpot.

2. Pinch off pieces of pork, about the size of a quarter, form into balls, and drop into boiling water.

3. Boil 5 minutes. Skim foam off top. (Foam will come to surface as meat cooks.) Discard foam.

4. Stir fish sauce and stevia into boiling broth. You can use more or less fish sauce, depending upon your taste preferences.

5. Add cabbage or bok choy and green onions.

6. Cover stockpot. Turn off burner. Let stand 15 minutes.

Serving suggestion: Serve over cauliflower rice.

- Calories 105
- Fat 8
- Sodium 481
- Carbs 4
- Sugar 1.5
- Protein 6

Shredded Pork Tortilla Soup

Hope Comerford
Clinton Township, MI

Makes 6-8 servings
Prep. Time: 10 minutes
Cooking Time: 8-10 hours
Ideal slow-cooker size: 5-qt.

3 large tomatoes, chopped

1 cup chopped red onion

1 jalapeño, seeded and minced

1 lb. pork loin

2 tsp. cumin

2 tsp. chili powder

2 tsp. onion powder

2 tsp. garlic powder

2 tsp. lime juice

8 cups chicken bone broth

garnish (*optional*):

    fresh chopped cilantro

    avocado slices

    freshly grated Mexican cheese

1. In your crock, place the tomatoes, onion, and jalapeños.

2. Place the pork loin on top.

3. Add all the seasonings and lime juice, and pour in the chicken broth.

4. Cover and cook on Low for 8–10 hours.

5. Remove the pork and shred it between two forks. Place it back into the soup and stir.

6. Serve each bowl of soup with fresh chopped cilantro, avocado slices, and freshly grated Mexican cheese, if desired, or any other garnishes you would like!

Tip: If you don't have time for freshly chopped tomatoes, use a can of diced or chopped tomatoes.

- Calories 154
- Fat 5
- Sodium 788
- Carbs 6
- Sugar 3
- Protein 18

Sausage, Tomato, Spinach Soup

Wendy B. Martzall
New Holland, PA

Makes 8 servings
Prep. Time: 15–20 minutes
Cooking Time: 5 hours
Ideal slow-cooker size: 3- to 4-qt.

½ lb. bulk pork or turkey sausage

1 medium onion, chopped

1 small green bell pepper, chopped

28-oz. can diced tomatoes

4 cups beef bone broth

8-oz. can no-salt-added tomato sauce

2 tsp. Frank's RedHot Original Cayenne
    Pepper Sauce

7 drops liquid stevia

1 tsp. dried basil

½ tsp. dried oregano

10-oz. box frozen spinach, thawed and squeezed dry

½ cup shredded mozzarella cheese

1. Brown sausage with onion and pepper in skillet. (If you use turkey sausage, you'll probably need to add 1–2 Tbsp. oil to the pan.) Stir frequently, breaking up clumps of meat. When no longer pink, drain off drippings.

2. Spoon meat and vegetables into slow cooker.

3. Add all remaining ingredients except spinach and cheese. Stir until well blended.

4. Cover. Cook on Low 4¾ hours.

5. Stir spinach into soup. Cover and continue cooking on Low another 15 minutes.

6. Top each individual serving with a sprinkling of mozzarella cheese.

- Calories 150
- Fat 6
- Sodium 946
- Carbs 11
- Sugar 3
- Protein 12

Sausage and Cabbage Soup

Donna Suter
Pandora, OH

Makes 6–8 servings
Prep. Time: 20 minutes
Cooking Time: 6–8 hours
Ideal slow-cooker size: 4-qt.

1 lb. loose sausage

4 cups vegetable broth

2 cups chicken bone broth

1 onion, chopped

½ head cabbage, chopped

4–6 stalks celery, sliced

14-oz. can diced tomatoes

4 cloves garlic, chopped

2 tsp. dried basil

1 tsp. salt

½ tsp. pepper

1. Brown sausage in skillet and drain off grease. Transfer sausage to slow cooker.

2. Add rest of ingredients to slow cooker.

3. Cover and cook on Low for 6–8 hours.

- Calories 200
- Fat 16
- Sodium 1041
- Carbs 5
- Sugar 2
- Protein 9

Zucchini Stew

Colleen Heatwole
Burton, MI

Makes 6 servings
Prep. Time: 30 minutes
Cooking Time: 5 hours
Ideal slow-cooker size: 6-qt.

1 lb. bulk Italian sausage

2 stalks celery, diced

2 medium green bell peppers, diced

1 medium onion, chopped

2 28-oz. cans diced tomatoes

2 lbs. zucchini, cut into ½-inch slices

2 cloves garlic, minced

5 drops liquid stevia

1 tsp. oregano

1 tsp. Italian seasoning

1 tsp. salt, *optional*

6 Tbsp. grated Parmesan cheese

1. Brown sausage in hot skillet until brown and crumbly, about 5–7 minutes. Drain and discard grease.

2. Mix celery, bell peppers, and onion into cooked sausage and cook and stir until they are softened, 10–12 minutes.

3. Combine remaining ingredients, except Parmesan cheese, and add to slow cooker. Taste before adding salt to see if needed.

4. Cook on Low 4–6 hours. Garnish each serving with 1 Tbsp. Parmesan cheese.

- Calories 250
- Fat 9
- Sodium 1044
- Carbs 24
- Sugar 8
- Protein 18

Ham and Green Bean Soup

Loretta Krahn
Mountain Lake, MN

Makes 6 servings
Prep. Time: 20 minutes
Cooking Time: 4–6 hours
Ideal slow-cooker size: 4-qt.

1 meaty ham bone

1½ qts. water

1 large onion, chopped

3 cups chopped green beans

2 stalks celery, chopped

1 cup chopped cauliflower

1 Tbsp. parsley

1 Tbsp. summer savory

¼ tsp. pepper

1 cup heavy cream

1. Combine all ingredients except heavy cream in slow cooker.

2. Cover. Cook on High 4–6 hours.

3. Remove ham bone. Cut off meat and return to slow cooker.

4. Turn to Low. Stir in cream. Heat through and serve.

- Calories 376
- Fat 24
- Sodium 2254
- Carbs 17
- Sugar 12
- Protein 26

Cabbage and Beef Soup

Colleen Heatwole
Burton, MI

Makes 6–8 servings
Prep. Time: 20 minutes
Cooking Time: 6–8 hours
Ideal slow-cooker size: 5-qt.

1 lb. ground beef

1 can tomatoes, 28–32-oz., or 1 qt. home-canned tomatoes

½ tsp. garlic salt

¼ tsp. onion powder

¼ tsp. garlic powder

¼ tsp. pepper

2 stalks celery, chopped

½ medium head cabbage, chopped

4 cups beef bone broth

chopped fresh parsley, for garnish

1. Brown beef in large skillet. Add tomatoes and chop coarsely. Transfer to slow cooker.

2. Add remaining ingredients, except parsley.

3. Cover and cook 6–8 hours on Low.

4. Serve in bowls garnished with fresh parsley.

- Calories 127
- Fat 5
- Sodium 458
- Carbs 6
- Sugar 4
- Protein 15

Cheeseburger Soup

Jean Hindal
Grandin, IA

Beverly High
Ephrata, PA

Sherlyn Hess
Millersville, PA

Makes 8 servings (¾ cup each)
Prep. Time: 30 minutes
Cooking Time: 20–30 minutes

1 lb. ground beef

¾ cup chopped onion

¾ cup shredded zucchini

¾ cup diced celery

¼ tsp. dried basil

1 tsp. dried parsley flakes

2 Tbsp. olive oil

3 cups chicken bone broth

2 cups diced cauliflower

1½ cups whole milk

¼–½ tsp. pepper

2 tsp. konjac flour

1 cup grated cheddar cheese

¼ cup sour cream

1. In a saucepan, brown beef. Drain. Set aside.

2. In the same saucepan, sauté onion, zucchini, celery, basil, and parsley in 2 Tbsp. olive oil until vegetables are tender.

3. Add broth, cauliflower, and beef. Bring to boil. Reduce heat, cover, and simmer for 10–12 minutes.

4. Reduce heat to low. Add milk and pepper. Sprinkle in konjac flour and whisk until mixture becomes smooth and thickens.

5. Slowly stir in grated cheese, about ½-cupful at a time. Continue to stir until cheese is fully melted and blended into white sauce.

6. Blend in sour cream. Heat, but do not boil.

7. When vegetables are tender and cheesy white sauce is finished, pour the white sauce into the vegetable mixture and gently stir together.

8. When well mixed and heated through, serve.

- Calories 320
- Fat 25
- Sodium 314
- Carbs 6
- Sugar 4
- Protein 17

Hamburger Soup

Chris Peterson
Green Bay, WI

Makes 8 servings
Prep. Time: 20 minutes
Cooking Time: 1–2 hours

1¾ lbs. ground beef

14½-oz. can stewed tomatoes

1 cup sliced mushrooms

2 cups sliced cabbage

1 cup sliced zucchini

2 cups chopped celery

2 cups fresh or frozen green beans

4 cups tomato juice

2 cups no-added-salt tomato juice

2 tsp. dried basil

2 tsp. dried oregano

1 Tbsp. Worcestershire sauce

1. In a soup pot, fry beef until brown and drain.

2. Add rest of ingredients.

3. Simmer 1–2 hours.

- Calories 374
- Fat 27
- Sodium 505
- Carbs 16
- Sugar 6
- Protein 19

Stuffed Pepper Soup

Shelia Heil
Lancaster, PA

Makes 8–10 servings
Prep. Time: 45 minutes
Cooking Time: 3–4 hours
Ideal slow-cooker size: 6-qt.

1 lb. ground beef

1 small onion, diced

1 large green bell pepper, diced

1 large red bell pepper, diced

26-oz. can diced tomatoes

8-oz. can tomato sauce

2 cups beef bone broth

15 drops liquid stevia

1 tsp. garlic powder

salt and pepper, to taste

1. In a large skillet, brown beef, cutting into small pieces as it browns.

2. Add onion and peppers and fry briefly. Drain off drippings. Transfer mixture to slow cooker.

3. Add rest of ingredients. Stir.

4. Cover and cook on Low 3–4 hours, to meld flavors.

- Calories 149
- Fat 9
- Sodium 381
- Carbs 6
- Sugar 2
- Protein 9

Stuffed Sweet Pepper Soup

Moreen Weaver
Bath, NY

Makes 10 servings
Prep. Time: 20 minutes
Cooking Time: 1¼ hours

1 lb. ground beef

2 qts. no-sugar-added tomato juice

3 medium sweet red, or green, bell peppers, diced

1½ cups chili sauce, no salt added

2 stalks celery, diced

1 large onion, diced

3 keto-friendly chicken bouillon cubes

2 cloves garlic, minced

2 cups cooked cauliflower rice

1. In a large kettle over medium heat, cook beef until no longer pink. Drain off drippings.

2. Add remaining ingredients, except cauliflower rice. Bring to a boil.

3. Reduce heat. Simmer, uncovered, for 1 hour.

4. Serve over cooked cauliflower rice, evenly divided among the bowls.

- Calories 206
- Fat 10
- Sodium 1185
- Carbs 18
- Sugar 11
- Protein 11

Hearty Beef Soup

Karen Gingrich
New Holland, PA

Makes 5 servings (¾ cup each)
Prep. Time: 5–10 minutes
Cooking Time: 35 minutes

1 lb. beef tips

2 cups sliced fresh mushrooms

¼ tsp. garlic powder

1 cup beef bone broth

1 cup chopped cauliflower

¼ tsp. dried thyme

dash pepper

½ tsp. konjac flour

1. Trim visible fat from beef.

2. Cook beef in nonstick saucepan until browned and juices evaporate, about 10 minutes, stirring often.

3. Add mushrooms and garlic powder and cook until mushrooms begin to wilt, about 5 minutes.

4. Add broth, cauliflower, thyme, and pepper.

5. Heat to boiling. Sprinkle in konjac flour and whisk until smooth. Cover and cook over low heat for 20 minutes, or until thickened.

- Calories 319
- Fat 20
- Sodium 192
- Carbs 7
- Sugar 1
- Protein 28

Country Fresh Soup

Susan Guarneri
Three Lakes, WI

Makes 4–6 servings
Prep. Time: 30 minutes
Cooking Time: 45 minutes

½ cup chopped onion

2 cloves garlic, minced

2 Tbsp. butter

1½ cups vegetable broth

2 cups cubed zucchini

2 cups cubed yellow squash

2 cups shredded cabbage

2 cups chopped cauliflower

16-oz. can whole tomatoes, chopped, undrained

¼ tsp. salt

½ tsp. dried thyme

½ tsp. dried oregano

dash pepper

1½ tsp. konjac flour

1. In a 6-qt. Dutch oven, over medium-high heat, sauté onion and garlic in butter until golden brown.

2. Add broth, zucchini, squash, cabbage, cauliflower, tomatoes, salt, thyme, oregano, and pepper.

3. Bring to boil. Reduce heat to low.

4. Sprinkle in konjac flour and whisk until smooth. Cover. Simmer for 30 minutes.

- Calories 89
- Fat 5
- Sodium 355
- Carbs 11
- Sugar 7
- Protein 3

Quick and Hearty Vegetable Soup

Berenice M. Wagner
Dodge City, KS

Sherri Grindle
Goshen, IN

Makes 8 servings
Prep. Time: 10 minutes
Cooking Time: 40–45 minutes

½ lb. ground beef

½ cup chopped onion

1 clove garlic, minced

5 cups beef bone broth

14½-oz. can diced tomatoes, undrained, no salt added

½ cup chopped broccoli

½ tsp. crushed dried basil

1 bay leaf

9-oz. pkg. frozen mixed green beans

¼ tsp. konjac flour

1. In a 4-qt. saucepan, brown meat. Drain off drippings.

2. Add onion and garlic. Cook until onion is tender.

3. Stir in remaining ingredients, except frozen green beans.

4. Cover and bring to a boil. Reduce heat. Simmer, covered, 10 minutes, stirring occasionally.

5. Add frozen green beans. Stir.

6. Sprinkle in the konjac flour and whisk until smooth. Cook 20 minutes longer or until thickened.

- Calories 125
- Fat 7
- Sodium 463
- Carbs 7
- Sugar 2
- Protein 8

Beef Mushroom Soup

Becky Frey
Lebanon, PA

Makes 8 servings
Prep. Time: 20 minutes
Cooking Time: 2½ hours

1 lb. boneless beef chuck, cubed

½ Tbsp. olive oil

2 cups chopped onion

½ cup sliced celery

1 cup chopped green beans

1 lb. fresh mushrooms, sliced

2 cloves garlic, crushed

½ tsp. dried thyme, *optional*

8 cups beef bone broth

½ tsp. freshly ground pepper

4 tsp. konjac flour

3 Tbsp. chopped fresh parsley, or 1 Tbsp.
   dried parsley

1. In a large saucepan brown beef on all sides in oil. Remove beef and set aside.

2. Add onion, celery, and green beans to oil in saucepan. Sauté over medium heat about 5 minutes.

3. Add mushrooms, garlic, and thyme (if using). Cook and stir about 2 minutes.

4. Add meat and all remaining ingredients, except the konjac flour and parsley, to saucepan. Bring to a boil.

5. Cover. Reduce heat and simmer about 2 hours, or until beef is tender.

6. Sprinkle in the konjac flour and whisk until smooth. Continue cooking 15 minutes or until soup is thickened.

7. Add parsley and serve piping hot.

- Calories 197
- Fat 10
- Sodium 626
- Carbs 11
- Sugar 2
- Protein 17

Springtime Soup

Clara L. Hershberger
Goshen, IN

Makes 12 servings (¾ cup each)
Prep. Time: 15 minutes
Cooking Time: about 1 hour

1 lb. ground beef

1 cup chopped onion

4 cups water

1 cup chopped green beans

1 cup diced celery

1 cup chopped cauliflower

2 tsp. salt, or less

1 tsp. Worcestershire sauce

¼ tsp. pepper

1 bay leaf

⅛ tsp. dried basil

6 tomatoes, chopped

fresh parsley, for garnish

1. In a large saucepan cook and stir ground beef until browned. Drain excess fat.

2. In a large, heavy soup pot cook and stir onion with meat until onion is clear and tender, about 5 minutes.

3. Stir in all remaining ingredients except parsley. Bring to a boil.

4. Reduce heat, cover, and simmer until vegetables are just tender.

5. Immediately before serving, add fresh parsley.

- Calories 134
- Fat 10
- Sodium 365
- Carbs 5
- Sugar 3
- Protein 7

Indian Tomato Lamb Soup

Valerie Drobel
Carlisle, PA

Makes 6 servings
Prep. Time: 15 minutes
Cooking Time: 55–60 minutes

2 cups chopped onion

3 cloves garlic, minced

1 Tbsp. olive oil

1 tsp. cumin

1 tsp. coriander

1 lb. ground lamb

4 cups chicken bone broth

2 cups chopped fresh tomatoes

2 Tbsp. chopped cilantro

3 cups cooked cauliflower rice

1. In a large stockpot, sauté onion and garlic in oil 10 minutes, or until onion is translucent.

2. Add seasonings and sauté 3 minutes.

3. Add in ground lamb and sauté until browed.

4. Add broth. Cover and bring to a boil.

5. Reduce heat and cook approximately 25 minutes.

6. Stir in tomatoes and heat through, about 5 minutes.

7. Add cilantro and serve over cooked cauliflower rice, evenly distributed among bowls.

- Calories 291
- Fat 20
- Sodium 325
- Carbs 10
- Sugar 4
- Protein 18

Great Fish Soup

Willard E. Roth
Elkhart, IN

Makes 10 servings (¾ cup each)
Prep. Time: 15 minutes
Cooking Time: 40 minutes

3 Tbsp. olive oil

1 onion, chopped

2 cloves garlic, minced

¼ tsp. pepper

1½ tsp. salt

1 bay leaf

¼ tsp. dried thyme

1 lb. pollock, cut into chunks

1 lb. red snapper, cut into chunks

½ lb. tilapia, cut into chunks

4 cups water

1 cup chicken bone broth

1 lb. scallops

12-oz. can evaporated milk

1. Combine oil, onion, and garlic in large stockpot. Sauté until onion and garlic begin to soften. Stir in pepper, salt, bay leaf, and thyme. Combine well.

2. Stir in pollock, red snapper, and tilapia. Simmer gently for about 10 minutes.

3. Add water and chicken broth. Bring to a boil. Simmer for 10 more minutes.

4. Add scallops. Cook about 15 minutes.

5. Stir in evaporated milk. Remove bay leaf before serving.

- Calories 243
- Fat 9
- Sodium 647
- Carbs
- Sugar 4
- Protein 35

Crab Bisque

Jere Zimmerman
Reinholds, PA

Makes 6 servings (¾ cup each)
Prep. Time: 15 minutes
Cooking Time: 20 minutes

4 Tbsp. olive oil, *divided*

½ cup finely chopped onion

½ cup finely chopped green pepper

2 green onions, finely chopped

¼ cup fresh parsley, chopped

8 oz. fresh mushrooms, chopped

2 cups whole milk

¼ tsp. salt

¼ tsp. pepper

3 cups half-and-half

16-oz. can (2½ cups) claw crabmeat

grated carrot for color, *optional*

2½ tsp. konjac flour

1. Heat 2 Tbsp. olive oil in stockpot. Add onion, green pepper, green onions, parsley, and mushrooms. Cook until tender. Remove vegetables from heat and set aside.

2. In the same stockpot, add remaining 2 Tbsp. olive oil and milk.

3. Add reserved vegetable mixture, salt, pepper, half-and-half, crabmeat, and grated carrot, if desired.

4. Sprinkle in konjac flour and whisk until smooth. Heat through over low heat, but do not boil.

- Calories 350
- Fat 25
- Sodium 541
- Carbs 14
- Sugar 10
- Protein 20

Stews

Ground Turkey Stew

Carol Eveleth
Cheyenne, WY

Makes 4–6 servings
Prep. Time: 5 minutes
Cooking Time: 25 minutes
Setting: Manual
Pressure: High
Release: Manual

1 Tbsp. oil

1 onion, chopped

1 lb. ground turkey

½ tsp. garlic powder

1 tsp. chili powder

¾ tsp. cumin

2 tsp. coriander

1 tsp. dried oregano

½ tsp. salt

1 green pepper, chopped

1 red pepper, chopped

1 tomato, chopped

1½ cups tomato sauce

1 Tbsp. soy sauce

1 cup water

2 handfuls cilantro, chopped

1. Press the Sauté function on the control panel of the Instant Pot.

2. Add the oil to the inner pot and let it get hot. Add onion, season with salt, and sauté for a few minutes, or until light golden.

3. Add ground turkey. Break the ground meat using a wooden spoon to avoid formation of lumps. Sauté for a few minutes, until the pink color has faded.

4. Add garlic powder, chili powder, cumin, coriander, dried oregano, and salt. Combine well. Add green pepper, red pepper, and chopped tomato. Combine well.

5. Add tomato sauce, soy sauce, and water; combine well.

6. Close and secure the lid. Click on the Cancel key to cancel the Sauté mode. Make sure the pressure release valve on the lid is in the sealing position.

7. Click on Manual function first and then select high pressure. Click the + button and set the time to 15 minutes.

8. You can either have the steam release naturally (it will take around 20 minutes) or, after 10 minutes, turn the pressure release valve on the lid to venting and release steam. Be careful as the steam is very hot. After the pressure has released completely, open the lid.

9. If the stew is watery, turn on the Sauté function and let it cook for a few more minutes with the lid off.

10. Add cilantro, combine well, and let cook for a few minutes.

- Calories 328
- Fat 3
- Sodium 608
- Carbs 21
- Sugar 6
- Protein 24

Chicken and Chili Stew

Susan Kasting
Jenks, OK

Makes 4 servings
Prep. Time: 20 minutes
Cooking Time: 30 minutes

1¾ cups chicken bone broth

1 lb. boneless, skinless chicken breasts, cut into bite-sized pieces

4 cloves garlic, minced

1–2 jalapeño peppers, seeded and diced

1 tsp. konjac flour

1 medium sweet red bell pepper, diced

1 medium zucchini, sliced

1 tsp. cumin

2 Tbsp. chopped cilantro

1. In good-sized stockpot, heat broth to boiling.

2. Add chicken to broth. Cook about 5 minutes, or until no longer pink.

3. Add garlic and jalapeño peppers. Cook 2 minutes.

4. Sprinkle the konjac flour into the stew and whisk until smooth. Cook, stirring, until thickened.

5. Stir in remaining ingredients.

6. Cover. Let simmer 20 minutes, stirring occasionally.

- Calories 166
- Fat 4
- Sodium 226
- Carbs 3
- Sugar 1
- Protein 29

Pork Thai Stew

Marilyn Mowry
Irving, TX

Makes 8 servings (½ cup cauliflower rice with ¾ cup stew each)
Prep. Time: 15 minutes
Cooking Time: 3¼ hours

2 lbs. pork tenderloin, visible fat trimmed, cubed

2 Tbsp. olive oil

2 cloves garlic, minced

2 cups sliced red bell pepper

2 Tbsp. rice wine vinegar

¼ cup keto-friendly teriyaki sauce

1 tsp. crushed red pepper flakes

½ cup water

¼ cup creamy no-sugar-added peanut butter

4 cups cooked cauliflower rice

sliced green onions, *optional*

chopped peanuts, *optional*

1. In a large skillet, brown meat in oil.

2. Add garlic, bell pepper, vinegar, teriyaki sauce, and red pepper flakes.

3. Simmer, covered, 1½ hours on stove. Stir in ½ cup water. Cover and continue simmering over low heat for another 1½ hours, or until meat is very tender.

4. Remove skillet from heat. While meat is still in skillet, shred the meat using 2 forks to pull it apart. Stir in peanut butter.

5. Serve over cooked cauliflower rice. Garnish with sliced green onions and chopped peanuts, if you wish.

- Calories 245
- Fat 11
- Sodium 458
- Carbs 10
- Sugar 5
- Protein 27

Beef Stew

Carol Eveleth
Cheyenne, WY

Makes 6 servings
Prep. Time: 10 minutes
Cooking Time: 65 minutes
Setting: Sauté and Manual
Pressure: High
Release: Manual

2 lbs. chuck steak, 1½-inch thickness

olive oil

2 tsp. salt, or to taste

½ tsp. black pepper

1 Tbsp. Worcestershire sauce

1 Tbsp. soy sauce

3 Tbsp. tomato paste

1¾ cups chicken bone broth, *divided*

2 small onions, thinly sliced

3 cloves garlic, crushed and minced

2 stalks celery, cut into 1½-inch chunks

2 zucchini, cut into 1½-inch chunks

2 bay leaves

¼ tsp. dried thyme

3 cups chopped cauliflower

1 tsp. konjac flour

1. Heat up your Instant Pot by pressing the Sauté button and click the adjust button to go to Sauté More function. Wait until the indicator says "hot."

2. Season one side of the chuck steak generously with salt and ground black pepper. Add olive oil into the inner pot. Be sure to coat the oil over whole bottom of the pot.

3. Carefully place the seasoned side of chuck steak in the inner pot. Generously season the other side

with salt and ground black pepper. Brown for 6–8 minutes on each side without constantly flipping the steak. Remove and set aside in a large mixing bowl.

4. While the chuck steak is browning, mix together the Worcestershire sauce, soy sauce, and tomato paste with 1½ cups of the chicken broth.

5. Add more olive oil into Instant Pot if necessary. Add thinly sliced small onions and sauté until softened and slightly browned. Add minced garlic cloves and stir for roughly 30 seconds until fragrant.

6. Add all celery and zucchini and sauté until slightly browned. Season with salt and freshly ground black pepper if necessary.

7. Pour in ¼ cup chicken broth and completely deglaze bottom of the pot by scrubbing the flavorful brown bits with a wooden spoon.

8. Add bay leaves, dried thyme, cauliflower, and the chicken broth mixture in the pot. Mix well. Close and secure lid and pressure-cook on Manual at high pressure for 4 minutes. When time is up, quick-release the pressure. Open the lid.

9. While the vegetables are pressure-cooking, cut the chuck steak into 1½–2-inch stew cubes on a large chopping board.

10. Place all chuck stew meat and the flavorful meat juice back in the large mixing bowl. Toss with the konjac flour.

11. Remove half of the vegetables from pressure cooker and set aside. Place beef stew meat and all its juice in the inner pot. Partially submerge the beef stew meat in the liquid without stirring, as you don't want too much flour in the liquid at this point.

12. Close and secure the lid and pressure-cook on Manual at high pressure for 32 minutes. When time is up, turn off the Instant Pot and quick-release any remaining pressure.

(Continued on next page)

13. On medium heat by pressing the Sauté button, break down the cauliflower with a wooden spoon. Stir to thicken the stew.

14. Add the reserved zucchini and celery back in the pot. Taste and season with salt and ground black pepper if necessary. Remove bay leaves before serving.

- Calories 445
- Fat 25
- Sodium 368
- Carbs 23
- Sugar 6
- Protein 33

Colorful Beef Stew

Hope Comerford
Clinton Township, MI

Makes 6 servings
Prep. Time: 20 minutes
Cooking Time: 8–9 hours
Ideal slow-cooker size: 4-qt.

2-lb. boneless beef chuck roast, trimmed of fat and cut into ¾-inch pieces

1 large red onion, chopped

2 cups beef bone broth

6-oz. can tomato paste

4 cloves garlic, minced

1 Tbsp. paprika

2 tsp. dried marjoram

½ tsp. black pepper

1 tsp. sea salt

1 red bell pepper, sliced

1 yellow bell pepper, sliced

1 orange bell pepper, sliced

1. Place all ingredients in the crock except the sliced bell peppers, and stir.

2. Cover and cook on Low for 8–9 hours. Stir in sliced bell peppers the last 45 minutes of cooking time.

- Calories 361
- Fat 22
- Sodium 643
- Carbs 11
- Sugar 6
- Protein 32

Beef and Kale Stew

Dora Martindale
Elk City, OK

Makes 6 servings
Prep. Time: 20 minutes
Cooking Time: 10 minutes
Setting: Sauté and Manual
Pressure: High
Release: Manual then Natural

1 cup sliced mushrooms

3 Tbsp. butter

2 lbs. ground beef

4 pieces nitrate-free bacon, chopped

2 bundles kale, finely chopped

4 cloves garlic, minced

2 onions, chopped

3–4 cups homemade beef bone broth, *divided*

2 Tbsp. dried thyme or 2 drops Young Living Thyme
    Vitality Essential Oil

3 tsp. salt (or more, to taste)

1 tsp. pepper (or more, to taste)

1 cup chopped cauliflower

2 tsp. konjac flour

1. In the inner pot of the Instant Pot, sauté mushrooms in the butter using the Sauté function, then place in a bowl.

2. Add the beef, chopped bacon, kale, garlic, and onions, and sauté until beef is brown and kale is reduced in size.

3. Add 2 cups bone broth, thyme, salt, and pepper. Secure the lid and make sure vent is at sealing, then cook on Manual at high pressure for 8 minutes.

4. Do a quick release of the pressure.

5. Add the rest of ingredients (except the konjac flour) and 1–2 more cups of bone broth.

6. Secure the lid and make sure vent is at sealing, then cook on Manual at high pressure 6 minutes. Let the pressure release naturally.

7. Sprinkle the contents of the Inner Pot with konjac flour and whisk until smooth. Let thicken on Sauté function. Add more salt or pepper as needed.

- Calories 580
- Fat 47
- Sodium 1491
- Carbs 10
- Sugar 3
- Protein 31

Pungent Beef Stew

Grace Ketcham
Marietta, GA

Makes 4–6 servings
Prep. Time: 15 minutes
Cooking Time: 10–12 hours
Ideal slow-cooker size: 4½-qt.

2 lbs. beef chuck, cubed

8-oz. can tomato sauce

1 tsp. liquid aminos

1 clove garlic, minced

1 medium onion, chopped

2 bay leaves

½ tsp. salt

½ tsp. paprika

¼ tsp. pepper

dash ground cloves or allspice

14-oz. can diced tomatoes

1 cup chopped green beans

2 cups chopped cauliflower

2 stalks celery, chopped

½ cup water

1. Combine all ingredients in slow cooker.

2. Cover. Cook on Low 10–12 hours. Remove bay leaves before serving.

- Calories 254
- Fat 11
- Sodium 386
- Carbs 7
- Sugar 2
- Protein 33

Jamaican Beef Stew

Andy Wagner
Quarryville, PA

Makes 6 servings
Prep. Time: 30 minutes
Cooking Time: 6–8 hours
Ideal slow-cooker size: 4-qt.

1 Tbsp. extra-virgin olive oil

2 cloves garlic, minced

1 lb. beef stew meat

2 cups sliced zucchini

3 green onions, chopped

½ cup chopped cauliflower

15-oz. can tomatoes, drained and diced

2 tsp. curry powder

½ tsp. dried thyme

¼ tsp. red pepper flakes

¼ tsp. ground allspice

salt and freshly ground black pepper, to taste

1 cup unsweetened coconut milk

1–2 cups vegetable broth

1. Pour the oil into a 4-qt. slow cooker and set the cooker on High. Add the garlic and put the lid on the cooker while you prepare the rest of the ingredients.

2. Add beef, zucchini, green onions, cauliflower, and tomatoes to the cooker.

3. Stir in the curry powder, thyme, red pepper flakes, allspice, and salt and pepper, to taste.

4. Add the coconut milk and broth.

5. Cover and cook on Low for 6–8 hours.

- Calories 202
- Fat 12
- Sodium 350
- Carbs 6
- Sugar 4
- Protein 18

Santa Fe Stew

Jeanne Allen
Rye, CO

Makes 4-6 servings
Prep. Time: 20 minutes
Cooking Time: 4½–6½ hours
Ideal slow-cooker size: 4-qt.

2 lbs. sirloin, or stewing meat, cubed

1 large onion, diced

2 cloves garlic, minced

2 Tbsp. olive oil

3 cups beef bone broth

1 Tbsp. dried parsley flakes

1 tsp. cumin

½ tsp. salt

3 zucchini squash, diced

14½-oz. can diced tomatoes

14½-oz. can green beans, drained, or 1 lb. frozen green
   beans

4-oz. can diced green chiles

1. Brown meat, onion, and garlic in oil in saucepan. Place in slow cooker.

2. Stir in remaining ingredients.

3. Cover. Cook on Low for 8 hours.

- Calories 334
- Fat 18
- Sodium 305
- Carbs 9
- Sugar 4
- Protein 35

Tomato and Beef Stew

Lizzie Ann Yoder
Hartville, OH

Makes 6 servings
Prep. Time: 20-30 minutes
Cooking Time: 1-1½ hours

1½ lbs. beef stew meat

1 cup chopped onion

2 stalks celery, including tops, cut up

3 cups chopped fresh tomatoes

2 Tbsp. fresh basil, or ½ tsp. dried basil

6 cups beef bone broth

1 cup sliced fresh mushrooms, *optional*

1. In a large stockpot combine all ingredients except mushrooms.

2. Bring to a boil and simmer, covered, 1–1½ hours.

3. If you wish, stir in mushrooms 30 minutes before end of cooking time.

- Calories 189
- Fat 5
- Sodium 679
- Carbs 7
- Sugar 3
- Protein 30

Meatball Stew

**Barbara Hershey
Lititz, PA**

Makes 8 servings
Prep. Time: 1 hour (includes preparing and baking meatballs)
Cooking Time: 4–5 hours
Ideal slow-cooker size: 4- or 6-qt.

Meatballs
  2 lbs. 90%-lean ground beef

  2 eggs, beaten

  2 Tbsp. dried onion

  ½ tsp. salt

  ¼ tsp. pepper

  1 tsp. Dijon mustard

  2 tsp. liquid aminos

4 cups chopped cauliflower

1 large onion, sliced

2 cups chopped broccoli

4 cups no-sugar-added tomato juice

1 tsp. dried basil

1 tsp. dried oregano

½ tsp. pepper

salt, to taste

1. In a bowl, thoroughly mix meatball ingredients together. Form into 1-inch balls.

2. Place meatballs on a lightly greased rimmed baking sheet. Bake at 400°F for 20 minutes.

3. Meanwhile, place all vegetables in slow cooker.

4. When finished baking, remove meatballs from pan.

5. Place meatballs on top of vegetables in slow cooker.

6. In a large bowl, combine tomato juice and seasonings. Pour over meatballs and vegetables in slow cooker.

7. Cover. Cook on High 4–5 hours, or until vegetables are tender.

- Calories 253
- Fat 13
- Sodium 343
- Carbs 7
- Sugar 3
- Protein 26

Oyster Stew

Dorothy Reise
Severna Park, MD

Makes 4 servings (¾ cup each)
Prep. Time: 10–15 minutes
Cooking Time: 15 minutes

2–3 doz. fresh oysters in liquid

2 Tbsp. olive oil

1 Tbsp. chopped onion

3 cups whole milk

1½ tsp. konjac flour

½ tsp. salt

½ tsp. pepper

½ tsp. chopped parsley

pinch celery seed, *optional*

dash paprika, *optional*

1. In a small skillet over medium heat, precook oysters in their own liquid until edges curl and oysters become plump. Set aside.

2. In a large stockpot, heat olive oil; add onion, and sauté until soft.

3. Slowly add milk. While stirring, sprinkle in the konjac flour. Continue stirring until smooth.

4. Add the precooked oysters and liquid, salt, pepper, parsley, and celery seed and paprika if you wish. Mix well.

5. Heat thoroughly and serve.

- Calories 210
- Fat 14
- Sodium 373
- Carbs 11
- Sugar 9
- Protein 9

Easy Oyster Stew

Clara Yoder Byler
Hartville, OH

Makes 8–10 servings
Prep. Time: 15 minutes
Cooking Time: 30 minutes

2 Tbsp. butter

1 qt. oysters with oyster liquor

1 qt. whole milk

2 cups cream

1½ tsp. salt

⅛–¼ tsp. pepper

1. Melt butter in large skillet or saucepan. Drain oysters (reserving liquor). One-by-one, place in butter.

2. Cook over medium heat until edges of oysters begin to curl. Remove immediately from heat.

3. Meanwhile, heat milk and cream in a large stockpot to boiling point.

4. Add oyster liquor to hot milk and bring to boiling point.

5. Immediately add oysters and seasonings.

- Calories 289
- Fat 25
- Sodium 415
- Carbs 9
- Sugar 6
- Protein 9

Gumbo

Dorothy Ealy
Los Angeles, CA

Makes 8 servings
Prep. Time: 30 minutes
Cooking Time: 4½–5½ hours
Ideal slow-cooker size: 5-qt.

2 onions, chopped

3 stalks celery, chopped

½ cup diced green bell pepper

2 cloves garlic, chopped

1 cup chopped fresh or frozen okra

½ cup diced andouille or chorizo sausage

2 15-oz. cans tomatoes, undrained

3 Tbsp. tomato paste

1 chicken bouillon cube

¼ tsp. freshly ground black pepper

¼ tsp. dried thyme

1½ lbs. raw shrimp, peeled and deveined, chopped if large

1. In the slow cooker, combine onions, celery, bell pepper, garlic, okra, sausage, tomatoes, tomato paste, bouillon cube, black pepper, and thyme.

2. Cover and cook on Low for 4–5 hours, until vegetables are soft.

3. Add shrimp. Cook for 15–20 more minutes on Low, until shrimp are just opaque and cooked through. Thin gumbo if necessary with a little water, broth, or wine. Taste and adjust salt.

Serving suggestion: Pass the hot sauce so people can make it really authentically spicy!

Note: If you are peeling the shrimp yourself, save the shells. Place them in a saucepan with water or chicken broth just to cover and simmer for 30 minutes. Strain out shells and discard. This makes a tasty seafood-infused broth for making other soups or thinning the gumbo.

- Calories 131
- Fat 3
- Sodium 837
- Carbs 10
- Sugar 5
- Protein 16

Oceanside Bisque

Jane Geigley
Lancaster, PA

Makes 8 servings
Prep. Time: 30 minutes
Cooking Time: 2½–3½ hours
Ideal slow-cooker size: 6-qt.

1 Tbsp. unsalted butter

1 Tbsp. olive oil

3 large shallots, minced (or 1 medium-sized Vidalia onion, minced)

5½ cups chicken bone broth

2 cups heavy cream

1 Tbsp. kosher salt

½ tsp. freshly ground white pepper

1 lb. fresh or thawed lump crabmeat (picked over for shell fragments), or canned crabmeat

fresh tarragon or flat-leaf parsley, for garnish

1. In a small saucepan, melt butter and oil over medium heat.

2. Add shallots and sauté until translucent (about 2–3 minutes).

3. Pour into slow cooker.

4. Add broth and cream.

5. Season with salt and pepper.

6. Cook on High for ½ hour.

7. Add crabmeat; stir.

8. Cook for another 2–3 hours.

9. Ladle into bowls and garnish with tarragon or parsley.

Serving suggestion: This is also delicious with fresh chopped parsley on top and a sprinkle of turmeric or paprika.

- Calories 334
- Fat 27
- Sodium 1232
- Carbs 8
- Sugar 5
- Protein 15

Italian Clam Chowder

Susan Guarneri
Three Lakes, WI

Makes 8 servings (¾ cup each)
Prep. Time: 30 minutes
Cooking Time: 4–5 hours

1 lb. lean turkey Italian sausage

1 onion, chopped

2 cups chopped cauliflower

4½ cups chicken bone broth

2½ cups half-and-half

1 dozen large fresh clams, chopped, or 6½-oz. can clams

8-oz. can minced clams

¼ tsp. salt

¼ tsp. pepper

1 tsp. dried basil

1. Cut sausage into ½-inch slices. Place in large Dutch oven and brown until no longer pink. Set sausage aside and remove drippings.

2. Add onion, cauliflower, broth, half-and-half, clams, salt, pepper, and basil. Stir until well mixed.

3. Heat oven to 275°F. Place Dutch oven in the oven. Bake for 4–5 hours. (Do not increase the temperature or the chowder may boil and then the cream will curdle.)

4. One hour before the end of the baking time, stir in the reserved sausage.

- Calories 295
- Fat 14
- Sodium 943
- Carbs 11
- Sugar 4
- Protein 31

KETO TIP:
Cooking in larger quantities and freezing meals may help you stick to your keto diet. Soups and stews are perfect for freezing! Particularly if you're freezing the soup in glass jars or containers, leave space at the top; the liquid will expand when frozen and can break the jar if there's nowhere for it to go.

Chilies

Chicken Chili

Sharon Miller
Holmesville, OH

Makes 6 servings
Prep. Time: 15 minutes
Cooking Time: 5–6 hours
Ideal slow-cooker size: 4-qt.

2 lbs. boneless, skinless chicken breasts, cubed

2 Tbsp. butter

2 14-oz. cans diced tomatoes, undrained, divided

1 cup diced onion

1 cup diced red bell pepper

1–2 Tbsp. chili powder, according to your taste preference

1 tsp. cumin

1 tsp. ground oregano

salt and pepper, to taste

1. In a skillet on high heat, brown chicken cubes in butter until they have some browned edges. Place in greased slow cooker.

2. Pour one of the cans of tomatoes with its juice into skillet to get all the browned bits and butter. Scrape and pour into slow cooker.

3. Add rest of ingredients, including other can of tomatoes, to cooker.

4. Cook on Low for 5–6 hours.

Serving suggestion: Can be served with shredded cheddar cheese, sour cream, and avocado slices.

- Calories 253
- Fat 7
- Sodium 335
- Carbs 11
- Sugar 3
- Protein 35

White Chicken Chili

Jewel Showalter
Landisville, PA

Makes 6–8 servings
Prep. Time: 25 minutes
Cooking Time: 7 hours
Ideal slow-cooker size: 5-qt.

2 whole skinless chicken breasts

6 cups water

2 onions, chopped

2 cloves garlic, minced

1 Tbsp. olive oil

2–4 4¼-oz. cans chopped green chiles, drained, depending on your taste preference

1–2 diced jalapeño peppers

2 tsp. cumin

1½ tsp. dried oregano

¼ tsp. cayenne pepper

½ tsp. salt

1–2 cups shredded cheese

sour cream

salsa

avocado chunks

1. Place all ingredients except the cheese, sour cream, salsa, and avocado into crock.

2. Cover. Cook on Low 7 hours.

3. Remove chicken from slow cooker and cube it. Place it back into the crock. Stir in the cheese.

4. Serve topped with sour cream, salsa, and avocado chunks.

- Calories 238
- Fat 10
- Sodium 237
- Carbs 7
- Sugar 3
- Protein 30

Scrumptious White Chili

Gloria L. Lehman
Singers Glen, VA

Lauren Bailey
Mechanicsburg, PA

Makes 6 servings (¾ cup each)
Prep. Time: 20–25 minutes
Cooking Time: 25 minutes

1 large onion, chopped

2 cloves garlic, minced

1½ Tbsp. olive oil

2 cups chopped cooked chicken

4-oz. can chopped mild green chiles

½–1 Tbsp. diced jalapeño pepper, *optional*

1½ tsp. cumin

1 tsp. dried oregano

10½-oz. can chicken bone broth

1 broth can water

1 cup chopped cauliflower

½ tsp. cayenne, or to taste

salt, to taste

2 oz. (½ cup) Monterey Jack cheese, shredded

½ cup sour cream

chopped green onions, *optional*

fresh cilantro, *optional*

1. In a large stockpot, sauté onion and garlic in oil over medium heat.

2. Add chicken, chiles, jalapeño pepper (if you want), cumin, oregano, chicken broth, water, and cauliflower to stockpot and stir well. Bring to a boil, reduce heat, and simmer, covered, 10–15 minutes.

3. Just before serving, add cayenne, salt, cheese, and sour cream. Heat just until cheese is melted, being careful not to let the chili boil.

4. Serve at once, garnished with chopped green onions and fresh cilantro, if desired.

- Calories 171
- Fat 8
- Sodium 261
- Carbs 5
- Sugar 2
- Protein 19

White Chili

Andrea Bjorlie
Grand Rapids, MI

SLOW COOKER

Makes 6 servings
Prep. Time: 20 minutes
Cooking Time: 4 hours
Ideal slow-cooker size: 5-qt.

1 onion, chopped

3 cloves garlic, minced

1 Tbsp. olive oil

1 lb. ground chicken

2 cups chopped cauliflower

15 oz. chicken bone broth

1 tsp. salt

1 tsp. cumin

1 tsp. dried oregano

½ tsp. black pepper

1 tsp. cayenne pepper

½ cup half-and-half

1 cup sour cream

fresh cilantro, to taste, *optional*

1. Sauté onion and garlic in oil in skillet until softened. Add in ground chicken and continue cooking until browned.

2. Put in slow cooker with cauliflower, broth, salt, cumin, oregano, pepper, and cayenne pepper.

3. Cook on Low for 4 hours.

4. Turn heat off for a bit near serving time. Add half-and-half and sour cream. Serve garnished with cilantro, if you wish.

- Calories 216
- Fat 15
- Sodium 502
- Carbs 5
- Sugar 2
- Protein 16

Turkey Chili

Julette Rush
Harrisonburg, VA

Makes 5 servings
Prep. Time: 15 minutes
Cooking Time: 30 minutes

1½ lbs. ground turkey breast

1 cup chopped onion

½ cup chopped sweet green bell pepper

½ cup chopped sweet red bell pepper

14-oz. can diced tomatoes

1¾ cups water

2 tsp. chili powder

½ tsp. garlic powder

¼ tsp. black pepper

¾ tsp. cumin

1 ¾ cups chicken bone broth

1 cup shredded cheddar cheese

1. In a large stockpot, sauté turkey, onion, and bell peppers until turkey is browned and vegetables are softened.

2. Mix in tomatoes, water, seasonings, and broth. Reduce heat to low.

3. Cover and simmer 20 minutes. Stir occasionally.

4. Top individual servings with cheese.

- Calories 286
- Fat 9
- Sodium 545
- Carbs 10
- Sugar 3
- Protein 41

Turkey Chili Con Carne

Jackie Stefl
East Bethany, NY

Makes 10 servings
Prep. Time: 15 minutes
Cooking Time: 2¼ hours

1 medium onion

1 medium sweet green bell pepper

1 medium sweet red bell pepper

1 medium sweet yellow bell pepper

2 lbs. ground turkey breast

2 Tbsp. extra-virgin olive oil

28-oz. can crushed tomatoes, no salt added, undrained

1 Tbsp. chili powder

1 tsp. cinnamon

1 tsp. cumin

2 cups beef bone broth

1½ cups grated cheddar cheese, *optional*

¾ cup sour cream, *optional*

1. Chop onion and bell peppers. Place in large stockpot, along with ground turkey and olive oil.

2. Sauté until meat is no longer pink and vegetables are tender.

3. Stir tomatoes, seasonings, and broth into pot.

4. Cover. Simmer 2 hours. Stir occasionally.

5. Garnish individual servings, if you wish, with 1 rounded Tbsp. cheese and sour cream.

- Calories 219
- Fat 8
- Sodium 487
- Carbs 9
- Sugar 5
- Protein 27

Pork Chili

Carol Duree
Salina, KS

SLOW COOKER

Makes 5 servings
Prep. Time: 15 minutes
Cooking Time: 4–8 hours
Ideal slow-cooker size: 4-qt.

1 lb. boneless pork ribs

2 14½-oz. cans diced tomatoes

4¼-oz. can diced green chiles, drained

½ cup chopped onion

1 clove garlic, minced

1 Tbsp. chili powder

1. Layer ingredients into slow cooker in order given.

2. Cover. Cook on High 4 hours or on Low 6–8 hours, or until pork is tender but not dry.

3. Cut up or shred meat. Stir through chili and serve.

- Calories 280
- Fat 15
- Sodium 368
- Carbs 11
- Sugar 3
- Protein 25

No-Beans Chili

Sharon Timpe
Jackson, WI

Makes 10–12 servings
Prep. Time: 35 minutes
Cooking Time: 6–10 hours
Ideal slow-cooker size: 5–6-qt.

2–3 Tbsp. olive oil

1½ lbs. round steak, cubed

1½ lbs. chuck steak, cubed

2 cups beef bone broth

1½ tsp. dried oregano

2 tsp. dried parsley

1 medium onion, chopped

1 cup chopped celery

1 cup diced bell pepper

28-oz. can stewed tomatoes

8-oz. can tomato sauce

1 Tbsp. vinegar

1½ tsp. Truvia Brown Sugar Blend

2 Tbsp. chili powder

1 tsp. cumin

¼ tsp. pepper

l tsp. salt

1. Heat oil in a skillet and brown the beef cubes. You may have to do this in two batches.

2. Put browned beef in slow cooker.

3. Add the beef bone broth to skillet and stir, scraping up browned bits. Scrape/pour mixture into slow cooker.

4. Add rest of ingredients to slow cooker.

5. Cook on Low 9–10 hours or High 6–7 hours, until meat is very tender.

Serving suggestion: Serve in bowls garnished with toppings like grated cheese, sour cream, blue cheese crumbles, and avocado chunks.

- Calories 260
- Fat 11
- Sodium 728
- Carbs 18
- Sugar 4
- Protein 27

Chunky Beef Chili

Ruth C. Hancock
Earlsboro, OK

Makes 4 servings
Prep. Time: 30 minutes
Cooking Time: 1¾–2¼ hours

2 Tbsp. olive oil, *divided*

1 lb. beef stew, cut into 1½-inch thick pieces

1 medium onion, chopped

1 medium jalapeño pepper with seeds, minced, *optional*

½ tsp. salt

2 14½-oz. cans chili-seasoned diced tomatoes (make sure there is no added sugar)

1. Heat 1 Tbsp. oil in stockpot over medium heat until hot.

2. Brown half of meat in oil. Remove meat from pot and keep warm.

3. Repeat with remaining beef. Remove meat from pot and keep warm.

4. Add remaining 1 Tbsp. oil to stockpot, along with the onion, and the jalapeño pepper if you wish.

5. Cook 5–8 minutes, or until vegetables are tender. Stir occasionally.

6. Return meat and juices to stockpot. Add salt and tomatoes.

7. Bring to a boil. Reduce heat. Cover tightly and simmer 1¾–2¼ hours, or until meat is tender but not dried out.

- Calories 247
- Fat 12
- Sodium 1186
- Carbs 9
- Sugar 6
- Protein 26

Adirondack Three-Alarm Chili

Joanne Kennedy
Plattsburgh, NY

Makes 8 servings
Prep. Time: 25 minutes
Cooking Time: 3 hours

2½ lbs. ground beef

3 medium onions, diced

4 cloves garlic, crushed

1 green pepper, chopped

28-oz. can crushed tomatoes

16-oz. can no-added-salt tomato sauce

1½ tsp. Truvia Brown Sugar Blend

1 tsp. dried oregano

¼–1 tsp. crushed red pepper

3 Tbsp. chili powder

1 tsp. salt, *optional*

1. Brown ground beef in large soup pot.

2. Add and sauté onions, garlic, and green pepper.

3. Add the rest of ingredients. Simmer on low heat for 3 hours.

- Calories 578
- Fat 43
- Sodium 971
- Carbs 17
- Sugar 8
- Protein 29

Steamy Beef Chili

Lavina Hochstedler
Grand Blanc, MI

Makes 12 servings
Prep. Time: 20 minutes
Cooking Time: 50–60 minutes

3 lbs. ground beef

1 large onion, chopped

1 large sweet green bell pepper

1 large sweet red bell pepper

3 medium zucchini, chopped

6 cloves garlic, minced

2 Tbsp. olive oil

28-oz. can no-salt-added crushed tomatoes undrained

2 cups water

8 oz. no-salt-added tomato paste

3 Tbsp. chili powder

2 Tbsp. Worcestershire sauce

1 Tbsp. cumin

2 tsp. dried thyme

2 tsp. dried parsley flakes

½ tsp. pepper

1. In Dutch oven or soup kettle, sauté ground beef, onion, peppers, zucchini, and garlic in oil for 15 minutes, or until vegetables are tender.

2. Stir in remaining ingredients. Bring to a boil.

3. Reduce heat. Cover and simmer 30–40 minutes, or until heated through.

- Calories 395
- Fat 31
- Sodium 171
- Carbs 8
- Sugar 4
- Protein 20

Hearty Chili

Joylynn Keener
Lancaster, PA

 SLOW COOKER

Makes 8 servings
Prep. Time: 20–25 minutes
Cooking Time: 8 hours
Ideal slow-cooker size: 5-qt.

1 onion, chopped

2 stalks celery, chopped

3 lbs. ground beef

1 Tbsp. olive oil

14-oz. can diced tomatoes

2 14-oz. cans tomato sauce

1 green bell pepper, chopped

15 drops liquid stevia

1 tsp. salt

1 tsp. dried thyme

1 tsp. dried oregano

1 Tbsp. chili powder, or to taste

1. Brown onion, celery, and beef in skillet in oil if needed. Stir frequently to break up clumps of meat. When meat is no longer pink, drain off drippings.

2. Spoon meat into slow cooker. Stir in all remaining ingredients, mixing well.

3. Cover. Cook on Low 8 hours.

- Calories 493
- Fat 36
- Sodium 922
- Carbs 10
- Sugar 5
- Protein 31

Beef Chili

Lois Hess
Lancaster, PA

Makes 8 servings
Prep. Time: 30 minutes
Cooking Time: 30 minutes

2½ lbs. ground beef

4 cloves garlic

1½ cups chopped onion

1 Tbsp. olive oil

1 cup chopped celery

1 cup chopped zucchini

1 cup chopped tomatoes

1 tsp. cumin

1 tsp. dried basil

1–1½ tsp. chili powder, depending upon your taste
    preferences

1 cup chopped sweet bell green pepper

1 cup no-sugar-added tomato juice

juice of ½ lemon

3 Tbsp. no-salt-added tomato paste

dash cayenne pepper, or ¼ tsp.
    coarsely ground black pepper

chopped fresh parsley, for garnish

1. Sauté ground beef, garlic, and onion in oil in large stockpot.

2. Add celery, zucchini, tomatoes, and spices.

3. When vegetables are almost tender, add pepper. Cook until tender.

4. Stir in all remaining ingredients except parsley. Cover and heat gently.

5. Top individual servings with parsley.

- Calories 454
- Fat 36
- Sodium 247
- Carbs 8
- Sugar 4
- Protein 24

Our Favorite Chili

Ruth Shank
Gridley, IL

Makes 10–12 servings
Prep. Time: 20 minutes
Cooking Time: 4–10 hours
Ideal slow-cooker size: 5-qt.

3 lbs. ground beef

¼ cup chopped onion

1 stalk celery, chopped

1 Tbsp. olive oil

29-oz. can stewed tomatoes

½ cup tomato sauce

1½ tsp. lemon juice

2 tsp. vinegar

¾ tsp. Truvia Brown Sugar Blend

1½ tsp. salt

1 tsp. liquid aminos

½ tsp. garlic powder

½ tsp. dry mustard

1 Tbsp. chili powder

2 6-oz. cans tomato paste

1. Brown ground beef, onion, and celery in skillet in oil. Stir frequently to break up clumps of meat. When meat is no longer pink, drain off drippings.

2. Place meat and vegetables in slow cooker. Add all remaining ingredients. Mix well.

3. Cover. Cook on Low 8–10 hours or on High 4–5 hours.

Serving Suggestion: Top with diced avocado and sprinkle with Colby or Monterey Jack cheese.

- Calories 408
- Fat 25
- Sodium 1255
- Carbs 24
- Sugar 11
- Protein 24

Texican Chili

Becky Oswald
Broadway, VA

Makes 15 servings
Prep. Time: 20 minutes
Cooking Time: 9–10 hours
Ideal slow-cooker size: 5- to 6-qt.

8 bacon strips, diced

2½ lbs. beef stewing meat, cubed

28-oz. can stewed tomatoes

14½-oz. can stewed tomatoes

2 8-oz. cans tomato sauce

1 medium onion, chopped

1 cup chopped celery

2 cups chopped bell pepper (any colors)

¼ cup minced fresh parsley

1 Tbsp. chili powder

1 tsp. salt

½ tsp. cumin

¼ tsp. pepper

1. Cook bacon in skillet until crisp. Drain on paper towel.

2. Brown beef in bacon drippings in skillet.

3. Combine all ingredients in slow cooker.

4. Cover. Cook on Low 9–10 hours, or until meat is tender. Stir occasionally.

- Calories 190
- Fat 11
- Sodium 723
- Carbs 7
- Sugar 4
- Protein 23

Favorite Chili

Carol Eveleth
Cheyenne, WY

Makes 4–6 servings
Prep. Time: 10 minutes
Cooking Time: 35 minutes
Setting: Manual
Pressure: High
Release: Natural

2 lbs. ground beef

1 tsp. salt

½ tsp. black pepper

1 Tbsp. olive oil

1 small onion, diced

2 cloves garlic, minced

1 green bell pepper, chopped

2 Tbsp. chili powder

½ tsp. cumin

1½ cups water

15-oz. can crushed tomatoes

1. Press Sauté button and adjust once to Sauté More function. Wait until indicator says "hot."

2. Season the ground beef with salt and black pepper.

3. Add the olive oil into the inner pot. Coat the whole bottom of the pot with the oil.

4. Add ground beef into the inner pot. The ground beef will start to release moisture. Allow the ground beef to brown and crisp slightly, stirring occasionally to break it up. Taste and adjust the seasoning with more salt and ground black pepper.

5. Add diced onion, minced garlic, chopped pepper, chili powder, and cumin. Sauté for about 5 minutes, until the spices start to release their fragrance. Stir frequently.

6. Add water. Mix well. Pour in crushed tomatoes.

7. Close and secure lid, making sure vent is set to sealing, and pressure-cook on Manual at high pressure for 10 minutes.

8. Let the pressure release naturally when cooking time is up. Open the lid carefully.

Serving suggestion: Garnish chili with sour cream, shredded cheese, jalapeño slices, or chopped onions.

- Calories 325
- Fat 18
- Sodium 436
- Carbs 7
- Sugar 3
- Protein 32

Chili Con Carne

Donna Conto
Saylorsburg, PA

Makes 4–6 servings
Prep. Time: 15 minutes
Cooking Time: 5–6 hours
Ideal slow-cooker size: 4-qt.

1½ lbs. ground beef

1 cup chopped onion

¾ cup chopped green pepper

1 clove garlic, minced

14½-oz. can chopped tomatoes

8-oz. can tomato sauce

2 tsp. chili powder

½ tsp. dried basil

1. Brown beef, onion, green pepper, and garlic in saucepan. Drain.

2. Combine all ingredients in slow cooker.

3. Cover. Cook on Low 5–6 hours.

- Calories 326
- Fat 23
- Sodium 372
- Carbs 9
- Sugar 5
- Protein 21

Dorothea's Slow Cooker Chili

Dorothea K. Ladd
Ballston Lake, NY

Makes 6–8 servings
Prep. Time: 15 minutes
Cooking Time: 8–10 hours
Ideal slow-cooker size: 6½-qt.

1 lb. ground beef

1 lb. bulk pork sausage

1 large onion, chopped

1 large green pepper, chopped

1 large red pepper, chopped

2–3 stalks celery, chopped

29-oz. can tomato purée

6-oz. can tomato paste

2 cloves garlic, minced

2 Tbsp. chili powder

2 tsp. salt

1. Brown ground beef and sausage in skillet. Drain.

2. Combine all ingredients in slow cooker.

3. Cover. Cook on Low 8–10 hours.

Serving suggestion: Top individual servings with shredded sharp cheddar cheese.

Variations:
1. For extra flavor, add 1 tsp. cayenne pepper.
2. For more zest, use mild or hot Italian sausage instead of regular pork sausage.

- Calories 356
- Fat 24
- Sodium 1041
- Carbs 14
- Sugar 7
- Protein 22

Main Dishes

Chicken & Turkey

Garlic Galore Rotisserie Chicken

Hope Comerford
Clinton Township, MI

Makes 4 servings
Prep. Time: 5 minutes
Cooking Time: 33 minutes
Setting: Sauté and Manual
Pressure: High
Release: Natural then Manual

3-lb. whole chicken

2 Tbsp. olive oil, *divided*

salt, to taste

pepper, to taste

20–30 cloves fresh garlic, peeled and left whole

1 cup chicken bone broth

2 Tbsp. garlic powder

2 tsp. onion powder

½ tsp. basil

½ tsp. cumin

½ tsp. chili powder

1. Rub chicken with one Tbsp. of the olive oil and sprinkle with salt and pepper.

2. Place the garlic cloves inside the chicken. Use butcher's twine to secure the legs.

3. Press the Sauté button on the Instant Pot then add the rest of the olive oil to the inner pot.

4. When the pot is hot, place the chicken inside. You are just trying to sear it, so leave it for about 4 minutes on each side.

5. Remove the chicken and set aside. Place the trivet at the bottom of the inner pot and pour in the chicken broth.

6. Mix together the remaining seasonings and rub it all over the entire chicken.

7. Place the chicken back inside the inner pot, breast side up, on top of the trivet and secure the lid to the sealing position.

8. Press the Manual button and use the +/- to set it for 25 minutes.

9. When the timer beeps, allow the pressure to release naturally for 15 minutes. If the lid will not open at this point, quick-release the remaining pressure and remove the chicken.

10. Let the chicken rest for 5–10 minutes before serving.

- Calories 801
- Fat 54
- Sodium 472
- Carbs 12
- Sugar 0
- Protein 69

Garlic and Lemon Chicken

Hope Comerford
Clinton Township, MI

SLOW COOKER

Makes 5 servings
Prep. Time: 5 minutes
Cooking Time: 5–6 hours
Ideal slow-cooker size: 3- or 5-qt.

4–5 lbs. boneless skinless chicken breasts or thighs

½ cup minced shallots

½ cup olive oil

¼ cup lemon juice

1 Tbsp. garlic paste (or use 1 medium clove garlic, minced)

1 Tbsp. no-salt seasoning

⅛ tsp. pepper

1. Place chicken in slow cooker.

2. In a small bowl, mix the remaining ingredients. Pour this mixture over the chicken in the crock.

3. Cover and cook on Low for 5–6 hours.

- Calories 641
- Fat 31
- Sodium 165
- Carbs 4
- Sugar 2
- Protein 82

Chicken Monterey

Sally Holzem
Schofield, WI

Makes 4 servings (1 chicken breast half each)
Prep. Time: 15 minutes
Baking Time: 30 minutes

4 4-oz. boneless, skinless chicken breast halves

⅛ tsp. pepper

⅓ cup keto-friendly barbecue sauce

2 slices bacon, cooked as crisp as you like

1 cup shredded cheddar cheese

4 green onions, trimmed and sliced

1 small tomato, chopped

1. Heat oven to 350°F.

2. Place chicken in a single layer in a greased baking dish.

3. Sprinkle with pepper. Spoon on the barbecue sauce.

4. Bake in oven for 25 minutes, or until all pink is gone.

5. Top each breast half with ½ slice of cooked bacon. Sprinkle with cheddar cheese.

6. Bake in oven 5 more minutes.

7. Top each breast half with fresh green onions and tomatoes just before serving.

- Calories 302
- Fat 14
- Sodium 543
- Carbs 7
- Sugar 3
- Protein 34

Bacon-Feta Stuffed Chicken

Tina Goss
Duenweg, MO

Makes 4 servings
Prep. Time: 10 minutes
Cooking Time: 1½–3 hours
Ideal slow-cooker size: 3-qt.

¼ cup crumbled cooked bacon
¼ cup crumbled feta cheese
4 boneless, skinless chicken breast halves
2 14½-oz. cans diced tomatoes
1 Tbsp. dried basil

1. In a small bowl, mix bacon and cheese together lightly.

2. Cut a pocket in the thicker side of each chicken breast. Fill each with ¼ of the bacon and cheese. Pinch shut and secure with toothpicks.

3. Place chicken in slow cooker. Top with tomatoes and sprinkle with basil.

4. Cover and cook on High 1½–3 hours, or until chicken is tender, but not dry or mushy.

- Calories 437
- Fat 14
- Sodium 857
- Carbs 11
- Sugar 2
- Protein 61

Basil Chicken Strips

Mary Fisher
Leola, PA

Makes 4 servings
Prep. Time: 10 minutes
Cooking Time: 10–12 minutes

1 lb. boneless skinless chicken strips
4 Tbsp. almond flour
4 Tbsp. butter
1 clove garlic, minced, *optional*
4 Tbsp. red wine vinegar
1 tsp. dried basil
¼ cup fresh parsley, *optional*
¼ cup fresh cilantro, chopped, *optional*

1. In a large resealable bag, shake chicken strips in flour until coated.

2. In a large skillet over medium-high heat, melt butter.

3. Add chicken, and garlic if you wish, and sauté 5 minutes.

4. Stir in vinegar and basil, and parsley and cilantro, if you wish. Cook until chicken juices run clear.

Serving suggestion: Serve over cauliflower rice.

- Calories 282
- Fat 18
- Sodium 57
- Carbs 2
- Sugar 0
- Protein 27

Ann's Chicken Cacciatore

Ann Driscoll
Albuquerque, NM

Makes 6–8 servings
Prep. Time: 10 minutes
Cooking Time: 3–9 hours
Ideal slow-cooker size: 4-qt.

1 large onion, thinly sliced

2½–3-lb. chicken, cut up

2 6-oz. cans tomato paste

4-oz. can sliced mushrooms

1 tsp. salt

¼ cup chicken bone broth

¼ tsp. pepper

1–2 cloves garlic, minced

1–2 tsp. dried oregano

½ tsp. dried basil

½ tsp. celery seed, *optional*

1 bay leaf

1. Place onion in slow cooker. Add chicken.

2. Combine remaining ingredients. Pour over chicken.

3. Cover. Cook on Low 7–9 hours, or on High 3–4 hours. Remove bay leaf before serving.

- Calories 218
- Fat 4
- Sodium 703
- Carbs 10
- Sugar 6
- Protein 35

Darla's Chicken Cacciatore

Darla Sathre
Baxter, MN

Makes 6 servings
Prep. Time: 5–10 minutes
Cooking Time: 8 hours
Ideal slow-cooker size: 4-qt.

2 onions, thinly sliced

4 boneless chicken breasts, cubed

3 cloves garlic, minced

¼ tsp. pepper

2 tsp. dried oregano

1 tsp. dried basil

1 bay leaf

2 15-oz. cans diced tomatoes

8-oz. can tomato sauce

4-oz. can sliced mushrooms

1. Place onions in bottom of slow cooker. Add remaining ingredients.

2. Cover. Cook on Low 8 hours. Remove bay leaf before serving.

- Calories 246
- Fat 4
- Sodium 374
- Carbs 11
- Sugar 2
- Protein 37

Italian Chicken and Broccoli

Liz Clapper
Lancaster, PA

Makes 6 servings
Prep. Time: 15–20 minutes
Cooking Time: 15–20 minutes

2 lbs. chicken tenderloins

2 Tbsp. olive oil

4 medium zucchini, chopped

2 cloves garlic, finely chopped

1 head broccoli, chopped into florets (about 4 cups)

½ cup chicken bone broth

1½ Tbsp. Italian seasoning, unsalted, like Mrs. Dash Italian Medley

3 cups cooked cauliflower rice

¼ cup shredded Parmesan cheese

1. In a large skillet or saucepan, cook chicken in olive oil about 7 minutes, or until cooked through.

2. Remove chicken from pan and keep warm.

3. Add zucchini to same pan. Sauté 2 minutes.

4. Add garlic and broccoli to zucchini. Sauté 2 minutes.

5. Add broth and Italian seasoning. Heat until broth simmers.

6. Cut chicken into bite-sized pieces. Stir into skillet with vegetables and cook 3 more minutes.

7. Add the cauliflower rice, sprinkle with Parmesan, and serve immediately.

- Calories 272
- Fat 9
- Sodium 169
- Carbs 9
- Sugar 3
- Protein 38

Chicken Dijon Dinner

Barbara Stutzman
Crossville, TN

SLOW COOKER

Makes 4–6 servings
Prep. Time: 20 minutes
Cooking Time: 4 hours
Ideal slow-cooker size: 6-qt.

2 lbs. boneless, skinless chicken thighs

2 cloves garlic, minced

1 Tbsp. olive oil

6 Tbsp. white wine vinegar

4 Tbsp. liquid aminos

4 Tbsp. Dijon mustard

1 lb. sliced mushrooms

1. Grease interior of slow-cooker crock.

2. Place thighs in crock. If you need to add a second layer, stagger the pieces so they don't directly overlap each other.

3. Stir together garlic, oil, vinegar, liquid aminos, and mustard until well mixed.

4. Gently stir in mushrooms.

5. Spoon sauce into crock, making sure to cover all thighs with some of the sauce.

6. Cover. Cook on Low for 4 hours, or until instant-read meat thermometer registers 160°F when stuck in center of chicken.

7. Serve chicken topped with sauce.

- Calories 218
- Fat 10
- Sodium 803
- Carbs 1
- Sugar 0
- Protein 30

Tarragon Chicken

Cassius L. Chapman
Tucker, GA

Makes 6 servings
Prep. Time: 15–20 minutes
Cooking Time: 4 hours
Ideal slow-cooker size: 5-qt.

6 boneless, skinless chicken thighs

¾ tsp. salt, *divided*

½ tsp. black pepper, coarsely ground

1 tsp. dried tarragon

2 Tbsp. chopped onion

½ cup chicken bone broth

2 Tbsp. butter

2 Tbsp. flaxseed

1 cup heavy cream

1 Tbsp. chopped fresh tarragon

1. Grease interior of slow-cooker crock.

2. Place thighs in cooker. If you need to create a second layer, stagger the pieces so they don't directly overlap each other.

3. In a small bowl, mix together ½ tsp. salt, pepper, dried tarragon, chopped onion, and broth.

4. Spoon over thighs, making sure to top those on both levels with the sauce.

5. Cover. Cook on Low for 4 hours, or until instant-read meat thermometer registers 160–165°F when stuck in the thighs.

6. Close to end of cooking time, melt butter in skillet or small saucepan. Blend in flaxseed and ¼ tsp. salt. Cook, stirring continuously over heat for 1–2 minutes until all clumps are broken up.

7. Gradually pour in cream, stirring continuously over medium heat until sauce thickens.

8. To serve, place thighs on platter. Spoon sauce over. Sprinkle with chopped fresh tarragon leaves.

- Calories 269
- Fat 22
- Sodium 349
- Carbs 2
- Sugar 1
- Protein 16

Butter Chicken

Pat Bishop
Bedminster, PA

SLOW COOKER

Makes 8 servings
Prep. Time: 20 minutes
Cooking Time: 6–8 hours
Ideal slow-cooker size: 5- to 6-qt.

2 onions, diced

3 cloves garlic, minced

3 Tbsp. butter, softened to room temperature

2 Tbsp. grated fresh ginger

1 Tbsp. Truvia Brown Sugar Blend

2 tsp. chili powder

¾ tsp. coriander

¾ tsp. turmeric

½ tsp. cinnamon

½ tsp. cumin

½ tsp. salt

¼ tsp. black pepper

28-oz. can diced tomatoes, undrained

1 cup chicken bone broth

¼ cup natural peanut butter, almond butter, or cashew butter (no sugar added)

3 lbs. boneless, skinless chicken thighs, halved

1 cup sour cream

2 Tbsp. chopped fresh cilantro

1. Grease interior of slow-cooker crock.

2. In the crock combine onions, garlic, butter, fresh ginger, brown sugar, chili powder, coriander, turmeric, cinnamon, cumin, salt, pepper, and tomatoes.

3. In a bowl, whisk broth with nut butter. Pour into crock. Stir everything together until well blended.

4. Settle chicken thighs into sauce, submerging as much as possible.

5. Cover. Cook on Low for 6-8 hours, or until instant-read meat thermometer registers 160°F when stuck in center of thigh pieces.

6. Remove chicken with slotted spoon and place in bowl. Cover and keep warm.

7. With immersion blender, puree sauce until smooth. Add chicken back into sauce.

8. Cover. Cook another 15 minutes, or until heated through.

9. Stir in sour cream.

10. Serve sprinkled with cilantro.

- Calories 394
- Fat 18
- Sodium 464
- Carbs 13
- Sugar 5
- Protein 42

Instant Pot Butter Chicken

Jessica Stoner
Arlington, OH

Makes 4 servings
Prep. Time: 10–15 minutes
Cooking Time: 20 minutes
Setting: Sauté and Poultry
Pressure: High
Release: Manual

1 Tbsp. olive oil

1 medium onion, diced

1–2 medium cloves garlic, minced

½ Tbsp. minced ginger

1 tsp. garam masala

½ tsp. turmeric

2 tsp. kosher salt

2 lbs. cubed boneless skinless chicken breast

¼ cup tomato paste

2 cups crushed tomatoes

½ cup water

15 drops liquid stevia

1½ cups heavy cream

1 Tbsp. butter

1. On Sauté function at high heat, heat oil in the inner pot of the Instant Pot. Add onion, garlic, and ginger and sauté for 1 minute, until fragrant and onion is soft.

2. Add garam masala, turmeric, and salt. Sauté quickly and add chicken. Stir to coat chicken. Add tomato paste and crushed tomatoes. Slowly add water, scraping the bottom of the pot with a spoon to make sure there are no bits of tomato stuck to the bottom. Stir in stevia.

3. Secure the lid, making sure vent is turned to sealing function. Use the Poultry high pressure function and set cook time to 15 minutes. Once done cooking, do a quick release of the pressure.

4. Remove lid and change to medium/normal Sauté function and stir in heavy cream and bring to a simmer. Simmer for 5 minutes, adding up to ¼ cup additional water if you need to thin the sauce out. Stir in butter until melted and turn off.

- Calories 394
- Fat 18
- Sodium 464
- Carbs 13
- Sugar 5
- Protein 42

Buttery Lemon Chicken

Judy Gascho
Woodburn, OR

Makes 4 servings
Prep. Time: 15 minutes
Cooking Time: 7 minutes
Setting: Poultry
Pressure: High
Release: Natural

2 Tbsp. butter

1 medium onion, chopped

4 cloves garlic, minced

½ tsp. paprika

½ tsp. pepper

1 tsp. dried parsley, or 1 Tbsp. chopped
fresh parsley

2 lbs. boneless chicken breasts or thighs

½ cup chicken broth

⅓ cup lemon juice

1 tsp. salt

1 tsp. konjac flour

1. Set the Instant Pot to Sauté. When it is hot, add butter to the inner pot and melt.

2. Add the onion, garlic, paprika, pepper, and parsley to melted butter and sauté until onion starts to soften. Push onion to side of pot.

3. With the Instant Pot still at Sauté, add the chicken and sear on each side 3–5 minutes.

4. Mix broth, lemon juice, and salt together. Pour over chicken and stir to mix all together.

5. Put on lid and set Instant Pot, move vent to sealing, and press Poultry. Set cook time for 7 minutes. Let depressurize naturally.

6. Remove chicken, leaving sauce in pot. Sprinkle in the konjac flour and whisk until smooth. Continue cooking on the Sauté function until the sauce has thickened.

7. Add the chicken back into the pot and stir.

- Calories 347
- Fat 12
- Sodium 633
- Carbs 4
- Sugar 1
- Protein 52

Jalapeno Poppers, page 65

Chicken Lettuce Wraps, page 66

Curried Almonds, page 76

Tomato Basil Soup, page 84

Turkey Sausage and Cabbage Soup, page 104

Shredded Pork Tortilla Soup, page 108

Stuffed Sweet Pepper Soup, page 114

Colorful Beef Stew, page 123

Chicken with Lemon

Colleen Heatwole
Burton, MI

Makes 4 servings
Prep. Time: 15 minutes
Cooking Time: 8 minutes
Setting: Manual
Pressure: High
Release: Natural

2 lbs. boneless skinless chicken thighs

3 Tbsp. olive oil, *divided*

1 tsp. rosemary

1 tsp. kosher salt

½ tsp. black pepper

1 lemon, organic preferred

1 medium onion, diced

2 cloves garlic, minced

2 Tbsp. water

1. Toss chicken with 1 Tbsp. oil, rosemary, salt, and pepper.

2. Wash lemon, trim ends, quarter lengthwise, and remove seeds. Slice quarters crosswise into ⅛-inch slices.

3. Heat remaining 2 Tbsp. oil in the inner pot using Sauté function of the Instant Pot.

4. Add onion and garlic and sauté 3 minutes, stirring frequently.

5. Add lemon and sauté an additional minute.

6. Add the 2 Tbsp. water.

7. Add chicken and stir to combine.

8. Secure the lid and set vent to sealing. Cook 8 minutes, using Manual at high pressure.

9. Allow pressure to release naturally.

- Calories 378
- Fat 16
- Sodium 584
- Carbs 6
- Sugar 2
- Protein 52

Lemon Chicken

Ruth Shank
Gridley, IL

Makes 10 servings (4 oz. each)
Prep. Time: 10–15 minutes
Baking Time: 40–50 minutes

3 lbs. boneless, skinless chicken breasts

¼ cup lemon juice

¼ tsp. garlic powder

¼ tsp. pepper

½ tsp. salt

2 tsp. dried oregano leaves

olive oil

1. Trim excess fat from chicken breasts and cut into 10 serving-sized pieces.

2. Arrange chicken pieces in a greased 9x13-inch baking dish.

3. In a small mixing bowl, combine lemon juice, garlic powder, pepper, salt, and oregano. Pour over chicken.

4. Bake, uncovered, at 375°F for 40–50 minutes. Brush with olive oil every 10 to 15 minutes, turning chicken pieces over occasionally.

- Calories 165
- Fat 4
- Sodium 157
- Carbs 1
- Sugar 0
- Protein 31

Savory Slow-Cooker Chicken

Sara Harter Fredette
Williamsburg, MA

Makes 4 servings
Prep. Time: 25 minutes
Cooking Time: 8–10 hours
Ideal slow-cooker size: 4- or 5-qt.

2½ lbs. chicken pieces, skinned

1 lb. fresh tomatoes, chopped, or 15-oz. can stewed tomatoes

1 bay leaf

¼ tsp. pepper

2 cloves garlic, minced

1 onion, chopped

½ cup chicken bone broth

1 tsp. dried thyme

¼ tsp. salt

2 cups broccoli, cut into bite-sized pieces

1. Combine all ingredients except broccoli in slow cooker.

2. Cover. Cook on Low 8–10 hours.

3. Add broccoli 30 minutes before end of cooking time.

- Calories 401
- Fat 8
- Sodium 312
- Carbs 11
- Sugar 5
- Protein 67

Lemony Chicken Thighs

Maria Shevlin
Sicklerville, NJ

Makes 3-5 servings
Prep. Time: 15 minutes
Cooking Time: 15 minutes
Setting: Poultry
Pressure: High
Release: Natural then Manual

1 cup chicken bone broth

5 frozen bone-in chicken thighs

1 small onion, diced

5-6 cloves garlic, diced

juice of 1 lemon

2 Tbsp. butter, melted

½ tsp. salt

¼ tsp. black pepper

1 tsp. True Lemon Lemon Pepper seasoning

1 tsp. parsley flakes

¼ tsp. oregano

rind of 1 lemon

1. Add the chicken bone broth into the inner pot of the Instant Pot.

2. Add the chicken thighs.

3. Add the onion and garlic.

4. Pour the fresh lemon juice in with the melted butter.

5. Add the seasonings.

6. Lock the lid, make sure the vent is at sealing, then press the Poultry button. Set to 15 minutes.

7. When cook time is up, let the pressure naturally release for 3–5 minutes, then manually release the rest.

8. You can place the chicken under the broiler for 2–3 minutes to brown.

9. Plate up and pour some of the sauce over top with fresh grated lemon rind.

- Calories 317
- Fat 24
- Sodium 646
- Carbs 3
- Sugar 1
- Protein 22

Chicken Asparagus Bake

Jean Butzer
Batavia, NY

Makes 4 servings
Prep. Time: 15–20 minutes
Chilling Time: 8–24 hours
Cooking/Baking Time: 1¼ hours

1 lb. boneless, skinless chicken breasts, cooked

¾ lb. fresh asparagus spears, or 10-oz. pkg. frozen
　asparagus spears

2 Tbsp. butter

1 cup whole milk

1 cup chicken bone broth

1 tsp. konjac flour

½ lb. fresh mushrooms, sliced, or 6-oz. can sliced
　mushrooms, drained

⅛ tsp. nutmeg

dash pepper

¼ cup almond flour

2 Tbsp. snipped parsley

2 Tbsp. slivered almonds

2 Tbsp. butter, melted

1. Slice breasts into ¼-inch-thick slices and set aside.

2. Cook asparagus lightly in microwave or in a saucepan on the stovetop. Drain.

3. In a skillet or saucepan, melt 2 Tbsp. butter spread. Whisk in milk and chicken broth. Cook, stirring constantly.

4. Sprinkle in the konjac flour and whisk until smooth. Continue cooking until thickened.

5. Stir in mushrooms, nutmeg, and pepper.

6. Arrange chicken slices in bottom of lightly greased 6×10-inch baking pan.

7. Spoon half of mushroom sauce over chicken.

8. Arrange asparagus over sauce.

9. Pour remaining sauce over asparagus spears.

10. Cover and refrigerate up to 24 hours.

11. In a bowl, almond flour, parsley, almonds, and 2 Tbsp. melted butter together. Set aside.

12. Bake casserole, covered, for 30 minutes at 375°F.

13. Remove cover.

14. Bake, uncovered, until heated through, about 15 minutes longer.

- Calories 374
- Fat 22
- Sodium 192
- Carbs 12
- Sugar 6
- Protein 35

Chicken Fajitas

Becky Frey
Lebanon, PA

Makes 12 servings
Prep. Time: 20–30 minutes
Marinating Time: 15 minutes
Cooking Time: 6–8 minutes

¼ cup lime juice

1-2 cloves garlic, minced

1 tsp. chili powder

½ tsp. cumin

3 lbs. boneless skinless chicken breasts,
    cut into ¼-inch slices

1 large onion, sliced

½ sweet green bell pepper, slivered

½ sweet red bell pepper, slivered

6 cups cooked cauliflower rice

½ cup no-sugar-added salsa

½ cup sour cream

½ cup shredded cheese

1. Combine first four ingredients in a large bowl.

2. Add chicken slices. Stir until chicken is well coated.

3. Marinate for 15 minutes.

4. Cook chicken mixture in large hot nonstick skillet for 3 minutes, or until no longer pink.

5. Stir in onion and peppers. Cook 3–5 minutes, or until done to your liking.

6. Divide cauliflower rice evenly between bowls.

7. Top each bowl with 2 tsp. salsa, 2 tsp. sour cream, and 2 tsp. shredded cheese.

- Calories 192
- Fat 6
- Sodium 182
- Carbs 6
- Sugar 2
- Protein 28

Southwestern Shredded Chicken

Hope Comerford
Clinton Township, MI

Makes 4 servings
Prep. Time: 8–10 minutes
Cooking Time: 5–6 hours
Ideal slow-cooker size: 3-qt.

1½ lbs. boneless skinless chicken breast

1 Tbsp. chili powder

2 tsp. garlic powder

1 tsp. cumin

1 tsp. onion powder

½ tsp. kosher salt

¼ tsp. pepper

1 medium onion, chopped

14½-oz. can diced tomatoes

4-oz. can diced green chiles

½ cup sour cream

optional toppings: lettuce, shredded cheese, sour
cream, and salsa

1. Place the chicken in the slow cooker.

2. Mix together the chili powder, garlic powder,
cumin, onion powder, kosher salt, and pepper.
Sprinkle this over both sides of the chicken.

3. Sprinkle the onions over the top of the chicken
and pour the cans of diced tomatoes and green chiles
over the top.

4. Cover and cook on Low for 5–6 hours.

5. Turn your slow cooker to Warm. Remove the
chicken and shred it between 2 forks.

6. Slowly whisk in the sour cream with the juices in
the crock. Replace the chicken in the crock and stir to
mix in the juices.

*Serving suggestion: Serve topped with some shredded
lettuce, shredded cheese, and fresh salsa.*

- Calories 309
- Fat 10
- Sodium 547
- Carbs 13
- Sugar 4
- Protein 41

Tasty Home-Style Chicken

Elaine Good
Lititz, PA

Makes 10 servings
Prep. Time: 15 minutes
Baking Time: 1¼–1¾ hours

4 lbs. chicken pieces, washed, dried, and skinned

1 cup chopped onion

1 cup chopped celery

¾ cup sliced fresh mushrooms

¾ tsp. salt

dash pepper

2½ cups water

1½ tsp. konjac flour

parsley flakes, or paprika, *optional*

1. Arrange chicken pieces in a greased 9×13-inch baking pan.

2. In a saucepan, sauté onion and celery in a few spoonfuls of water until somewhat tender.

3. Add mushrooms. Continue to cook until mushrooms give off a bit of liquid.

4. Add salt, pepper, and 2½ cups water, stirring until well mixed.

5. Sprinkle in the konjac flour and whisk, cooking and stirring continually until thickened and smooth.

6. Remove from heat. Pour sauce over chicken in baking pan.

7. If you wish, sprinkle chicken with parsley or paprika.

8. Bake, covered, at 350°F for 45 minutes.

9. Uncover, and continue baking 30–45 more minutes, or until chicken is tender.

10. Remove chicken to a warm platter and serve.

- Calories 227
- Fat 5
- Sodium 235
- Carbs 2
- Sugar 0.5
- Protein 41

Chicken Dinner in a Packet

Bonnie Whaling
Clearfield, PA

Makes 4 servings
Prep. Time: 25 minutes
Baking Time: 30–35 minutes

4 5-oz. boneless skinless chicken breast halves

2 cups sliced fresh mushrooms

1 cup sliced onion

3 medium zucchini, sliced

2 Tbsp. olive oil

2 Tbsp. lemon juice

4 tsp. fresh basil, or 1 tsp. dried basil

¼ tsp. salt

¼ tsp. black pepper

1. Preheat oven to 375°F.

2. Fold four 12×28-inch pieces of foil in half to make four 12×14-inch rectangles. Place one chicken breast half on each piece of foil.

3. Top with mushrooms, onion, and zucchini, dividing vegetables equally among chicken bundles.

4. In a small bowl, stir together oil, lemon juice, basil, salt, and pepper.

5. Drizzle oil mixture over vegetables and chicken.

6. Pull up two opposite edges of foil. Seal with a double fold. Then fold in remaining edges, leaving enough space for steam to build.

7. Place bundles side-by-side in a shallow baking pan.

8. Bake 30–35 minutes, or until chicken reaches 170°F on an instant-read thermometer.

9. Serve dinners in foil packets, or transfer to serving plate.

- Calories 273
- Fat 11
- Sodium 202
- Carbs 9
- Sugar 4
- Protein 35

Chicken in Tomato Vegetable Sauce

Irene Klaeger
Inverness, FL

Makes 6 servings
Prep. Time: 15 minutes
Cooking Time: 25–30 minutes

1 Tbsp. olive oil

1 cup sliced leeks

2 cloves garlic, minced

1 lb. boneless skinless chicken breast, cut into thin strips

1 tsp. dried basil

1 tsp. dried oregano

14½-oz. can tomatoes, no salt added, undrained and chopped

1 medium zucchini, unpeeled and sliced

¾ cup chicken bone broth

¼ tsp. salt

¼ cup tomato paste, no salt added

3 cups cooked cauliflower rice

2 Tbsp. grated Parmesan cheese

fresh basil sprigs, *optional*

1. Heat oil in large skillet over medium heat until hot. Add leeks and garlic. Sauté 3 minutes, or until tender.

2. Add chicken. Sauté 7 minutes, or until done.

3. Stir in basil and oregano.

4. Remove chicken and seasonings. Set aside and keep warm.

5. Add next 5 ingredients to skillet. Stir well.

6. Cover skillet. Reduce heat and simmer 10 minutes.

7. Add chicken and cook until thoroughly heated.

8. Serve chicken over cauliflower rice, evenly divided between plates, and sprinkle with the Parmesan cheese and, if desired, fresh basil.

- Calories 168
- Fat 5
- Sodium 441
- Carbs 10
- Sugar 9
- Protein 21

Savory Stir-Fried Chicken Breast

Carolyn Baer
Conrath, WI

Makes 8 servings (1 chicken breast half each)
Prep. Time: 10 minutes
Cooking Time: 6–8 minutes

1 cup almond flour

2½ tsp. seasoning salt

1 tsp. paprika

1 tsp. poultry seasoning

1 tsp. ground mustard

½ tsp. pepper

4 8-oz. whole boneless, skinless chicken breasts, cubed into 1½-inch pieces

¼ cup olive oil

1. In a plastic bag, combine flour, seasoning salt, paprika, poultry seasoning, ground mustard, and pepper.

2. Add chicken breast cubes and shake bag until chicken is well coated.

3. In a large skillet, sauté coated chicken in olive oil for 6–8 minutes. Stir constantly while sautéing.

- Calories 266
- Fat 16
- Sodium 70
- Carbs 3
- Sugar 0.5
- Protein 28

Szechuan-Style Chicken and Broccoli

Jane Meiser
Harrisonburg, VA

Makes 4 servings
Prep. Time: 30 minutes
Cooking Time: 1–3 hours
Ideal slow-cooker size: 4-qt.

2 whole boneless, skinless chicken breasts

1 Tbsp. olive oil

½ cup chicken bone broth

10 drops Frank's RedHot Original Cayenne Pepper Sauce

2 Tbsp. liquid aminos

2 drops liquid stevia

2 tsp. flaxseed

1 medium onion, chopped

2 cloves garlic, minced

½ tsp. ground ginger

2 cups broccoli florets

1 medium red bell pepper, sliced

1. Cut chicken into 1-inch cubes and brown lightly in oil in skillet. Place in slow cooker.

2. Stir in remaining ingredients.

3. Cover. Cook on High 1–1½ hours or on Low 2–3 hours.

- Calories 219
- Fat 7
- Sodium 171
- Carbs 8
- Sugar 6
- Protein 29

Mild Chicken Curry with Coconut Milk

Brittney Horst
Lititz, PA

Makes 4–6 servings
Cooking time: 14 minutes
Setting: Manual
Pressure: High
Release: Manual

1 large onion, diced

6 cloves garlic, crushed

¼ cup coconut oil (butter or avocado oil would work fine too)

½ tsp. black pepper

½ tsp. turmeric

½ tsp. paprika

¼ tsp. cinnamon

¼ tsp. cloves

¼ tsp. cumin

¼ tsp. ginger

½ tsp. salt

1 Tbsp. curry powder (more if you like more flavor)

½ tsp. chili powder

24-oz. can diced or crushed tomatoes

13½-oz. can of no-sugar-added coconut milk (I prefer a brand that has no unwanted ingredients, like guar gum or sugar)

4 lbs. boneless skinless chicken breasts, cut into chunks

1. Sauté onion and garlic in oil, either with Sauté setting in the inner pot of the Instant Pot, or on stove top and then add to pot.

2. Combine spices in a small bowl, then add to the inner pot.

3. Add tomatoes and coconut milk and stir.

4. Add chicken and stir to coat the pieces with the sauce.

5. Secure the lid and make sure vent is at sealing. Set to Manual mode (or Pressure Cook on newer models) for 14 minutes.

6. Let pressure release naturally (if you're crunched for time, you can do a quick release).

7. Serve with your favorite sides, and enjoy!

- Calories 535
- Fat 21
- Sodium 315
- Carbs 10
- Sugar 5
- Protein 71

Chicken with Spiced Sesame Sauce

Colleen Heatwole
Burton, MI

Makes 4–6 servings
Prep. Time: 20 minutes
Cooking Time: 8 minutes
Setting: Manual
Pressure: High
Release: Manual

2 Tbsp. tahini (sesame sauce)

¼ cup water

1 Tbsp. soy sauce

¼ cup chopped onion

1 tsp. red wine vinegar

2 tsp. minced garlic

1 tsp. shredded fresh ginger (Microplane works best)

2 lbs. chicken breasts, chopped into 8 portions

1. Place first seven ingredients in bottom of the inner pot of the Instant Pot.

2. Add coarsely chopped chicken on top.

3. Secure the lid and make sure vent is at sealing. Set for 8 minutes using Manual setting. When cook time is up, let the pressure release naturally for 10 minutes, then perform a quick release.

4. Remove ingredients and shred chicken with forks. Combine with other ingredients in pot for a tasty sandwich filling or sauce.

- Calories 217
- Fat 7
- Sodium 234
- Carbs 1
- Sugar 0
- Protein 35

Traditional Turkey Breast

Hope Comerford
Clinton Township, MI

Makes 10–12 servings
Prep. Time: 10 minutes
Cooking Time: 8 hours
Ideal slow-cooker size: 7-qt.

7-lb. or less turkey breast

olive oil

4 Tbsp. (½ stick) butter, cut in 8 pieces

Rub:
2 tsp. garlic powder

1 tsp. onion powder

1 tsp. salt

¼ tsp. pepper

1 tsp. poultry seasoning

1. Remove the gizzards from the turkey breast, rinse it, and pat dry. Place the breast into the crock.

2. Rub the turkey breast all over with olive oil.

3. Mix together all the rub ingredients. Rub this all over the turkey breast and press it in.

4. Place the pieces of butter all over the top of the breast.

5. Cover and cook on Low for 8 hours.

- Calories 348
- Fat 12
- Sodium 352
- Carbs 1
- Sugar 0
- Protein 55

Turkey Stir-Fry

Arianne Hochstetler
Goshen, IN

Makes 6 servings (¾ cup each)
Prep. Time: 15–20 minutes
Cooking Time: 20 minutes

1½ lbs. boneless turkey, cut into strips

1 Tbsp. olive oil

1 large onion, chopped

1 medium zucchini, chopped

½ green pepper, sliced

2 cups fresh, sliced mushrooms

1 cup chicken bone broth

1 tsp. konjac flour

3 Tbsp. soy sauce

½ tsp. ginger

1 tsp. curry powder

1 cup frozen green beans

1 cup frozen broccoli

3 cups cooked cauliflower rice

⅓ cup cashews, *optional*

1. In a large skillet or wok, stir-fry turkey in oil over medium-high heat until no longer pink, about 5–6 minutes. Remove turkey from pan and keep warm.

2. Stir-fry the onion, zucchini, green pepper, and mushrooms until crisp-tender, about 5 minutes.

3. In a small bowl, combine chicken broth, konjac flour, soy sauce, ginger, and curry powder until smooth.

4. Add to the skillet. Cook and stir until thickened and bubbly.

5. Return turkey to skillet with frozen green beans and broccoli. Cook and stir until heated through.

6. Serve over cooked cauliflower rice. Top with cashews, if desired.

- Calories 199
- Fat 9
- Sodium 726
- Carbs 9
- Sugar 4
- Protein 30

Cheesy Stuffed Cabbage

Maria Shevlin
Sicklerville, NJ

Makes 6–8 servings
Prep. Time: 30 minutes
Cooking Time: 18 minutes
Setting: Manual
Pressure: High
Release: Manual

1–2 heads savoy cabbage

1 lb. ground turkey

1 egg

1 cup shredded cheddar cheese

2 Tbsp. heavy cream

¼ cup shredded Parmesan cheese

¼ cup shredded mozzarella cheese

¼ cup finely diced onion

¼ cup finely diced bell pepper

¼ cup finely diced mushrooms

1 tsp. salt

½ tsp. black pepper

1 tsp. garlic powder

6 basil leaves, fresh and cut chiffonade

1 Tbsp. fresh parsley, chopped

1 qt. of your favorite keto-friendly pasta sauce

1. Remove the core from the cabbages.

2. Boil water and place 1 head at a time into the water for approximately 10 minutes.

3. Allow cabbage to cool slightly. Once cooled, remove the leaves carefully and set aside. You'll need about 15 or 16.

4. Mix together the meat and all remaining ingredients except the pasta sauce.

5. One leaf at a time, put a heaping Tbsp. of meat mixture in the center.

6. Tuck the sides in and then roll tightly.

7. Add ½ cup sauce to the bottom of the inner pot of the Instant Pot.

8. Place the rolls, fold side down, into the pot and layer them, putting a touch of sauce between each layer and finally on top. (You may want to cook the rolls half a batch at a time.)

9. Lock lid and make sure vent is at sealing. Set timer on 18 minutes on Manual at high pressure, then manually release the pressure when cook time is over.

- Calories 198
- Fat 8
- Sodium 678
- Carbs 14
- Sugar 7
- Protein 20

Savory Turkey

Clara Newswanger
Gordonville, PA

Makes 12 servings (3 oz. turkey with sauce each)
Prep. Time: 15 minutes
Baking Time: 35–45 minutes

½ cup chopped onion

2 Tbsp. olive oil

2 9-oz. cans mushrooms, drained

½ tsp. konjac flour

1 cup beef bone broth

2 Tbsp. soy sauce

2 lbs. boneless skinless turkey thighs, cut in 2-inch chunks

1. In a medium-sized saucepan, sauté onion in olive oil.

2. Add mushrooms and flour. Stir until well mixed.

3. Add beef broth and soy sauce. Mix well and bring to a boil.

4. Meanwhile, place turkey thighs in a greased baking dish. Pour sauce over thighs.

5. Bake uncovered at 350°F for 35-45 minutes, or until tender.

- Calories 157
- Fat 5
- Sodium 469
- Carbs 3
- Sugar 1
- Protein 23

KETO TIP
Whenever possible, buy grass-fed organic poultry and meat. You're likely consuming more meat than you were when you were eating carbs regularly, so you want to make sure it's high quality.

Pork

Garlic Pork Roast in the Slow-Cooker

Earnie Zimmerman
Mechanicsburg, PA

Makes 10 servings
Prep. Time: 15–20 minutes
Cooking Time: 7–8 hours
Ideal slow-cooker size: 6- to 8-qt.

3-lb. boneless pork loin roast, short and wide rather
    than long and narrow

1 Tbsp. butter

1 tsp. salt

½ tsp. coarsely ground black pepper

1 medium onion, sliced

6 cloves garlic, peeled

8 strips (each 3 inches long, ½ inch wide) fresh lemon
    peel

1 head cauliflower, broken up

1 lb. celery sticks

½ tsp. dried thyme

1 cup chicken bone broth

1. Grease interior of slow-cooker crock.

2. If you have time, heat butter in 12-inch skillet over medium-high heat until hot. Place pork roast in skillet and brown on all sides. Move meat to crock.

3. If you don't have time, place pork in crock directly.

4. Sprinkle all over with salt and pepper.

5. In a large bowl, mix together onion, garlic, lemon peel, cauliflower, celery, and thyme. Stir in chicken broth.

6. Spoon mixture into crock alongside meat and over top.

7. Cover. Cook on Low 4 hours, or until instant-read meat thermometer registers 140–145°F when stuck in center of roast. Remove roast to cutting board. Cover to keep warm. Let stand for 10 minutes.

8. Check if onion, cauliflower, and celery are as tender as you like them. If not, cover crock and continue cooking another 30–60 minutes, or until veggies are as done as you want.

9. Slice pork into ½-inch-thick slices. Place on deep platter. Serve topped with vegetables and broth.

- Calories 352
- Fat 19
- Sodium 381
- Carbs 5
- Sugar 2
- Protein 38

Savory Pork Roast

Mary Louise Martin
Boyd, WI

Makes 4–6 servings
Prep. Time: 15 minutes
Cooking Time: 3½–4½ hours
Ideal slow-cooker size: oval 6-qt.

4-lb. boneless pork butt roast

1 tsp. ground ginger

1 Tbsp. fresh minced rosemary

½ tsp. mace or nutmeg

1 tsp. coarsely ground black pepper

2 tsp. salt

2 cups water

1. Grease interior of slow-cooker crock.

2. Place roast in slow cooker.

3. In a bowl, mix spices and seasonings together. Sprinkle half on top of roast, pushing down on spices to encourage them to stick.

4. Flip roast and sprinkle with rest of spices, again pushing down to make them stick.

5. Pour 2 cups water around the edge, being careful not to wash spices off meat.

6. Cover. Cook on Low 3½–4½ hours, or until instant-read meat thermometer registers 140°F when stuck into center of roast.

- Calories 513
- Fat 34
- Sodium 1111
- Carbs 1
- Sugar 0
- Protein 52

Pork Butt Roast

Marla Folkerts
Batavia, IL

Makes 6–8 servings
Prep. Time: 10 minutes
Cooking Time: 9 minutes
Setting: Manual
Pressure: High
Release: Natural

3-4-lb. pork butt roast

2-3 Tbsp. of your favorite keto-friendly rub

2 cups water

1. Place pork in the inner pot of the Instant Pot.

2. Sprinkle in the rub all over the roast and add the water, being careful not to wash off the rub.

3. Secure the lid and set the vent to sealing. Cook for 9 minutes on the Manual setting.

4. Let the pressure release naturally.

- Calories 598
- Fat 39
- Sodium 152
- Carbs 0
- Sugar 0
- Protein 57

Pork Tenderloin with Mustard Sauce

Bobbie Jean Weidner Muscarella
State College, PA

Makes 10-12 servings
Prep. Time: 20 minutes
Cooking Time: 3–4 hours
Marinating Time: 2–3 hours
Ideal slow-cooker size: oval 6- or 7-qt.

Roast Pork:

½ cup liquid aminos

½ cup beef bone broth

⅛ cup Truvia Brown Sugar Blend

3-lb. boneless pork loin roast (wide and short; not
  skinny and long)

Mustard Sauce:

1 Tbsp. dry mustard

¼ cup Dijon mustard

30 drops liquid stevia

½ tsp. salt

2 Tbsp. apple cider vinegar

4 egg yolks, beaten

1 cup cream

1. Grease interior of slow-cooker crock.

2. In a bowl, mix together liquid aminos, beef bone broth, and brown sugar blend.

3. Place pork in bowl. Pour marinade over it. Cover.

4. Marinate at room temperature for 2–3 hours, turning meat over occasionally.

5. Place meat in crock. Pour marinade over top.

6. Cover. Cook on Low 3–4 hours, or until instant-read meat thermometer registers 140–145°F when stuck into center.

7. While roast is cooking, place dry mustard, Dijon mustard, liquid stevia, salt, vinegar, and egg yolks in top of double boiler.

8. Cook over simmering water, stirring constantly until thickened.

9. Cool slightly. Then stir in cream. Set aside. (You can serve it at room temperature or heated slightly.)

10. Lift roast out of cooker with sturdy tongs or 2 sturdy metal spatulas onto cutting board. Cover and keep warm. Let stand 10 minutes.

11. Slice into thin, diagonal slices and serve with mustard sauce.

Tips: You can make the Mustard Sauce ahead of time and keep it in the fridge for up to 3 days. The sauce is also delicious on ham.

- Calories 232
- Fat 12
- Sodium 939
- Carbs 3
- Sugar 3
- Protein 26

Barbara Jean's Whole Pork Tenderloin

Barbara Jean Fabel
Wausau, WI

Makes 8 servings
Prep. Time: 20 minutes
Cooking Time: 3–5 hours
Ideal slow-cooker size: 4- or 5-qt.

½ cup sliced celery

¼ lb. fresh mushrooms, quartered

1 medium onion, sliced

3 Tbsp. butter, *divided*

2 1¼-lb. pork tenderloins, trimmed of fat

1 Tbsp. olive oil

½ cup beef bone broth

¾ tsp. salt

¼ tsp. pepper

1 Tbsp. flaxseed

1. Place celery, mushrooms, onion, and 2 Tbsp. butter in slow cooker.

2. Brown tenderloins in skillet in 1 Tbsp. olive oil. Layer over vegetables in slow cooker.

3. Pour beef broth over tenderloins. Sprinkle with salt and pepper.

4. Combine 1 Tbsp. butter and flaxseed until smooth. Pour over tenderloins.

5. Cover. Cook on High 3 hours or Low 4–5 hours.

- Calories 227
- Fat 11
- Sodium 414
- Carbs 2
- Sugar 1
- Protein 30

Pork and Cabbage Dinner

Mrs. Paul Gray
Beatrice, NE

Makes 8 servings
Prep. Time: 25 minutes
Cooking Time: 5–6 hours
Ideal slow-cooker size: 4- or 5-qt.

2 lbs. pork steaks, or chops, or shoulder, bone in, trimmed of fat

¾ cup chopped onions

¼ cup chopped fresh parsley, or 2 Tbsp. dried parsley

4 cups shredded cabbage

1 tsp. salt

⅛ tsp. pepper

½ tsp. caraway seeds

⅛ tsp. allspice

½ cup beef bone broth

1. Place pork in slow cooker. Layer onions, parsley, and cabbage over pork.

2. Combine salt, pepper, caraway seeds, and allspice. Sprinkle over cabbage. Pour broth over cabbage.

3. Cover. Cook on Low 5–6 hours.

- Calories 156
- Fat 4
- Sodium 381
- Carbs 4
- Sugar 2
- Protein 28

Teriyaki Pork Steak with Sugar Snap Peas

Hope Comerford
Clinton Township, MI

Makes 4-6 servings
Prep. Time: 10 minutes
Cooking Time: 7–9 hours
Ideal slow-cooker size: 5-qt.

2½ lbs. pork shoulder blade steaks

1 Tbsp. onion powder, *divided*

1 Tbsp. garlic powder, *divided*

salt and pepper, to taste

1 cup liquid aminos

15 drops liquid stevia

½ Tbsp. flaxseed

½ medium onion, sliced into half rings

1½-2 cups sugar snap peas

1. Place the pork steaks in your crock and sprinkle them with half the onion powder and garlic powder, and a bit of salt and pepper.

2. Mix together the liquid aminos, liquid stevia, and flaxseed.

3. Pour half of the liquid aminos sauce over the contents of the crock.

4. Place your onion on top and sprinkle with more salt, pepper, and the rest of the garlic powder and onion powder. Pour the rest of the liquid aminos sauce over the top.

5. Cover and cook on Low for 7–9 hours.

6. About 40 minutes before the cook time is up, add in the sugar snap peas.

7. Serve the pork with some of the sugar snap peas on top and sauce from the crock drizzled over the top.

- Calories 440
- Fat 29
- Sodium 1875
- Carbs 5
- Sugar 2
- Protein 43

Pork Baby Back Ribs

Marla Folkerts
Batavia, IL

Makes 6–8 servings
Prep. Time: 20 minutes
Cooking Time: 30 minutes
Setting: Meat
Pressure: High
Release: Natural then Manual

3 racks of ribs

½ cup Truvia Brown Sugar blend

⅓ cup stevia baking blend

1 tsp. garlic powder

1 tsp. garlic salt

1 cup water

½ cup apple cider vinegar

1 tsp. liquid smoke

½ cup keto-friendly barbecue sauce

1. Take the membrane/skin off the back of the ribs.

2. Mix together the remaining ingredients (except the barbecue sauce) and slather it on the ribs.

3. Place the ribs around the inside of the inner pot instead of stacking them. Secure the lid in place and make sure vent is at sealing.

4. Use the Meat setting and set for 30 minutes on high pressure.

5. When cooking time is up, let the pressure release naturally for 10 minutes, then do a quick release of the remaining pressure.

6. Place the ribs on a baking sheet and cover them with the barbecue sauce. Broil for 7–10 minutes (watching so they don't burn).

- Calories 183
- Fat 8
- Sodium 304
- Carbs 18
- Sugar 13
- Protein 11

Tasty Tender Ribs

Carol Eveleth
Cheyenne, WY

Makes 2–3 servings
Prep. Time: 5 minutes
Cooking Time: 35 minutes
Setting: Manual
Pressure: High
Release: Natural

2 tsp. salt

2 tsp. black pepper

1 tsp. garlic powder

1 tsp. onion powder

1 slab baby back ribs

1 cup water

1 cup keto-friendly barbecue sauce, *divided*

1. Mix salt, pepper, garlic powder, and onion powder together. Rub seasoning mixture on both sides of slab of ribs. Cut slab in half if it's too big for your Instant Pot.

2. Pour water into inner pot of the Instant Pot. Place ribs into pot, drizzle with ¼ cup of sauce, and secure lid. Make sure the vent is set to sealing.

3. Set it to Manual for 25 minutes. It will take a few minutes to heat up and seal the vent. When cook time is up, let it sit 5 minutes, then release steam by turning valve to venting. Turn oven on to broil (or heat your grill) while you're waiting for the 5-minute resting time.

4. Remove ribs from Instant Pot and place on a baking sheet. Slather on both sides with remaining ¾ cup sauce.

5. Place under broiler (or on grill) for 5–10 minutes, watching carefully so they don't burn. Remove and brush with a bit more sauce. Pull apart and dig in!

- Calories 932
- Fat 45
- Sodium 2570
- Carbs 36
- Sugar 28
- Protein 95

Pulled Pork

Colleen Heatwole
Burton, MI

Makes 8 servings
Prep. Time: 15 minutes
Cooking Time: 75 minutes
Setting: Meat/Stew
Pressure: High
Release: Natural

2 Tbsp. olive oil

4-lb. boneless pork shoulder, cut into two pieces

2 cups keto-friendly barbecue sauce, *divided*

½ cup water

1. Add oil to the inner pot of the Instant Pot and select Sauté.

2. When oil is hot, brown pork on both sides, about 3 minutes per side. Brown each half of roast separately. Remove to platter when browned.

3. Add 1 cup barbecue sauce and ½ cup water to the inner pot. Stir to combine.

4. Add browned pork and any accumulated juices to the inner pot. Secure the lid and set vent to sealing.

5. Using Meat/Stew mode, set timer to 60 minutes, on high pressure.

6. When cook time is up, allow the pressure to release naturally.

7. Carefully remove meat and shred with two forks, discarding excess fat as you shred.

8. Strain cooking liquid, reserving ½ cup. If possible, use fat separator to separate fat from juices.

9. Place shredded pork in the inner pot with remaining 1 cup barbecue sauce and reserved ½ cup

cooking liquid. Using Sauté function, stir to combine and bring to a simmer, stirring frequently.

Serving suggestion: Try using pulled pork as a topping on your favorite keto pizza crust, along with pizza sauce, shredded cheddar cheese, and some diced red onions.

- Calories 370
- Fat 11
- Sodium 687
- Carbs 10
- Sugar 5
- Protein 52

BBQ Pork

Carol Eveleth
Cheyenne, WY

Makes 4 servings
Prep. Time: 20 minutes
Cooking Time: 1 hour
Setting: Manual and Sauté
Pressure: High
Release: Manual

2 tsp. salt

1 tsp. onion powder

1 tsp. garlic powder

2-lb. pork shoulder roast, cut into 3-inch pieces

1 Tbsp. olive oil

2 cups keto-friendly barbecue sauce

1. In a small bowl, combine the salt, onion powder, and garlic powder. Season the pork with the rub.

2. Turn the Instant Pot on to Sauté. Heat the olive oil in the inner pot.

3. Add the pork to the oil and turn to coat. Lock the lid and set vent to sealing.

4. Press Manual and cook on high pressure for 45 minutes.

5. When cooking is complete, release the pressure manually, then open the lid.

6. Using 2 forks, shred the pork, pour barbecue sauce over the pork, then press Sauté. Simmer, 3–5 minutes. Press Cancel. Toss pork to mix.

- Calories 628
- Fat 38
- Sodium 2214
- Carbs 21
- Sugar 11
- Protein 46

Ginger Pork Chops

Mary Fisher
Leola, PA

Makes 2 servings
Prep. Time: 10 minutes
Cooking/Broiling Time: 15 minutes

2 6-oz. (4 oz. meat) bone-in pork chops

¼ tsp. konjac flour

2 Tbsp. soy sauce

½ tsp. liquid stevia

1 clove garlic, minced

dash ground ginger

1 Tbsp. sliced green onion

1. Broil pork chops 3–4 inches from heat for 5–6 minutes on each side.

2. In a small saucepan, combine flour and soy sauce until smooth.

3. Stir in stevia, garlic, and ginger.

4. Bring to a boil. Cook and stir for 1 minute, or until thickened.

5. Drizzle over cooked chops.

6. Sprinkle with green onion just before serving.

- Calories 262
- Fat 10
- Sodium 1115
- Carbs 3
- Sugar 0.5
- Protein 38

Spicy Pork Chops

Mary Puskar
Forest Hill, MD

Makes 5 servings
Prep. Time: 15 minutes
Cooking Time: 6–8 hours
Ideal slow-cooker size: 4-qt.

5–6 center-cut loin pork chops

3 Tbsp. olive oil

1 onion, sliced

1 green pepper, cut in strips

8-oz. can tomato sauce

1½ Tbsp. Truvia Brown Sugar Blend

1 Tbsp. vinegar

1½ tsp. salt

1 tsp. liquid aminos

1. Brown chops in oil in skillet. Transfer to slow cooker.

2. Add remaining ingredients to cooker.

3. Cover. Cook on Low 6–8 hours.

- Calories 215
- Fat 11
- Sodium 910
- Carbs 8
- Sugar 6
- Protein 21

Spiced Pork Chops

Mary Jane Hoober
Shipshewana, IN

Makes 4 servings (1 pork chop each)
Prep. Time: 15 minutes
Cooking/Baking Time: 75 minutes

½ cup almond flour

1½ tsp. garlic powder

1½ tsp. dry mustard

1½ tsp. paprika

½ tsp. celery salt

¼ tsp. ground ginger

⅛ tsp. dried oregano

⅛ tsp. dried basil

⅛ tsp. salt

pinch pepper

4 6-oz. pork loin chops, approximately ¾-inch-thick, bone in, visible fat removed

1–2 Tbsp. olive oil

1 cup no-sugar-added ketchup

1 cup water

¼ cup Splenda Brown Sugar Blend

1. In a medium-sized mixing bowl, combine the first 10 ingredients (through pepper).

2. Dredge pork chops on both sides in dry mixture.

3. Heat oil in a skillet. Brown chops on both sides. (Do not crowd the skillet. The chops will brown better if they're not tight against each other.) Place in a greased 9x13-inch baking dish.

4. In a small bowl, combine ketchup, water, and brown sugar blend. Pour over chops.

5. Bake uncovered, at 350°F for 1 hour, or until tender.

- Calories 348
- Fat 12
- Sodium 908
- Carbs 20
- Sugar 13
- Protein 43

Sweet Pork Chops

Angie Clemens
Dayton, VA

Makes 6 servings (1 pork chop each)
Prep. Time: 15 minutes
Cooking/Baking Time: 75 minutes

2 Tbsp. olive oil

6 4-oz. boneless pork chops, visible fat trimmed

1 onion, sliced

1 green pepper, sliced into rings

6 Tbsp. Splenda Brown Sugar Blend

6 Tbsp. no-sugar-added ketchup

6 Tbsp. lemon juice

1. Brown pork chops in oil in large skillet. (Do not crowd the skillet. The chops will brown more fully if they're not squeezed in the pan.) Place browned chops in a greased 9x13-inch baking dish.

2. On top of each chop, place 1 onion slice and 1 green pepper slice.

3. In a small mixing bowl, combine brown sugar blend, ketchup, and lemon juice. Top each chop with about 3 Tbsp. of the mixture.

4. Cover and bake at 350°F for 30 minutes. Uncover and bake 30 minutes more.

5. Baste occasionally during the final 30 minutes.

- Calories 330
- Fat 13
- Sodium 201
- Carbs 19
- Sugar 16
- Protein 31

Pork Chops and Cabbage

Shirley Hedman
Schenectady, NY

Makes 4 servings (1 pork chop each)
Prep. Time: 10 minutes
Cooking Time: 1–2 hours

4 6-oz. pork chops, bone in, visible fat removed

2 Tbsp. oil

dash salt

dash pepper

dash garlic powder

1 medium-sized head of cabbage, shredded

8-oz. can tomato sauce

¼ cup water

1. In a large skillet or saucepan, brown pork chops on one side in oil. Turn.

2. Season with salt, pepper, and garlic powder.

3. Top chops with cabbage.

4. In a small bowl, mix together tomato sauce and water until smooth. Pour over cabbage. Cover pan.

5. Cook slowly over low heat for 1½ hours, stirring occasionally, until chops and cabbage are tender, but not overdone.

- Calories 380
- Fat 24
- Sodium 726
- Carbs 7
- Sugar 4
- Protein 35

Pork Kabobs

Susan Kasting
Jenks, OK

Makes 8 servings
Prep. Time: 20 minutes
Marinating Time: 8 hours, or overnight
Grilling Time: 8–10 minutes

2 lbs. boneless pork loin, cut into 1-inch cubes

Marinade:

¼ cup olive oil

¼ cup chopped onion

3 Tbsp. lemon juice

1 Tbsp. chopped parsley

1 clove garlic, minced

½ tsp. dried marjoram

⅛ tsp. pepper

Sauce:

1 cup plain yogurt or sour cream

½ cup chopped cucumber

1 Tbsp. chopped onion

1 Tbsp. chopped parsley

1 clove garlic, minced

1 tsp. lemon juice

1. Mix pork and marinade ingredients in a resealable plastic bag.

2. Place bag with meat and marinade in a bowl (in case of leaks). Refrigerate 8 hours, or overnight.

3. Mix sauce ingredients in a bowl.

4. Drain pork. Place on skewers or on a grill pan.

5. Grill 8–10 minutes, turning over at least once.

6. Serve topped with sauce.

- Calories 263
- Fat 16
- Sodium 95
- Carbs 5
- Sugar 3
- Protein 25

Healthy Joes

Gladys M. High
Ephrata, PA

Makes 4 servings
Prep. Time: 20 minutes
Cooking Time: 20 minutes

¾ lb. ground pork loin

1 cup chopped onion

1 medium sweet bell pepper, chopped

1½ cups diced tomatoes

1 medium zucchini, shredded, *optional*

1 Tbsp. chili powder

1 tsp. paprika

½ tsp. minced garlic

pepper, to taste

3 Tbsp. tomato paste

1. In a large skillet, cook ground pork, onion, and bell pepper until meat is brown and onion is tender. Drain off drippings.

2. Stir in diced tomatoes, zucchini if you wish, chili powder, paprika, garlic, and pepper. Cover and bring to a boil. Reduce heat.

3. Add tomato paste to thicken. Simmer, uncovered, for 5 minutes.

Serving suggestion: Serve spooned onto keto-friendly buns or bread.

- Calories 251
- Fat 14
- Sodium 365
- Carbs 14
- Sugar 5
- Protein 17

Mother's Baked Ham

Dawn Ranck
Lansdale, PA

Makes 8 servings
Prep. Time: 10 minutes
Baking Time: 60–75 minutes

2 1-lb. slices boneless, ham steaks, each 1¼-inch thick

1 tsp. dry mustard

4 Tbsp. Splenda Brown Sugar Blend

whole milk to cover ham

1. Place ham in large baking pan.

2. Rub with mustard.

3. Sprinkle with brown sugar blend.

4. Add enough milk to barely cover ham. (Pour milk in along the side of the meat slices so as not to wash off the mustard and sugar.)

5. Cover with foil.

6. Bake at 325°F for 60–75 minutes, or until milk is absorbed.

- Calories 187
- Fat 9
- Sodium 1459
- Carbs 8
- Sugar 8
- Protein 23

Beef

Corned Beef

**Margaret Jarrett
Anderson, IN**

Makes 6-7 servings
Prep. Time: 5 minutes
Cooking Time: 4-5 hours
Ideal slow-cooker size: 5-qt.

2-3-lb. cut of marinated corned beef

2-3 cloves garlic, minced

10-12 peppercorns

1. Place meat in bottom of cooker. Top with garlic and peppercorns. Cover with water.

2. Cover. Cook on High 4–5 hours, or until tender.

- Calories 326
- Fat 25
- Sodium 1261
- Carbs 1
- Sugar 0
- Protein 24

Corned Beef and Cabbage

**Rhoda Burgoon
Collingswood, NJ**

**Jo Ellen Moore
Pendleton, IN**

**Kathi Rogge
Alexandria, IN**

Makes 6-8 servings
Prep. Time: 5 minutes
Cooking Time: 7-13 hours
Ideal slow-cooker size: 5- to 6-qt.

½ head cauliflower, broken into pieces

3-4-lb. corned beef brisket

2-3 medium onions, quartered

¾-1¼ cups water

½ small head of cabbage, cut in wedges

1. Layer all ingredients, except cabbage, in slow cooker.

2. Cover. Cook on Low 8–10 hours, or on High 5–6 hours.

3. Add cabbage wedges to liquid, pushing down to moisten. Turn to High and cook an additional 2–3 hours.

Note: To cook more cabbage than slow cooker will hold, cook separately in skillet. Remove 1 cup broth from slow cooker during last hour of cooking. Pour over cabbage wedges in skillet. Cover and cook slowly for 20–30 minutes.

Serving suggestion: Top individual servings with mixture of sour cream and horseradish.

- Calories 463
- Fat 34
- Sodium 2766
- Carbs 4
- Sugar 3
- Protein 34

Pot Roast

Carol Eveleth
Cheyenne, WY

Makes 4 servings
Prep. Time: 20 min
Cooking Time: 2 hours
Setting: Manual
Pressure: High
Release: Manual

2-lb. beef roast, boneless

¼ tsp. salt

¼ tsp. pepper

1 Tbsp. olive oil

2 stalks celery, chopped

4 Tbsp. butter

2 cups no-sugar-added tomato juice

2 cloves garlic, finely chopped, or 1 tsp. garlic powder

1 tsp. thyme

1 bay leaf

2 zucchini, chopped

1 medium onion, chopped

1 small head of cabbage, sliced into large chunks

1. Pat beef dry with paper towels; season on all sides with ¼ tsp. each salt and pepper.

2. Select Sauté function on the Instant Pot and adjust heat to "more." Put the oil in the inner pot, then cook the beef in oil for 6 minutes, until browned, turning once. Set on plate.

3. Add celery and butter to the inner pot; cook 2 minutes. Stir in tomato juice, garlic, thyme, and bay leaf. Hit Cancel to turn off Sauté function.

4. Place beef on top of the contents of the inner pot and press into sauce. Cover and lock lid and make sure vent is at sealing. Select Manual and cook at high pressure for 1 hour 15 minutes.

5. Once cooking is complete, release pressure by using natural release function. Transfer beef to cutting board. Discard bay leaf.

6. Skim off any excess fat from surface. Choose Sauté function and adjust heat to "more." Cook 18 minutes, or until reduced by about half (2½ cups). Hit Cancel to turn off Sauté function.

7. Add zucchini, onion, and cabbage. Cover and lock lid and make sure vent is at sealing. Select Manual and cook at high pressure for 10 minutes.

8. Once cooking is complete, release pressure by using a quick release. Using Sauté function, keep at a simmer.

9. Season with more salt and pepper, to taste.

- Calories 438
- Fat 20
- Sodium 581
- Carbs 10
- Sugar 6
- Protein 54

Herbed Pot Roast

Sarah Herr
Goshen, IN

Makes 6 servings
Prep. Time: 20 minutes
Cooking Time: 6–8 hours
Ideal slow-cooker size: oval 6-qt.

2 lbs. boneless beef chuck roast

½ head cauliflower, broken/chopped into pieces

2 cups brussels sprouts

2 stalks celery, cut into small chunks

½ tsp. salt

½ tsp. dried rosemary

½ tsp. dried thyme

¼ tsp. garlic powder

¼ tsp. onion powder

¼ tsp. paprika

¼ tsp. coarsely ground pepper

3 Tbsp. balsamic vinegar

1. Grease interior of slow-cooker crock.

2. Place roast in crock.

3. Place veggies around roast.

4. Sprinkle herbs and spices evenly over all.

5. Drizzle balsamic vinegar over top.

6. Cover. Cook on Low 6–8 hours.

- Calories 234
- Fat 9
- Sodium 312
- Carbs 5
- Sugar 2
- Protein 33

Spicy Beef Roast

Karen Ceneviva
Seymour, CT

Makes 10 servings
Prep. Time: 15–20 minutes
Cooking Time: 3–8 hours
Ideal slow-cooker size: 4- or 5-qt.

1–2 Tbsp. cracked black peppercorns

2 cloves garlic, minced

3-lb. eye of round roast, trimmed of fat

3 Tbsp. balsamic vinegar

⅓ cup liquid aminos

2 tsp. dry mustard

1. Rub cracked pepper and garlic onto roast. Put roast in slow cooker.

2. Make several shallow slits in top of meat.

3. In a small bowl, combine remaining ingredients. Spoon over meat.

4. Cover and cook on Low for 6–8 hours, or on High for 3–4 hours, just until meat is tender, but not dry.

- Calories 178
- Fat 4
- Sodium 424
- Carbs 2
- Sugar 1
- Protein 33

Marinated Chuck Roast

Susan Nafziger
Canton, KS

Makes 7–8 servings
Prep. Time: 15 minutes
Cooking Time: 5–6 hours
Marinating Time: 2–3 hours
Ideal slow-cooker size: oval 5-qt.

1 cup olive oil

1 cup liquid aminos

¼ cup red wine vinegar

½ cup chopped onions

⅛ tsp. garlic powder

¼ tsp. ground ginger

½ tsp. black pepper (coarsely ground is best)

½ tsp. dry mustard

3–4-lb. boneless chuck roast

1. Mix all ingredients except roast, either by whisking together in a bowl or whirring the mixture in a blender.

2. Place roast in a low baking or serving dish and pour marinade over top. Cover and refrigerate for 2–3 hours.

3. Grease interior of slow-cooker crock.

4. Place roast in crock. Pour marinade over top.

5. Cover. Cook on Low 5–6 hours, or until instant-read meat thermometer registers 140–145°F when stuck into center of meat.

6. When finished cooking, use a sturdy pair of tongs, or 2 metal spatulas, to move roast onto a cutting board. Cover to keep warm and allow to stand 15 minutes.

7. Cut into slices or chunks. Top with marinade and serve.

- Calories 552
- Fat 47
- Sodium 1461
- Carbs 2
- Sugar 0.5
- Protein 36

Hungarian Beef with Paprika

Maureen Csikasz
Wakefield, MA

Makes 9 servings
Prep. Time: 15 minutes
Cooking Time: 3–6 hours
Ideal slow-cooker size: oval 5- or 6-qt.

3-lb. boneless chuck roast

2–3 medium onions, coarsely chopped

5 Tbsp. sweet paprika

¾ tsp. salt

¼ tsp. black pepper

½ tsp. caraway seeds

1 clove garlic, chopped

½ green bell pepper, sliced

¼ cup water

½ cup sour cream

fresh parsley

1. Grease interior of slow cooker crock.

2. Place roast in crock.

3. In a good-sized bowl, mix all remaining ingredients together, except sour cream and parsley.

4. Spoon evenly over roast.

5. Cover. Cook on High 3–4 hours, or on Low 5–6 hours, or until instant-read meat thermometer registers 140–145°F when stuck in center of meat.

6. When finished cooking, use sturdy tongs or 2 metal spatulas to lift meat to cutting board. Cover with foil to keep warm. Let stand 10–15 minutes.

7. Cut into chunks or slices.

8. Just before serving, dollop with sour cream. Garnish with fresh parsley.

- Calories 313
- Fat 20
- Sodium 289
- Carbs 5
- Sugar 2
- Protein 30

Carol's Italian Beef

Carol Findling
Princeton, IL

Makes 6–8 servings
Prep. Time: 5–10 minutes
Cooking Time: 4–12 hours
Ideal slow-cooker size: 4-qt.

3–4-lb. lean rump roast

2 tsp. salt, *divided*

4 cloves garlic

2 tsp. Romano or Parmesan cheese, *divided*

1½ cups beef bone broth

1 tsp. dried oregano

1. Place roast in slow cooker. Cut 4 slits in top of roast. Fill each slit with ½ tsp. salt, 1 garlic clove, and ½ tsp. cheese.

2. Pour broth over meat. Sprinkle with oregano.

3. Cover. Cook on Low 10–12 hours, or on High 4–6 hours.

4. Remove meat and slice or shred.

- Calories 246
- Fat 11
- Sodium 713
- Carbs 1
- Sugar 0
- Protein 37

Four-Pepper Steak

Renee Hankins
Narvon, PA

Makes 14 servings
Prep. Time: 30 minutes
Cooking Time: 5–8 hours
Ideal slow-cooker size: 4- or 5-qt.

1 yellow pepper, sliced into ¼-inch-thick pieces

1 red pepper, sliced into ¼-inch-thick pieces

1 orange pepper, sliced into ¼-inch-thick pieces

1 green pepper, sliced into ¼-inch-thick pieces

2 cloves garlic, sliced

2 large onions, sliced

1 tsp. cumin

½ tsp. dried oregano

1 bay leaf

3-lb. flank steak, cut in ¼–½-inch-thick slices across the grain

salt, to taste

2 14½-oz. cans low-sodium diced tomatoes in juice

jalapeño chiles, sliced, *optional*

1. Place sliced bell peppers, garlic, onions, cumin, oregano, and bay leaf in slow cooker. Stir gently to mix.

2. Put steak slices on top of vegetable mixture. Season with salt.

3. Spoon tomatoes with juice over top. Sprinkle with jalapeño slices if you wish. Do not stir.

4. Cover and cook on Low 5–8 hours, depending on your slow cooker. Check after 5 hours to see if meat is tender. If not, continue cooking until tender but not dry. Remove bay leaf before serving.

- Calories 191
- Fat 8
- Sodium 160
- Carbs 7
- Sugar 2
- Protein 22

Slow-Cooked Pepper Steak

Carolyn Baer
Conrath, WI

Ann Driscoll
Albuquerque, NM

Makes 8 servings
Prep. Time: 25 minutes
Cooking Time: 6¼–7¼ hours
Ideal slow-cooker size: 4-qt.

1½–2 lbs. beef round steak, cut in 3×1-inch strips,
  trimmed of fat

2 Tbsp. olive oil

¼ cup liquid aminos

1 clove garlic, minced

1 cup chopped onion

5 drops liquid stevia

¼ tsp. pepper

¼ tsp. ground ginger

2 large green peppers, cut in strips

4 medium tomatoes cut in eighths, or 16 oz. can diced
  tomatoes

½ cup cold water

1 Tbsp. flaxseed

1. Brown beef in oil in saucepan. Transfer to slow cooker.

2. Combine liquid aminos, garlic, onion, stevia, pepper, and ginger. Pour over meat.

3. Cover. Cook on Low 5–6 hours.

4. Add green peppers and tomatoes. Cook 1 hour longer.

5. Combine water and flaxseed. Stir into slow cooker. Cook on High until thickened, about 10 minutes.

- Calories 213
- Fat 11
- Sodium 415
- Carbs 5
- Sugar 2
- Protein 26

Three-Pepper Steak

Renee Hankins
Narvon, PA

Makes 10 servings
Prep. Time: 15 minutes
Cooking Time: 5–8 hours
Ideal slow-cooker size: 4- or 5-qt.

3 bell peppers—one red, one orange, and one yellow
  pepper (or any combination of colors), cut into
  ¼-inch-thick slices

2 cloves garlic, sliced

1 large onion, sliced

1 tsp. cumin

½ tsp. dried oregano

1 bay leaf

3-lb. beef flank steak, cut in ¼–½-inch-thick slices
  across the grain

salt, to taste

14½-oz. can diced tomatoes in juice

jalapeño chilies, sliced, *optional*

1. Place sliced peppers, garlic, onion, cumin, oregano, and bay leaf in slow cooker. Stir gently to mix.

2. Put steak slices on top of vegetable mixture. Season with salt.

3. Spoon tomatoes with juice over top. Sprinkle with jalapeño pepper slices if you wish. Do not stir.

4. Cover. Cook on Low 5–8 hours, depending on your slow cooker. Check after 5 hours to see if meat is tender. If not, continue cooking until tender but not dry. Remove bay leaf before serving.

- Calories 260
- Fat 13
- Sodium 154
- Carbs 4
- Sugar 1
- Protein 30

Asian Pepper Steak

Donna Lantgen
Rapid City, SD

Makes 6 servings
Prep. Time: 20 minutes
Cooking Time: 6–8 hours
Ideal slow-cooker size: 4-qt.

1-lb. round steak, sliced thin, trimmed of fat

3 Tbsp. liquid aminos

½ tsp. ground ginger

1 clove garlic, minced

1 medium green pepper, thinly sliced

1 cup sliced fresh mushrooms

1 medium onion, thinly sliced

½ tsp. crushed red pepper

1. Combine all ingredients in slow cooker.

2. Cover. Cook on Low 6–8 hours.

- Calories 118
- Fat 5
- Sodium 388
- Carbs 3
- Sugar 1
- Protein 17

Slow Cooker Sirloin Steak

Amy Troyer
Garden Grove, IA

Makes 4–5 servings
Prep. Time: 10 minutes
Cooking Time: 6–8 hours
Ideal slow-cooker size: 2- to 3-qt.

2½-lb. sirloin steak, cut into ½-inch strips.

1 large onion, sliced

2 bell peppers, sliced

1 tsp. ginger

15 drops liquid stevia

2 Tbsp. olive oil

½ cup liquid aminos

2 cloves garlic, minced

1. Place steak in slow cooker, and top with the sliced onion and peppers.

2. Mix together remaining ingredients.

3. Pour sauce over meat, onion, and peppers.

4. Cook on Low 6–8 hours.

- Calories 350
- Fat 16
- Sodium 1191
- Carbs 4
- Sugar 1
- Protein 53

Herb Marinated Steak

Linda E. Wilcox
Blythewood, SC

Makes 4 servings
Prep. Time: 10 minutes
Marinating Time: 6–8 hours, or overnight
Cooking/Broiling Time: 12–18 minutes
Standing Time: 10 minutes

¼ cup chopped onion

2 Tbsp. fresh parsley

2 Tbsp. balsamic vinegar

1 Tbsp. olive oil

2 tsp. Dijon-style mustard

1 clove garlic, minced

1-lb. London broil, or chuck steak

1. Combine onion, parsley, vinegar, oil, mustard, and garlic in a bowl.

2. Place London broil or chuck steak in a sturdy plastic bag. Add onion mixture, spreading it on both sides of the meat. Close bag securely.

3. Place filled bag in a long dish in case of any leaks. Marinate in refrigerator 6–8 hours, or overnight. Turn it over at least once while marinating.

4. Pour off marinade. Place steak on rack in broiler pan so meat is about 5 inches from heat source. Broil about 6–8 minutes on each side for rare; 9 minutes on each side for medium.

5. When finished broiling, allow meat to stand for 10 minutes.

6. Carve meat diagonally across the grain into thin slices.

- Calories 295
- Fat 22
- Sodium 135
- Carbs 3
- Sugar 2
- Protein 22

Quick Steak Tacos

Hope Comerford
Clinton Township, MI

Makes 6 servings
Prep. Time: 5 minutes
Cooking Time: 10 minutes
Setting: Sauté

1 Tbsp. olive oil

8-oz. sirloin steak

2 Tbsp. steak seasoning

1 tsp. Worcestershire sauce

½ red onion, sliced

6 large leaves lettuce (romaine or iceberg work well)

¼ cup chopped tomatoes

¾ cup shredded Mexican cheese

2 Tbsp. sour cream

6 Tbsp. no-sugar-added garden fresh salsa

¼ cup chopped fresh cilantro

1. Turn the Instant Pot on the Sauté function. When the pot displays "hot," add the olive oil to the pot.

2. Season the steak with the steak seasoning.

3. Add the steak to the pot along with the Worcestershire sauce.

4. Cook each side of the steak for 2–3 minutes until the steak turns brown.

5. Remove the steak from the pot and slice thinly.

6. Add the onion slices to the pot and cook them until translucent with the remaining olive oil and steak juices.

7. Remove the onion from the pot.

8. Assemble the steak, onion, tomatoes, cheese, sour cream, salsa, and cilantro on top of each piece of lettuce.

- Calories 189
- Fat 9
- Sodium 254
- Carbs 14
- Sugar 2
- Protein 14

Philly Cheese Steaks

Michele Ruvola
Vestal, NY

Makes 6 servings
Prep. Time: 15 minutes
Cooking Time: 55 minutes
Setting: Slow Cook
Pressure: Low
Release: Natural then Manual

1 red pepper, sliced

1 green pepper, sliced

1 onion, sliced

2 cloves garlic, minced

2½ lbs. thinly sliced steak

1 tsp. salt

½ tsp. black pepper

0.7-oz. pkg. dry keto-friendly Italian Dressing Mix (recipe on pg. 326)

1 cup beef bone broth

6 slices provolone cheese

6 slices keto-friendly bread

1. Put all ingredients in the inner pot of the Instant Pot, except the provolone cheese and bread.

2. Seal the lid, make sure vent is at sealing, and cook for 40 minutes on the Slow Cook setting.

3. Let the pressure release naturally for 10 minutes, then do a quick release.

4. Scoop meat and vegetables onto keto-friendly bread.

5. Top with provolone cheese and put on a baking sheet.

6. Broil in oven for 5 minutes.

7. Pour remaining juice in pot into cups for dipping.

- Calories 738
- Fat 39
- Sodium 1142
- Carbs 25
- Sugar 5
- Protein 69

Barbecue Beef Strips

Doris Ranck
Gap, PA

Makes 10 servings (¾ cup each)
Prep. Time: 30 minutes
Cooking Time: 40–45 minutes

2 lbs. steak or London broil, trimmed of visible fat

2 Tbsp. olive oil

1 medium-sized onion, chopped

1 cup no-sugar-added ketchup

1 cup no-salt-added tomato sauce

⅓ cup water

1½–2 tsp. Truvia Brown Sugar Blend

1 Tbsp. prepared mustard

1 Tbsp. Worcestershire sauce

1. Slice steak into strips about 3 inches long and ⅛ inch wide.

2. Place oil in large skillet. Add strips of meat and chopped onion. Brown quickly over high heat, stirring so that all sides of beef brown well. Pour off all but 2 Tbsp. drippings.

3. Combine remaining ingredients in a mixing bowl. When well mixed, pour over beef strips and onion in skillet.

4. Cover and cook slowly for 35–40 minutes, or until beef is tender. Stir occasionally.

Serving suggestion: Serve over cooked cauliflower rice.

- Calories 163
- Fat 7
- Sodium 216
- Carbs 3
- Sugar 1
- Protein 20

Nadine and Hazel's Swiss Steak

Nadine Martinitz
Salina, KS

Hazel L. Propst
Oxford, PA

Makes 6-8 servings
Prep. Time: 20 minutes
Cooking Time: 6–8 hours
Ideal slow-cooker size: 6-qt.

3-lb. round steak

⅓ cup almond flour

2 tsp. salt

½ tsp. pepper

3 Tbsp. butter

1 large onion, or more, sliced

1 large pepper, or more, sliced

14½-oz. can stewed tomatoes, or 3-4 fresh tomatoes, chopped

water

1. Sprinkle meat with almond flour, salt, and pepper. Pound both sides. Cut into 6 or 8 pieces. Brown meat in butter over medium heat on top of stove, about 15 minutes. Transfer to slow cooker.

2. Brown onion and pepper. Add tomatoes and bring to boil. Pour over steak. Add water to completely cover steak.

3. Cover. Cook on Low 6–8 hours.

Variation: To add some flavor, stir in your favorite dried herbs when beginning to cook the steak, or add fresh herbs in the last hour of cooking.

- Calories 349
- Fat 19
- Sodium 835
- Carbs 9
- Sugar 2
- Protein 38

Beef Broccoli

Anita Troyer
Fairview, MI

Makes 6 servings
Prep. Time: 15 minutes
Cooking Time: 20 minutes
Setting: Manual and Sauté
Pressure: High
Release: Manual

1 Tbsp. olive oil

1½ lbs. boneless beef, trimmed and sliced thinly (round steak or chuck roast)

¼ tsp. black pepper

½ cup diced onion

3 cloves garlic, minced

¾ cup beef bone broth

½ cup soy sauce

⅛ cup Truvia Brown Sugar Blend

2 Tbsp. coconut oil

⅛ tsp. red pepper flakes

1 lb. broccoli, chopped

3 Tbsp. water

½ tsp. konjac flour

1. Put oil into the inner pot of the Instant Pot and select Sauté. When oil begins to sizzle, brown the beef in several small batches, taking care to brown well. After browning, remove and put into another bowl. Season with black pepper.

2. Sauté onion in pot for 2 minutes. Add garlic and sauté another minute. Add beef broth, soy sauce, brown sugar blend, coconut oil, and red pepper flakes. Stir to mix well.

3. Add beef to mixture in inner pot. Secure lid and make sure vent is at sealing. Set on Manual at high pressure and set timer for 12 minutes.

4. After beep, turn cooker off and use quick pressure release. Remove lid.

5. In a microwave-safe bowl, steam the broccoli for 3 minutes or until desired doneness.

6. In a small bowl, stir together water and konjac flour. Add to pot and stir. Put on Sauté setting and stir some more. After mixture becomes thick, add broccoli and turn pot off.

- Calories 390
- Fat 25
- Sodium 991
- Carbs 16
- Sugar 6
- Protein 27

Pounded Swiss Steak in a Yummy Sauce

Robbin Poetzl
Springfield, OR

Makes 12 servings (4 oz. meat each)
Prep. Time: 20–30 minutes
Browning/Baking Time: 50 minutes

4-5 lbs. skirt or flank beef steak, about ½-inch thick, trimmed of visible fat

1½-2 cups almond flour

1 Tbsp. Italian seasoning

1 tsp. garlic powder

1 tsp. pepper

1 tsp. onion powder

1 tsp. pepper herb seasoning

2 Tbsp. olive oil

Sauce:
2 tsp. olive oil

½ tsp. crushed garlic

½-1 cup beef bone broth

⅓ cup keto-friendly teriyaki sauce

1 tsp. Italian seasoning

1½ cups sliced fresh mushrooms

1 cup chopped celery

2 14½-oz. cans diced tomatoes, undrained

1. Cut the steak into serving-size pieces. Pound each piece to about ¼-inch thick. In a small bowl, mix flour with seasonings. Flour all sides of pounded steak pieces.

2. Brown floured meat, a few pieces at a time, in hot oil in a large skillet. Brown 2–3 minutes on one side and then the other side for 2–3 minutes. Place browned steak in a shallow baking dish.

3. To make the sauce, heat 2 tsp. oil in a large, heavy skillet over medium-high heat. Stir in garlic. When garlic begins to "pop," add the beef broth.

4. Simmer for 2–3 minutes. Then add the teriyaki sauce, Italian seasoning, mushrooms, celery, and canned tomatoes. Bring to a light boil.

5. Turn down heat and continue to cook the sauce, uncovered, until it thickens. Pour the sauce over prepared steaks.

6. Cover and bake at 350°F for 15 minutes. Remove lid and bake an additional 15 minutes.

- Calories 392
- Fat 22
- Sodium 573
- Carbs 10
- Sugar 3
- Protein 38

Slow-Cooker Cabbage Lasagna

Sylvia Eberly
Reinholds, PA

Makes 4–5 servings
Prep. Time: 30 minutes
Cooking Time: 5 hours
Ideal slow-cooker size: 5-qt.

1 medium to large head cabbage, about 6 inches in diameter

1 lb. ground beef

2 cloves garlic, minced or pressed

1 medium onion, chopped

1 green sweet bell pepper, chopped

6-oz. can tomato paste

8-oz. can tomato sauce

1–3 tsp. dried oregano, according to your taste preference

2 tsp. dried basil, *optional*

1 tsp. black pepper

1 cup mozzarella cheese, grated, *divided*

½ cup ricotta or cottage cheese, *divided*

½ cup Parmesan cheese, grated

1. Wash cabbage and remove tough outer leaves. Cut head in half and slice thinly.

2. Arrange finely sliced cabbage in a steamer basket and steam about 3–5 minutes. (You might need to do this in 2 batches.)

3. Drain cabbage well. Set aside.

4. Grease interior of slow-cooker crock.

5. If you have time, brown beef, garlic, onion, and green pepper together in a skillet. Drain off any drippings. If you don't have time, place beef in bowl and use a sturdy spoon to break up into small clumps. Mix in garlic, onion, and green pepper.

6. Add tomato paste, tomato sauce, and seasonings to beef mixture. Combine well.

7. Drain cabbage again.

8. Make layers in crock, starting with half the cabbage leaves, half the meat mixture, ⅓ of the mozzarella, and half the ricotta.

9. Repeat layers, using remaining cabbage and meat mixture, ½ the remaining mozzarella, and all of the ricotta.

10. Top with remaining mozzarella.

11. Cover. Cook on Low 5 hours, or until vegetables are as tender as you like them.

12. Uncover. Sprinkle with Parmesan cheese.

13. Let stand 10 minutes so that Parmesan cheese can melt and lasagna firm up.

- Calories 460
- Fat 28
- Sodium 880
- Carbs 25
- Sugar 13
- Protein 31

Baked Cabbage Lasagna

Sylvia Eberly
Reinholds, PA

Makes 8 servings
Prep. Time: 15 minutes
Cooking/Baking Time: 45–50 minutes

1 medium to large head of cabbage, about 6 inches in diameter
1 Tbsp. olive oil
2 cloves garlic, minced or pressed
1 medium onion, chopped
1 sweet green bell pepper
¾ lb. ground beef
6-oz. can tomato paste, no salt added
8-oz. can tomato sauce, no salt added
1–3 tsp. dried oregano, according to your taste preference
2 tsp. dried basil, *optional*
1 tsp. black pepper
1 cup grated mozzarella cheese, *divided*
½ cup ricotta, or cottage cheese, *divided*
½ cup freshly grated Parmesan cheese

1. Preheat oven to 350°F.

2. Wash cabbage and remove tough outer leaves. Cut head in half and slice.

3. Arrange finely sliced cabbage in a steamer basket and steam about 3–5 minutes. (You may need to do this in 2 batches.)

4. Drain cabbage well. Set aside.

5. Sauté garlic, onion, and green pepper in olive oil in large skillet over medium heat.

6. Add ground beef to skillet and brown thoroughly. Drain off any drippings.

7. Add tomato paste, tomato sauce, and seasonings to beef mixture. Combine well.

8. Lightly grease a 9×13-inch baking pan. Drain cabbage again. Make layers starting with half the cabbage leaves, half the meat mixture, a third of the mozzarella, and half the ricotta cheese.

9. Add another layer with remaining cabbage, then the meat mixture, half the mozzarella, and all the remaining ricotta cheese.

10. Top with remaining mozzarella.

11. Finish by scattering Parmesan on top.

12. Bake, covered, for 20 minutes.

13. Uncover and bake 5–10 minutes more, or until lightly browned.

- Calories 170
- Fat 9
- Sodium 515
- Carbs 15
- Sugar 8
- Protein 9

Oven Zucchini Lasagna

Ruth Ann Hoover
New Holland, PA

Makes 8 servings, (2¾ x3½-inch rectangle each)
Prep. Time: 20 minutes
Cooking/Baking Time: 55 minutes

6 cups sliced raw zucchini, unpeeled

1 lb. ground beef

6-oz. can tomato paste

½ tsp. dried basil

½ tsp. dried oregano

½ tsp. salt

¼ tsp. garlic powder

1 cup cottage cheese

1 egg

¼ cup grated Parmesan cheese

¼ cup shredded cheddar cheese

1 cup shredded mozzarella cheese

1. Spread slices of zucchini into a long microwave-safe dish. Sprinkle with 2 Tbsp. water. Cover and cook on high for 3½ minutes. Stir. Cover and return to microwave and cook on High an additional 3½ minutes. Stir. Cover and return to microwave and cook on High 1½ minutes more. Drain zucchini and set aside.

2. Meanwhile, in large stockpot, brown ground beef. Drain off drippings.

3. Add tomato paste, basil, oregano, salt, garlic powder, cottage cheese, egg, grated Parmesan, cheddar cheese, and cooked zucchini to browned beef in stockpot. Stir gently together until well mixed.

4. Spoon mixture into greased 7x11-inch baking dish.

5. Bake uncovered at 350°F for 25 minutes.

6. Sprinkle mozzarella cheese over lasagna. Return to oven and continue baking 20 more minutes.

- Calories 300
- Fat 22
- Sodium 464
- Carbs 4
- Sugar 3
- Protein 21

Zucchini and Beef Lasagna

Carolyn Snader
Ephrata, PA

Makes 4 servings
Prep. Time: 15–20 minutes
Cooking Time: 4 hours
Ideal slow-cooker size: 4- or 5-qt.

1 lb. ground beef

½ tsp. dried basil

½ tsp. dried oregano

⅛ tsp. garlic powder

6-oz. can tomato paste

1 cup cottage cheese

1 egg

2 cups mozzarella cheese, shredded, *divided*

6 cups sliced, unpeeled zucchini

1. Grease interior of slow-cooker crock.

2. If you have time, brown beef in a skillet. Using a slotted spoon, lift beef out of drippings and place in good-sized bowl. If you don't have time, place beef in bowl and use a sturdy spoon to break into small clumps.

3. Mix basil, oregano, and garlic powder with beef.

4. Stir tomato paste into beef mixture.

5. In a separate bowl, combine cottage cheese, egg, and 1 cup mozzarella.

6. Cover bottom of crock with half the zucchini slices.

7. Top with half the meat mixture.

8. Spoon half the cheese mixture over meat.

9. Repeat layers.

10. Cover. Cook on Low 4 hours, or until zucchini is as tender as you like.

11. Uncover crock. Sprinkle in remaining mozzarella cheese. Allow to stand 10 minutes so cheese can melt and lasagna can firm up.

- Calories 620
- Fat 40
- Sodium 1171
- Carbs 18
- Sugar 13
- Protein 50

Beef and Zucchini Casserole

Judi Manos
West Islip, NY

Makes 6 servings
Prep. Time: 15 minutes
Cooking/Baking Time: 50–65 minutes

2 tsp. olive oil

½ cup finely chopped onion

1 lb. (3 small) zucchini, cut into ¼-inch-thick slices

¼ lb. fresh mushrooms, sliced

1 lb. ground beef

14½-oz. can sliced tomatoes, undrained, no salt added

½ tsp. garlic powder

½ tsp. dried oregano

½ cup grated Parmesan cheese

1. Preheat oven to 350°F.

2. Heat oil in large skillet. Add onion and stir until tender and light golden in color.

3. Add zucchini and mushrooms to skillet. Cook over medium heat 3–4 minutes, stirring lightly.

4. Put zucchini mixture into lightly greased 2-qt. baking dish.

5. Place ground beef in skillet. Cook over medium heat until no longer pink, stirring frequently. Drain off drippings.

6. Add tomatoes, garlic powder, and oregano to meat in skillet. Mix well.

7. Spoon meat mixture over zucchini in baking dish.

8. Sprinkle cheese on top.

9. Bake, uncovered, 35–45 minutes, or until cheese is lightly browned and dish is heated through.

- Calories 245
- Fat 16
- Sodium 228
- Carbs 9
- Sugar 3
- Protein 16

Mild Indian Curry

Vic and Christina Buckwalter
Keezletown, VA

Makes 6 servings (¾ cup each)
Prep. Time: 10 minutes
Cooking Time: 15–20 minutes

1 lb. ground beef

1 onion, chopped

3 cloves garlic, finely chopped

½ tsp. ground ginger

2 tsp. coriander

2 tsp. cumin

1 tsp. turmeric

¼ tsp. ground cloves

¼ tsp. cayenne pepper

¾ cup tomato sauce

½ tsp. salt

30 drops liquid stevia

¼ cup plain yogurt

cooked cauliflower rice

topping options: grated cheeses; chopped fresh onions; orange sections; sliced bananas; chopped papaya, mango, and/ or tomatoes; peanuts; raisins

1. In a large skillet, brown beef, onion, and garlic together. Drain off any drippings.

2. Add ginger, coriander, cumin, turmeric, ground cloves, and cayenne pepper to beef mixture. Cook 1 minute.

3. Stir in tomato sauce, salt, and stevia. Cook 10 minutes.

4. Just before serving, blend in yogurt.

5. Serve over cauliflower rice.

6. Send small bowls of each topping that you choose around the table after the rice and curry have been passed.

- Calories 249
- Fat 20
- Sodium 360
- Carbs 5
- Sugar 2
- Protein 14

Succulent Meatloaf

Lizzie Ann Yoder
Hartville, OH

Makes 6 servings (1 slice per serving)
Prep. Time: 20 minutes
Baking Time: 1–1½ hours

1 lb. ground beef

⅔ cup almond meal

½ cup whole milk

1 egg

⅓ cup chopped onion

1 Tbsp. prepared mustard

1 Tbsp. Worcestershire sauce

½ tsp. black pepper

¼ cup no-sugar-added ketchup

1. In a large bowl, mix together beef, almond meal, milk, egg, onion, mustard, Worcestershire sauce, pepper, and ketchup. Blend well.

2. Shape into a loaf and place in well-greased loaf pan.

3. Bake at 350°F for 1–1½ hours. Check with meat thermometer in center of loaf after 1 hour of baking to see if loaf is finished. If temperature registers 160°F, it's done baking. Continue baking if it hasn't reached that temperature.

4. Allow to stand 10 minutes before slicing.

- Calories 334
- Fat 27
- Sodium 221
- Carbs 8
- Sugar 4
- Protein 17

Grandma's Best Meatloaf

Nanci Keatley
Salem, OR

Makes 10 servings (1 slice per serving)
Prep. Time: 15–25 minutes
Baking Time: 1 hour and 5 minutes

2 lbs. ground beef

2 Tbsp. fresh Italian parsley, chopped

1 tsp. dried oregano

1 small onion, chopped fine

4 cloves garlic, minced

¼ cup, plus 2 Tbsp., Romano cheese, *optional*

½ cup almond flour

½ cup no-sugar-added ketchup

2 eggs

1 tsp. black pepper

1 tsp. kosher salt

1. In a large mixing bowl, mix together ground beef, parsley, oregano, onion, garlic, optional cheese, almond flour, ketchup, eggs, pepper, and salt.

2. Roll mixture into a large ball.

3. Place in well-greased 9×13-inch baking dish or roaster, flattening slightly.

4. Bake at 375°F for 1 hour. Keep in oven 5 more minutes with oven off and door closed.

5. Remove meatloaf from oven. Let stand 10 minutes before slicing to allow meatloaf to gather its juices and firm up.

- Calories 342
- Fat 27
- Sodium 233
- Carbs 6
- Sugar 3
- Protein 18

Cheesy Meat Loaf

Jean Turner
Williams Lake, BC

Makes 8 servings (1 slice per serving)
Prep. Time: 20–30 minutes
Baking Time: 1½ hours

½ cup chopped onion

½ cup chopped green pepper

1 tsp. olive oil

8-oz. can tomato sauce

2 eggs

1 cup shredded white cheddar cheese

1 cup almond flour

¼ tsp. salt

dash pepper

¼ tsp. dried thyme

1½ lbs. ground beef

½ lb. ground pork tenderloin

1. In a small saucepan, sauté onion and green pepper in olive oil just until tender.

2. In a large mixing bowl, combine all ingredients and mix well.

3. Shape into a loaf. Place in greased 9x5-inch loaf pan.

4. Bake at 350°F for 1½ hours.

- Calories 538
- Fat 44
- Sodium 423
- Carbs 6
- Sugar 2
- Protein 31

Mexican Meatloaf

Jennifer Freed
Rockingham, VA

Makes 4-6 servings
Prep. Time: 20 minutes
Cooking Time: 5–7 hours
Ideal slow-cooker size: 3- to 4-qt.

2 lbs. ground beef

2 cups ground pork rinds

1 cup shredded cheddar cheese

⅔ cup salsa

2 eggs, beaten

4 Tbsp. taco seasoning

1. Combine all ingredients in large bowl; mix well.

2. Shape meat mixture into loaf and place in slow cooker.

3. Cover; cook on Low for 5–7 hours, or until internal temperature is 165°F.

- Calories 532
- Fat 38
- Sodium 1022
- Carbs 9
- Sugar 2
- Protein 40

Nutritious Meatloaf

Elsie Russett
Fairbank, IA

Makes 6 servings
Prep. Time: 10 minutes
Cooking Time: 3–4 hours
Ideal slow-cooker size: 4-qt.

1 lb. ground beef

2 cups finely shredded cabbage

1 medium green pepper, diced

1 Tbsp. dried onion

½ tsp. caraway seeds

1 tsp. salt

1. Combine all ingredients. Shape into loaf and place on rack in slow cooker.

2. Cover. Cook on High 3–4 hours.

- Calories 133
- Fat 6
- Sodium 313
- Carbs 3
- Sugar 1.5
- Protein 16

Teriyaki Burgers

Susan Kasting
Jenks, OK

Makes 4 servings (1 burger each)
Prep. Time: 10 minutes
Cooking Time: 10 minutes

1 lb. ground beef

2 Tbsp. soy sauce

1 Tbsp. peeled fresh ginger, grated

1 clove garlic, minced

¼ cup chopped green onions

pinch pepper

1. Combine all ingredients in bowl.

2. Form into 4 patties.

3. Grill or broil for 10 minutes, flipping to brown both sides.

- Calories 341
- Fat 28
- Sodium 570
- Carbs 1
- Sugar 0
- Protein 19

Meatless & Seafood

Eggplant Italian

Melanie Thrower
McPherson, KS

SLOW COOKER

Makes 6–8 servings
Prep. Time: 30 minutes
Cooking Time: 4 hours
Ideal slow-cooker size: 4- or 5-qt. oval

2 eggplants

1 egg

24 oz. cottage cheese

¼ tsp. salt

black pepper, to taste

14-oz. can tomato sauce

2–4 Tbsp. Italian seasoning, according to your taste
preference

1. Peel eggplants and cut in ½-inch thick slices. Soak in salt water for about 5 minutes to remove bitterness. Drain well.

2. Spray slow cooker with cooking spray.

3. Mix egg, cottage cheese, salt, and pepper together in bowl.

4. Mix tomato sauce and Italian seasoning together in another bowl.

5. Spoon a thin layer of tomato sauce into bottom of slow cooker. Top with about one-third of eggplant slices, and then one-third of egg/cheese mixture, and finally one-third of remaining tomato sauce mixture.

6. Repeat those layers twice, ending with seasoned tomato sauce.

7. Cover. Cook on High 4 hours. Allow to rest 15 minutes before serving.

- Calories 124
- Fat 3
- Sodium 569
- Carbs 15
- Sugar 10
- Protein 12

Exceptional Eggplant Casserole

Lisa Good
Harrisonburg, VA

Makes 8 servings (¾ cup each)
Prep. Time: 15–20 minutes
Baking Time: 45–50 minutes

½ cup chopped onion

½ cup chopped green pepper

½ cup chopped celery

1 tsp. olive oil

2 8-oz. cans tomato sauce

2½ Tbsp. Splenda Brown Sugar Blend

1½ tsp. dried oregano

½ tsp. minced garlic

1 medium-sized eggplant, peeled or unpeeled, sliced in ⅛-inch-thick slices

1 cup mozzarella cheese

1. In a large skillet or sauce pan, sauté the onion, green pepper, and celery in the oil.

2. Add the tomato sauce, brown sugar blend, oregano, and garlic to the sautéed vegetables. Mix well.

3. Layer one-third of the sauce mixture, one-third of the eggplant, and one-third of the cheese into a greased 2-qt. baking dish. Repeat the layers twice.

4. Bake uncovered at 350°F for 45–50 minutes.

- Calories 95
- Fat 4
- Sodium 363
- Carbs 11
- Sugar 8
- Protein 4

Tomato-Artichoke Scallop

Clara Earle Baskin
Quinton, NJ

Makes 8 servings (¾ cup each)
Prep. Time: 20 minutes
Baking Time: 10–15 minutes

2 Tbsp. olive oil

½ cup finely chopped onion

2 Tbsp. finely chopped green onion

14-oz. can artichoke hearts, drained

35-oz. can whole plum tomatoes, drained

½ tsp. fresh, or pinch dried, basil

5–10 drops liquid stevia

salt and pepper, to taste

¼ cup grated Parmesan cheese

1. In a large skillet or saucepan, heat oil. Sauté onion and green onion until tender.

2. Rinse artichokes and cut into quarters. Add to skillet.

3. Stir in tomatoes and basil. Heat 2–3 minutes, stirring occasionally.

4. Season with stevia, salt, and pepper. Turn into greased shallow baking dish. Sprinkle with Parmesan cheese.

5. Bake at 325°F for 10–15 minutes, or until vegetables are tender.

- Calories 94
- Fat 4.5
- Sodium 142
- Carbs 12
- Sugar 4
- Protein 3

Baked Salmon

Erma Brubaker
Harrisonburg, VA

Makes 4 servings (3½ oz. salmon each)
Prep. Time: 5 minutes
Baking Time: 30–45 minutes

1 lb. fresh salmon, cut into 4 pieces

2 Tbsp. butter, melted

seasoning salt

¼ cup mayonnaise

parsley

1. Coat baking dish with melted butter. Arrange salmon in baking dish, coating each side with the butter in the dish.

2. Sprinkle with seasoning salt, spread with mayonnaise, and top with parsley.

3. Bake, uncovered, at 350°F for 30–45 minutes.

- Calories 293
- Fat 21
- Sodium 262
- Carbs 0
- Sugar 0
- Protein 26

Roasted Salmon

Gloria Julien
Gladstone, MI

Makes 2 servings
Prep. Time: 7–10 minutes
Baking Time: 10–12 minutes

2 5-oz. pieces salmon with skin

2 tsp. extra-virgin olive oil

1 Tbsp. chopped chives

1 Tbsp. fresh tarragon leaves, *optional*

1. Preheat oven to 425°F.

2. Line a baking sheet with foil.

3. Rub salmon all over with 2 tsp. oil.

4. Roast skin side down on foil-lined baking sheet until fish is cooked through, about 12 minutes. (Check if fish flakes easily with fork after it bakes 10 minutes. Continue baking only if it doesn't.)

5. Using a metal spatula, lift salmon off skin and place salmon on serving plate. Discard skin.

6. Sprinkle salmon with herbs and serve.

- Calories 248
- Fat 14
- Sodium 64
- Carbs 1
- Sugar 0
- Protein 28

Baked Fish

Patricia Howard
Green Valley, AZ

Makes 4 servings
Prep. Time: 5 minutes
Baking Time: 10–15 minutes

2 Tbsp. butter, melted

4 4-oz. fish fillets (hake, cod, or mahi-mahi)

juice of ½ lemon

1 tsp. dill weed

1 tsp. dried basil

1 tsp. original Mrs. Dash

1½ tsp. parsley flakes

4 thin slices lemon

1. Preheat oven to 350°F.

2. Coat baking dish with melted butter. Add fish fillets to dish in one layer.

3. Squeeze lemon juice over fish.

4. Sprinkle fish with dill weed, basil, Mrs. Dash, and parsley.

5. Place lemon slices on top. Cover with foil.

6. Bake 10–15 minutes. Do not over-bake. The thinner the fillet, the faster it cooks, and the less time it takes. Check for flakiness with the tines of a fork after 10 minutes. Continue baking only if needed.

- Calories 205
- Fat 12
- Sodium 60
- Carbs 1
- Sugar 0
- Protein 22

Salmon in a Skillet

Bernita Boyts
Shawnee Mission, KS

Makes 4 servings
Prep. Time: 10 minutes
Cooking Time: 10-15 minutes

1 lb. wild salmon fillet, cut to fit in your skillet

1 tsp. olive oil

dash pepper

2 Tbsp. butter

1 clove garlic, chopped fine

¼ cup water

2 Tbsp. capers

2 green onions, finely chopped

1 tsp. fresh, or ¼ tsp. dried dill weed

1 medium tomato, chopped

1 Tbsp. lemon juice

1. Rinse salmon in cool water; pat dry.

2. Heat oil in skillet.

3. Pepper fillet and place carefully in skillet, skin side up. Cook over medium heat 3–5 minutes. Allow longer time for a thick fillet.

4. Turn fillet over. Cook another 3–5 minutes, or until fish flakes when prodded with a fork. Don't overcook in skillet; it will finish on serving platter.

5. Remove fish from skillet. Place on platter and cover.

6. Melt butter in skillet. Add garlic. Stir and cook about 30 seconds.

7. Add water and heat until bubbling, scraping brown bits into liquid.

8. Add capers, green onions, and dill. Cook another minute.

9. Stir in chopped tomato. Heat through.

10. Sprinkle lemon juice over salmon.

11. Top with sauce and serve.

- Calories 207
- Fat 11
- Sodium 155
- Carbs 3
- Sugar 1
- Protein 23

Lemon Dijon Fish

June S. Groff
Denver, PA

SLOW COOKER

Makes 4 servings
Prep. Time: 10 minutes
Cooking Time: 3 hours
Ideal slow-cooker size: 2-qt.

1½ lbs. orange roughy fillets

2 Tbsp. Dijon mustard

3 Tbsp. butter, melted

1 tsp. liquid aminos

1 Tbsp. lemon juice

1. Cut fillets to fit in slow cooker.

2. In a bowl, mix remaining ingredients together. Pour sauce over fish. (If you have to stack the fish, spoon a portion of the sauce over the first layer of fish before adding the second layer.)

3. Cover and cook on Low 3 hours, or until fish flakes easily but is not dry or overcooked.

- Calories 36
- Fat 19
- Sodium 316
- Carbs 0.5
- Sugar 0
- Protein 33

Easy Tilapia

Karen Ceneviva
New Haven, CT

Makes 4 servings
Prep. Time: 2 minutes
Cooking Time: 6–7 minutes

1 Tbsp. olive oil

4 6-oz. tilapia fillets

lemon pepper

1. Heat oil in large skillet.

2. Lay fish in hot skillet, being careful not to splash yourself with hot oil.

3. Sprinkle fish lightly with lemon pepper.

4. Cook 3 minutes.

5. Flip fish carefully. Sprinkle lightly with lemon pepper.

6. Cook another 3 minutes, or just until fish flakes when pricked with a fork.

- Calories 193
- Fat 6
- Sodium 109
- Carbs 0
- Sugar 0
- Protein 34

Baked Halibut Steaks

Kristi See
Weskan, KS

Makes 4 servings
Prep. Time: 15 minutes
Cooking/Baking Time: 25 minutes

1 tsp. olive oil

1 cup unpeeled diced zucchini

½ cup minced onion

1 clove garlic, peeled and minced

2 cups diced fresh tomatoes

2 Tbsp. chopped fresh basil

¼ tsp. salt

¼ tsp. pepper

4 6-oz. halibut steaks

⅓ cup crumbled feta cheese

1. Preheat oven to 450°F. Lightly grease shallow baking dish.

2. Heat olive oil in a medium saucepan over medium heat. Stir in zucchini, onion, and garlic.

3. Cook for 5 minutes, or until tender. Stir now and then.

4. Remove saucepan from heat. Mix in tomatoes, basil, salt, and pepper.

5. Arrange halibut steaks in a single layer in the prepared baking dish.

6. Spoon equal amounts of zucchini mixture over each steak.

7. Top each steak with feta cheese.

8. Bake 15 minutes in the preheated oven, or until fish is easily flaked with a fork.

- Calories 225
- Fat 6
- Sodium 375
- Carbs 7
- Sugar 4
- Protein 35

Crab-Topped Catfish

Vicki J. Hill
Memphis, TN

Makes 6 servings (1 fillet with topping each)
Prep. Time: 5–10 minutes
Baking Time: 27 minutes

6 4-oz. catfish fillets

6-oz. can white crabmeat, drained and flaked

½ cup mayonnaise

1 tsp. lemon juice

paprika

⅓ cup sliced almonds

1. Place catfish on greased cookie sheet.

2. Bake, uncovered, at 350°F for 22 minutes, or until fish flakes easily with a fork. Drain.

3. Meanwhile, combine crab, mayonnaise, and lemon juice in a bowl.

4. After fish has baked for 22 minutes, spoon crab mix evenly over fish. Sprinkle with paprika and sliced almonds.

5. Return to oven and bake uncovered at 350°F for 5 minutes more.

- Calories 328
- Fat 25
- Sodium 360
- Carbs 2
- Sugar 0.5
- Protein 24

Shrimp Stir-Fry

Jean Binns Smith
Bellefonte, PA

Makes 4 servings
Prep. Time: 10 minutes
Cooking Time: 8–10 minutes

1–2 cloves garlic, chopped

⅛ tsp. grated, or finely chopped, fresh ginger

1 Tbsp. olive oil

2½ cups chopped broccoli

½ cup chopped sweet red bell pepper, *optional*

12 oz. medium-sized raw shrimp, peeled and deveined

2 cups cooked cauliflower rice

1. Sauté garlic and ginger in oil in large skillet until fragrant.

2. Stir in broccoli and chopped pepper, if using. Sauté until crisp-tender.

3. Stir in shrimp. Cook over medium heat 3–4 minutes until shrimp are just opaque in centers.

4. Serve with cooked cauliflower rice.

- Calories 129
- Fat 5
- Sodium 516
- Carbs 8
- Sugar 3
- Protein 14

Shrimp with Ginger and Lime

Joy Uhler
Richardson, TX

Makes 4 servings
Prep. Time: 15–20 minutes
Cooking Time: 10 minutes

3 Tbsp. lime juice

4 Tbsp. olive oil, *divided*

1 Tbsp. minced fresh ginger

1½ tsp. Truvia Brown Sugar Blend

1 tsp. grated lime zest

1 tsp. coconut oil

1 large clove garlic, minced

1 lb. cooked shrimp, peeled and deveined

cooked cauliflower rice

2 Tbsp. cilantro, chopped

1. In a large mixing bowl, stir together lime juice, 3 Tbsp. olive oil, ginger, brown sugar blend, lime zest, coconut oil, and garlic clove.

2. Stir in shrimp and mix well so that they're covered with the marinade. Allow shrimp to marinate for 15 minutes.

3. Pour remaining 1 Tbsp. olive oil into large skillet or wok. Spoon in shrimp mixture and stir-fry until heated through.

4. Serve over prepared cauliflower rice. Sprinkle with chopped cilantro.

- Calories 277
- Fat 17
- Sodium 1074
- Carbs 5
- Sugar 2
- Protein 26

Shrimp Curry

Margaret Thorpe
Lancaster, PA

Makes 5 servings
Prep. Time: 10 minutes
Cooking Time: 14 minutes

¼ cup olive oil

1 medium sweet green bell pepper, cut into ½-inch squares

½ cup sliced celery

2 Tbsp. sliced green onion

2 tsp. curry powder

½ tsp. salt

1 tsp. konjac flour

2 cups chicken bone broth

8-oz. can sliced water chestnuts, drained

1½ cups cooked shrimp

2 Tbsp. chopped pimento

2 cups cooked cauliflower rice

1. Place olive oil, green pepper, celery, and onion in 2-qt. baking dish. Cover loosely. Microwave 2 minutes on High. Stir. Cover and continue microwaving another 2 minutes at 100 percent power.

2. Stir curry powder and salt into vegetable mixture.

3. Mix together the konjac flour and chicken broth, whisking until smooth.

4. Add chicken broth mixture, drained water chestnuts, and shrimp to vegetables to baking dish. Mix well.

5. Cover loosely. Microwave 2–3 minutes on 100 percent power. Stir.

6. Microwave, covered, another 2–3 minutes on 100 percent power. Stir.

7. Microwave, covered, yet another 2–3 minutes on 100 percent power, or until sauce thickens.

8. Stir in pimento. Serve over cauliflower rice.

- Calories 284
- Fat 13
- Sodium 666
- Carbs 29
- Sugar 7
- Protein 15

Sesame Shrimp and Asparagus

Karen Kay Tucker
Manteca, CA

Makes 6 servings (¾ cup each)
Prep. Time: 30 minutes
Cooking Time: 10 minutes

1½ lbs. fresh asparagus

1 Tbsp. sesame seeds

3 Tbsp. olive oil

2 small red onions, sliced in rings

1½ lbs. large shrimp, peeled and deveined

4 tsp. soy sauce

¼ tsp. salt

1. About 30 minutes before serving, prepare asparagus. Hold base of each stalk firmly and bend. The end will break off at the spot where it becomes too tough to eat. Discard ends or freeze and use when making stock.

2. Wash and trim asparagus. Then cut into 2-inch pieces and steam in a ½ inch of water in saucepan until crisp-tender. Plunge asparagus into cold water to stop cooking. Set aside.

3. In a large skillet or wok, over medium heat, toast sesame seeds until golden brown, stirring seeds and shaking skillet often. Remove seeds to small bowl.

4. In the same skillet or wok, over medium-high heat, heat oil until hot. Add onions and shrimp. Cook until shrimp are pink, about 5 minutes.

5. Drain asparagus. Add to skillet with shrimp. Stir in sesame seeds, soy sauce, and salt. Heat until asparagus is warm.

- Calories 178
- Fat 9
- Sodium 945
- Carbs 7
- Sugar 3
- Protein 19

Cajun Shrimp

Mary Ann Potenta
Bridgewater, NJ

Makes 5 servings (4 oz. shrimp each)
Prep. Time: just minutes!
Cooking Time: 10–12 minutes

3 Tbsp. olive oil, *divided*

½ cup chopped green onion

1 tsp. minced garlic

1 tsp. cayenne pepper

½ tsp. white pepper

½ tsp. black pepper

¼ tsp. dry mustard

¼ tsp. salt

1 tsp. Frank's RedHot Original Cayenne Pepper Sauce

2 lbs. shrimp, peeled and cleaned

cooked cauliflower rice

1. Heat 2 Tbsp. olive oil in large skillet. Add onion and garlic and sauté till clear, but not brown, about 1 minute.

2. Add peppers, mustard, and salt. Cook and stir for 3 minutes.

3. Mix in 1 Tbsp. olive oil and Frank's RedHot sauce until blended.

4. Add shrimp. Cook just until pink. Do not overcook.

5. Serve over cooked cauliflower rice.

- Calories 208
- Fat 10
- Sodium 1149
- Carbs 3
- Sugar 0
- Protein 25

Grilling

Grilled Chicken Breasts

Gloria Mumbauer
Singers Glen, VA

Thelma F. Good
Harrisonburg, VA

Makes 2½–2¾ cups marinade; 10-12 chicken breast halves
Prep. Time: 5 minutes
Marinating Time: 6-8 hours, or overnight
Grilling Time: 15-18 minutes

10-12 boneless skinless chicken breast halves,
⠀⠀½–¾ inches thick

¾ cup olive oil

¾ cup soy sauce

½ cup apple cider vinegar

¼ cup Worcestershire sauce

⅓ cup lemon juice

2 tsp. prepared mustard

1 tsp. black pepper

2 cloves garlic, minced, or 1½ tsp. garlic powder

1. Place chicken breasts in a single layer in a nonmetallic dish.

2. In a bowl, mix together rest of ingredients.

3. When well blended, pour over chicken.

4. Cover. Marinate 6–8 hours or overnight. Turn chicken over about halfway through, if it's not the middle of the night and you're able to, to coat both sides.

5. Remove from marinade. Grill over medium heat until cooked through, about 15–18 minutes. Do not overcook or meat will dry out!

- Calories 273
- Fat 17
- Sodium 1105
- Carbs 3
- Sugar 1
- Protein 27

Subtly Wonderful Grilled Chicken

Joyce Zuercher
Hesston, KS

Makes 6-8 servings
Prep. Time: 5 minutes
Marinating Time: 2 hours
Grilling Time: 10-15 minutes, depending on type and size of chicken pieces

½ cup oil

½ cup lemon juice, or vinegar of your choice

¼ cup water

2 tsp. salt

¼ tsp. pepper

15 drops liquid stevia

1 tsp. paprika

1 Tbsp. minced onion

chicken breasts, or legs and/or thighs, to serve 6-8 people

1. Measure ingredients into bowl except for chicken, and mix well.

2. Let sauce stand 1 hour to allow flavors to blend.

3. Place chicken in single layer in nonmetallic bowl.

4. Pour sauce over chicken. Cover. Marinate chicken 1 hour in fridge.

5. Turn pieces over during grilling, allowing about 5–10 minutes total for breasts and 10–15 minutes total for legs and/or thighs.

- Calories 202
- Fat 10
- Sodium 531
- Carbs 2
- Sugar 0.5
- Protein 26

Grilled or Broiled Chicken Breasts

Judy Houser
Hershey, PA

Makes 8 servings
Prep. Time: 15 minutes
Marinating Time: 2-4 hours
Grilling/Broiling Time: 10-15 minutes

4 Tbsp. olive oil

4 Tbsp. soy sauce

3 Tbsp. lemon juice, or wine vinegar

8 boneless, skinless chicken breast halves

3 cloves garlic, sliced

1 tsp. dried thyme, or basil leaves, *optional*

1. For marinade, blend together oil, soy sauce, and lemon juice.

2. Place chicken breasts in single layer in glass dish. Sprinkle with garlic and, if using, herbs. Pour marinade over chicken.

3. Cover and refrigerate for 2–4 hours, turning breasts over from time to time.

4. Preheat grill. Place chicken breasts on grill. Grill for 5 minutes on one side.

5. Turn and grill for 5–9 minutes on other side. Juices should run clear when pierced with a fork.

6. To broil instead of grilling, preheat broiler for 10 minutes. Place breasts on tray. Pour marinade over breasts.

7. Broil close to heat for 3–5 minutes on each side. Juices should run clear when pierced with a fork.

- Calories 136
- Fat 10
- Sodium 545
- Carbs 1
- Sugar 0
- Protein 27

Lemon Grilled Chicken Breasts

Wilma J. Haberkamp
Fairbank, IA

Makes 4 servings
Prep. Time: 15 minutes
Grilling Time: 4-5 minutes

1¼ lbs. boneless, skinless chicken breasts

2 lemons

2 Tbsp. olive oil

½ tsp. salt

½ tsp. coarsely ground pepper

1. Prepare grill for direct grilling over medium heat.

2. Pound chicken to uniform ¼-inch thickness.

3. Grate 1½ Tbsp. lemon peel and squeeze 3 Tbsp. lemon juice into a small bowl.

4. Add oil, salt, and pepper. Whisk until well blended.

5. In a large bowl, toss chicken with marinade.

6. Place on grill. Cook 2–2½ minutes.

7. Turn over. Cook 2–2½ minutes more, or until juices run clear.

- Calories 241
- Fat 11
- Sodium 306
- Carbs 6
- Sugar 1
- Protein 33

Grilled Chicken Caesar

Deborah Heatwole
Waynesboro, GA

Makes 4 servings
Prep. Time: 5 minutes
Grilling Time: 15 minutes

4 boneless, skinless chicken breast halves

4 tsp. olive oil

½ tsp. Italian seasoning

½ tsp. garlic salt

½ tsp. black pepper

½ tsp. paprika, *optional*

1. Drizzle oil over chicken. Sprinkle with seasonings.

2. Grill, covered, over medium-hot coals for 12–15 minutes, or until juices run clear. Turn over several times.

- Calories 179
- Fat 8
- Sodium 172
- Carbs 0.5
- Sugar 0
- Protein 26

Thai Peanut Chicken

Susan Kasting
Jenks, OK

Makes 4 servings
Prep. Time: 10 minutes
Marinating Time: 1 hour
Cooking Time: 15 minutes

½ cup no-sugar-added peanut butter

¾ tsp. liquid stevia

¼ cup soy sauce

2 Tbsp. curry powder

4 boneless, skinless chicken breasts

1. Combine peanut butter, stevia, soy sauce, and curry powder.

2. Marinate chicken breasts in mixture for 1 hour.

3. Grill chicken breasts until juices run clear when pierced with a fork.

- Calories 345
- Fat 19
- Sodium 1191
- Carbs 9
- Sugar 3
- Protein 34

Grilled Pork Chops

Laura R. Showalter
Dayton, VA

Makes 4 servings
Prep. Time: 10 minutes
Marinating Time: 2 hours
Grilling Time: 20 minutes

1 large onion, sliced

¾ cup lime, or lemon, juice

½ tsp. cayenne pepper

1 clove garlic, minced

½ tsp. salt, *optional*

4 pork chops

1. Combine all ingredients except the pork chops in a large resealable bag or container with tight-fitting lid. Combine well.

2. Submerge chops in marinade.

3. Seal bag or container and refrigerate at least 2 hours.

4. Remove chops from marinade and grill, covered, over medium-hot heat, 8–10 minutes on each side.

5. Bring the marinade to a full rolling boil in a small saucepan. Use it to baste the chops while they grill, if you wish.

- Calories 175
- Fat 5
- Sodium 309
- Carbs 8
- Sugar 2.5
- Protein 25

Fill and Grill Sizzlers

Shanon Swartz Lambert
Harrisonburg, VA

Makes 6 servings
Prep. Time: 30 minutes
Grilling Time: 10–15 minutes

2 lbs. smoked sausage or kielbasa

1 cup grated Muenster cheese

½ cup sauerkraut, drained well

6 bacon slices, *optional*

1. Cut sausage into six 6-inch pieces. Split lengthwise ¾ of the way through.

2. Mix grated cheese and drained sauerkraut together in a small mixing bowl.

3. Fill each sausage piece with mixture of 2 Tbsp. grated cheese and 1 Tbsp. sauerkraut.

4. Wrap each filled piece with a strip of bacon, if you wish. Secure with a toothpick.

5. Grill or broil 4 inches from heat until done.

6. Garnish with additional Muenster cheese just before serving.

- Calories 351
- Fat 23
- Sodium 1894
- Carbs 12
- Sugar 3
- Protein 27

Tender Flank Steak

Kayla Snyder
North East, PA

Makes 6 servings
Prep. Time: 15 minutes
Marinating Time: 6–8 hours, or overnight
Grilling Time: 20 minutes

1 cup soy sauce

¼ cup lemon juice

½ tsp. liquid stevia

6 cloves garlic, minced, or less if you prefer

1–1½ lbs. beef flank steak

1. In a large resealable plastic bag, combine soy sauce, lemon juice, stevia, and garlic.

2. Add steak. Seal bag and turn to coat. Place in shallow dish with sides to catch any leaks.

3. Refrigerate 6–8 hours or overnight to marinate in sauce.

4. When ready to grill, drain meat and discard marinade.

5. Grill over medium heat 8–10 minutes on each side or until meat reaches desired doneness (for medium-rare, a meat thermometer should read 145°F; medium 160°F; well-done 170°F).

6. Allow to stand off heat 10 minutes before slicing.

7. Slice steak into thin slices across the grain.

- Calories 156
- Fat 6
- Sodium 2685
- Carbs 4
- Sugar 0.5
- Protein 21

Flank Steak

Sharon Swartz Lambert
Harrisonburg, VA

Makes 2–4 servings
Prep. Time: 10 minutes
Marinating Time: 5–24 hours, or overnight
Grilling Time: 15 minutes

½–2-lb. flank steak

1 Tbsp. white wine vinegar

2 Tbsp. soy sauce

1 tsp. minced fresh garlic

5 drops liquid stevia

1. Diamond-cut ¼-inch-wide slashes on both sides of flank steak.

2. Mix remaining ingredients together in a small bowl.

3. Place steak in a long dish. Pour marinade over top. Cover and refrigerate 5–24 hours, or overnight.

4. Grill 5 minutes per side over high heat. (You may need a bit more time, depending on thickness of the meat.)

5. Cut into thin slices on the diagonal.

- Calories 128
- Fat 6
- Sodium 378
- Carbs 0
- Sugar 6
- Protein 17

Peppered Rib-Eye Steaks

Meredith Miller
Dover, DE

Makes 4 servings
Prep. Time: 10 minutes
Marinating Time: 1 hour or more
Grilling Time: 8–10 minutes

1 Tbsp. olive oil

1 Tbsp. garlic powder

1 Tbsp. paprika

2 tsp. dried thyme

2 tsp. dried oregano

1½ tsp. black pepper

1 tsp. salt

1 tsp. lemon pepper seasoning

1 tsp. cayenne pepper

4 beef rib-eye steaks, 1½-inch thick

1. In a bowl, mix together oil, garlic powder, paprika, thyme, oregano, pepper, salt, lemon pepper, and cayenne pepper.

2. Brush each steak well on both sides with mixture.

3. Lay steaks in single layer in nonmetallic baking dish. Pour remaining marinade over top.

4. Cover. Refrigerate at least 1 hour.

5. Grill, uncovered, over medium-high heat, 4-5 minutes on first side.

6. Turn and grill 4-5 minutes on other side.

- Calories 234
- Fat 17
- Sodium 534
- Carbs 4
- Sugar 0
- Protein 18

Grilled Burgers

Deborah Heatwole
Waynesboro, GA

Makes 12 servings
Prep. Time: 10–15 minutes
Grilling Time: 10–15 minutes

2 lbs. ground beef

¾ cup almond flour

2 eggs

⅓ cup no-sugar-added ketchup

1½ tsp. dried onion, *optional*

1 tsp. Worcestershire sauce, *optional*

salt and pepper, to taste

1. Mix ground beef thoroughly with the rest of the ingredients.

2. Shape ⅓ cupfuls into patties.

3. Place patties on hot grill. Grill, covered, 5–7 minutes per side, or until centers of burgers are no longer pink.

Serving suggestion: Serve on keto-friendly buns with toppings of your choice.

- Calories 196
- Fat 16
- Sodium 95
- Carbs 2
- Sugar 1 Protein 11

Simply Grilled Salmon

Leann Brown
Lancaster, PA

Makes 3 servings
Prep. Time: 5 minutes
Grilling Time: 15 minutes

2 lbs. salmon steaks or fillets

½ cup lemon juice

1½ Tbsp. butter

seasoned salt

1. Lay salmon on large piece of foil.

2. Pour lemon juice over top.

3. Lay butter in several slivers over top.

4. Sprinkle evenly with seasoned salt, to taste.

5. Close foil and wrap again in second layer so lemon juice will not escape.

6. Grill over medium heat for 15 minutes, or until salmon is flaky but not dry.

- Calories 689
- Fat 46
- Sodium 180
- Carbs 3
- Sugar 1
- Protein 62

Grilled Veggies

Tim Smith
Rutledge, PA

Makes 6 servings (¾ cup each)
Prep. Time: 10–20 minutes
Grilling Time: 20–40 minutes

2 cups chopped cauliflower

1 medium zucchini, sliced ¼-inch thick

1 medium yellow squash, sliced ¼-inch thick

1 small red onion, sliced

1 small white onion, sliced

2 Tbsp. crushed garlic

1 tsp. pepper

½ tsp. white pepper

1 Tbsp. fresh basil leaves

3 Tbsp. olive oil

1. Combine all ingredients in a large mixing bowl.

2. Cut a piece of heavy-duty foil large enough to hold all ingredients. Spoon vegetables into center of foil. Close tightly.

3. Place on preheated grill. Grill over medium heat for 20 minutes, turning every 5 minutes. Open and poke vegetables after 20 minutes to see if the vegetables are done to your liking. Close up and continue grilling if you want them more tender, checking again after 10 minutes. Continue until they are as tender as you want them, up to about 40 minutes.

- Calories 92
- Fat 7
- Sodium 14
- Carbs 7
- Sugar 2
- Protein 1

Grilled Asparagus Spears

Dale and Shari Mast
Harrisonburg, VA

Makes 6–8 servings
Prep. Time: 7 minutes
Grilling Time: 12 minutes

2 lbs. fresh asparagus spears

1 Tbsp. olive oil

seasoned salt

1. Break woody ends off washed asparagus.

2. In a large bowl or resealable bag, toss asparagus spears with oil and salt, to taste.

3. Place spears directly onto preheated grill on low heat.

4. Grill for 12 minutes, turning spears 2–3 times.

5. Serve hot or at room temperature.

- Calories 37
- Fat 2
- Sodium 2
- Carbs 4
- Sugar 2
- Protein 2

Zucchini on the Grill

Judy Buller
Bluffton, OH

Makes as many servings as you wish
Prep. Time: 5 minutes
Grilling Time: 5–6 minutes

medium-sized zucchini

olive oil

pepper

seasoning salt

garlic powder

1. Wash, but do not peel zucchini. Slice into long strips about ¼-inch thick.

2. Brush both sides with olive oil. Gently sprinkle both sides with pepper, seasoning salt, and garlic powder.

3. Place on grill, turning frequently. Each side takes about 3 minutes, but watch carefully so as not to overdo or burn the slices.

- Calories 26
- Fat 2
- Sodium 52
- Carbs 2
- Sugar 1
- Protein 1

Grilled Cabbage

Jenelle Miller
Marion, SD

Makes 4 servings
Prep. Time: 5–10 minutes
Grilling Time: 40–45 minutes

1 small head cabbage

4 Tbsp. (½ stick) butter

seasoned salt

4 slices bacon, uncooked

1. Remove outer leaves of cabbage head. Cut cabbage into 4 wedges.

2. Lay each wedge on a square of aluminum foil.

3. Spread 1 Tbsp. of butter over side of wedge.

4. Sprinkle each generously with seasoned salt.

5. Wrap a piece of bacon around each wedge.

6. Wrap tightly in foil.

7. Lay over hot coals. Grill 40–45 minutes, or until tender when jagged with a fork.

- Calories 150
- Fat 15
- Sodium 285
- Carbs 1
- Sugar 1
- Protein 3

Grilled Mushrooms

Doyle Rounds
Bridgewater, VA

Makes 4 servings
Prep. Time: 5 minutes
Grilling Time: 10–15 minutes

½ lb. whole fresh medium-sized mushrooms

4 Tbsp. (½ stick) butter, melted

½ tsp. dill weed

½ tsp. garlic salt

1. Thread mushrooms onto skewers.

2. Combine butter, dill, and garlic salt. Brush over mushrooms.

3. Grill over hot coals for 10–15 minutes, basting and turning every 5 minutes.

Note: If using wooden skewers, soak them in water for 30 minutes before threading on the mushrooms.

- Calories 123
- Fat 12
- Sodium 123
- Carbs 4
- Sugar 0
- Protein 2

Grilled Onions

Loretta Weisz
Auburn, WA

Makes 2 servings
Prep. Time: 5 minutes
Grilling Time: 35–45 minutes

2 medium white, or yellow, sweet onions

dab butter

dash pepper

sprinkling salt

1. Slice each onion into 4 wedges, but without slicing through the bottom, so that each onion stays whole.

2. Add a dab of butter and sprinklings of pepper and salt between each wedge.

3. Wrap stuffed onions tightly in foil.

4. Grill until soft and tender, 35–45 minutes.

- Calories 247
- Fat 23
- Sodium 247
- Carbs 10
- Sugar 5
- Protein 1

Grilled Vegetables

Deborah Heatwole
Waynesboro, GA

Makes 4 servings
Prep. Time: 15–30 minutes, depending on how fast you slice veggies
Grilling Time: 15–25 minutes

4 cups sliced fresh summer squash and/or zucchini

4 cups sliced sweet onions, such as Vidalia

3–4 Tbsp. olive oil

1–2 Tbsp. red wine vinegar

salt and pepper, to taste

1. Toss all ingredients in a large bowl until vegetables are evenly coated with oil and vinegar.

2. Spray a grill basket with nonstick cooking spray. Place on grill rack over hot coals.

3. Pour vegetables into basket, replace grill lid, and cook 15–25 minutes, until vegetables reach desired doneness, stirring every 4–5 minutes.

- Calories 202
- Fat 14
- Sodium 129
- Carbs 19
- Sugar 9
- Protein 3

Brooks White Sauce Marinade

Deb Herr
Montaintop, PA

Makes 3¼ cups
Prep. Time: 5 minutes
Marinating Time: 3–4 hours

2 cups white vinegar

1 cup olive oil

½ tsp. pepper

2 Tbsp. salt

3 Tbsp. poultry seasoning

1 egg, beaten

1. Pour all ingredients into a 1-qt. covered container. Shake vigorously.

2. Use to marinate chicken breasts for 3–4 hours, and then grill.

- Calories 253
- Fat 28
- Sodium 1449
- Carbs 1
- Sugar 0
- Protein 1

Marinade for Beef or Venison

Alta Metzler
Willow Street, PA

Makes 6-8 servings
Prep. Time: 10 minutes
Marinating Time: 24 hours
Grilling Time: 30-40 minutes

½ cup soy sauce

2 Tbsp. water

¼ cup olive oil

1 tsp. minced garlic

¼ tsp. pepper

1 tsp. Truvia Brown Sugar Blend

2 lbs. venison or beef steak

1. Mix all marinade ingredients together well in a small bowl.

2. Place 2 lbs. venison or beef steak in a long bowl.

3. Marinate, covered, in refrigerator for 24 hours, turning meat 1 or 2 times.

4. Grill according to the thickness of the meat and your preferred doneness.

- Calories 231
- Fat 14
- Sodium 1068
- Carbs 2
- Sugar 0.5
- Protein 25

Steak Marinade

Sharon Shank
Bridgewater, VA

Makes 2+ cups
Prep. Time: 5 minutes
Marinating Time: 8–12 hours

1 cup red wine vinegar

1 Tbsp. garlic powder

½ cup olive oil

½ cup soy sauce

2 Tbsp. minced onion

1. Mix all ingredients together in a small bowl.

2. Use to marinate steaks for 8–12 hours before grilling.

- Calories 139
- Fat 14
- Sodium 992
- Carbs 2
- Sugar 0
- Protein 2

Marinade for Grilling

Samuel and Sadie Mae Stoltzfus
Bird-In-Hand, PA

Makes ¾ cup
Prep. Time: 2–3 minutes

¼ cup soy sauce

⅓ cup water

2 Tbsp. olive oil

1 tsp. lemon juice

1 clove garlic, minced

1½ tsp. Truvia Brown Sugar Blend

½ tsp. black pepper

1 tsp. vinegar

1. Mix ingredients together in a small bowl.

2. Use as marinade for turkey fillets, turkey cutlets, boneless skinless chicken breasts, or beef steaks.

- Calories 54
- Fat 4
- Sodium 1978
- Carbs 3
- Sugar 1
- Protein 3

Sirloin or Chuck Steak Marinade

Susan Nafziger
Canton, KS

Makes marinade for 4 steaks
Prep. Time: 15 minutes

1 cup olive oil

1 cup soy sauce

¼ cup wine vinegar

½ cup chopped onion

⅛ tsp. garlic powder

¼ tsp. ground ginger

½ tsp. pepper

½ tsp. dry mustard

1. Mix all ingredients together, either by whisking together in a bowl, or whirring the mixture in a blender.

2. Place sirloin or chuck steak in marinade mixture and marinate for at least 1 hour per 1-inch thickness of meat.

3. When ready to grill or broil meat, drain off marinade and discard. Cook steak.

- Calories 265
- Fat 27
- Sodium 1982
- Carbs 3
- Sugar 1
- Protein 3

Southern Pork Marinating/Basting Sauce

Barbara Sparks
Glen Burnie, MD

Makes 2¾ cups
Prep. Time: 35 minutes
Marinating Time: 2 hours
Grilling/Broiling Time: about 15 minutes on each side

1 cup water

2 cups cider vinegar

1–1½ (½–¾ cup) sticks butter

1 tsp. salt

1 tsp. ground red pepper, or cayenne

1. Combine all ingredients in a saucepan. Simmer for 30 minutes.

2. Marinate pork chops or ribs in the sauce for 2 hours before grilling or broiling. (Discard sauce used for marinating. Make fresh sauce for basting.)

3. Baste pork chops or ribs with sauce on the grill, or under the broiler.

- Calories 115
- Fat 12
- Sodium 245
- Carbs 1
- Sugar 0
- Protein 0

Side Dishes & Vegetables

Broccoli with Garlic and Lemon

Jan Moore
Wellsville, KS

Leona Yoder
Hartville, OH

Makes 4-5 servings
Prep. Time: 10 minutes
Cooking Time: 10-15 minutes

4½ cups fresh broccoli florets

¼-½ cup water

1 Tbsp. extra-virgin olive oil

1 clove garlic, crushed, or 1½ tsp. jarred minced garlic

juice and grated peel from ½ lemon

grated Parmesan cheese, *optional*

1. Place broccoli and water in a good-sized skillet. Cover and cook over medium-high heat, stirring occasionally for several minutes until broccoli is crisp-tender. Add more water if necessary to prevent scorching, but only a small amount.

2. Drain excess liquid from skillet. Push broccoli to one side and add olive oil and garlic to the other side. Cook for about 10–20 seconds, or until garlic begins to turn color and smell fragrant.

3. Toss all together.

4. Stir in lemon juice and peel.

5. When ready to serve, top with Parmesan cheese if you wish.

- Calories 54
- Fat 3
- Sodium 30
- Carbs 6
- Sugar 2
- Protein 2

Italian Broccoli

Linda Gebo
Plattsburgh, NY

Makes 4 servings
Prep. Time: 25–30 minutes
Cooking Time: 10–15 minutes

1 large head of broccoli

1 clove garlic

½ cup water

1 Tbsp. or more vegetable broth

salt and pepper, to taste

2-oz. jar pimientos

1. Remove leaves and peel lower part of broccoli stalks. Cut into florets and ½-inch slices.

2. Steam cut-up broccoli and whole garlic clove in water in a skillet for about 4 minutes. Discard garlic and add broth.

3. Salt and pepper, to taste.

4. Cover and cook over low heat 10–15 minutes, or until broccoli is tender. You may need to add more broth if skillet gets dry.

5. Sprinkle with pimientos and serve.

- Calories 59
- Fat 1
- Sodium 257
- Carbs 9
- Sugar 2
- Protein 4

White Chicken Chili, page 134

Garlic and Lemon Chicken, page 149

Chicken Dijon Dinner, page 152

Buttery Lemon Chicken, page 156

Eggplant Italian, page 212

Broccoli and Bell Peppers, page 237

Cheesy Broccoli Casserole, page 238

Golden Cauliflower, page 241

Broccoli and Bell Peppers

Frieda Weisz
Aberdeen, SD

Makes 8 servings
Prep. Time: 20 minutes
Cooking Time: 4–5 hours
Ideal slow-cooker size: 3½- or 4-qt.

2 lbs. fresh broccoli, trimmed and chopped into bite-sized pieces

1 clove garlic, minced

1 green or red bell pepper, cut into thin slices

1 onion, peeled and cut into slices

4 Tbsp. liquid aminos

½ tsp. salt

dash black pepper

1 Tbsp. sesame seeds, as garnish, *optional*

1. Combine all ingredients except sesame seeds in slow cooker.

2. Cook on Low for 4–5 hours. Top with sesame seeds, if using.

- Calories 20
- Fat 0.5
- Sodium 460
- Carbs 4
- Sugar 1
- Protein 2

Stir-Fried Broccoli

Vicki Dinkel
Sharon Springs, KS

Makes 4 servings (¾ cup each)
Prep. Time: 15 minutes
Cooking Time: 5 minutes

1 onion, diced

1 Tbsp. olive oil

1 lb. broccoli florets, cut in pieces, fresh or frozen

½ cup chicken bone broth

¼ tsp. konjac flour

2 Tbsp. soy sauce

5 drops liquid stevia

cooked cauliflower rice

1. Brown onion in oil in a large skillet. Add broccoli. Stir-fry 3 minutes.

2. In a small bowl, combine chicken broth, konjac flour, soy sauce, and stevia. Add to broccoli. Cook 1-2 minutes until sauce clears.

3. Serve over cooked cauliflower rice.

- Calories 88
- Fat 4
- Sodium 581
- Carbs 10
- Sugar 3
- Protein 5

Cheesy Broccoli Casserole

**Dorothy VanDeest
Memphis, TN**

SLOW
COOKER

Makes 3–4 servings
Prep. Time: 10–15 minutes
Cooking Time: 3–5 hours
Ideal slow-cooker size: 3-qt.

10-oz. pkg. frozen chopped broccoli

6 eggs, beaten

24 oz. small-curd cottage cheese

6 Tbsp. almond flour

8 oz. mild cheese of your choice, diced

4 Tbsp. (½ stick) butter, melted

2 green onions, chopped

salt, to taste

1. Place frozen broccoli in colander. Run cold water over it until it thaws. Separate into pieces. Drain well.

2. Combine broccoli and all other ingredients in greased slow cooker. Mix together gently but well.

3. Cover. Cook on High 1 hour. Stir well, then continue cooking on Low 2–4 hours.

- Calories 785
- Fat 61
- Sodium 1098
- Carbs 15
- Sugar 7
- Protein 46

Broccoli Custard

**Judy Wantland
Menomonee Falls, WI**

Makes 4 servings
Prep. Time: 20 minutes
Baking Time: 40–50 minutes

1¼ cups whole milk

10-oz pkg. frozen broccoli

3 eggs, lightly beaten

½ tsp. salt

½ tsp. nutmeg

½ cup grated cheese of your choice

1. Heat milk to boiling in small saucepan. Set aside to cool to lukewarm.

2. Meanwhile, cook broccoli for 3 minutes in small amount of water. Drain.

3. Mix eggs with salt and nutmeg.

4. Add cooled milk and cheese to eggs, beating constantly.

5. Pour into greased 8×8-inch glass baking dish. Add broccoli.

6. Bake at 350°F for 40–50 minutes, or until knife inserted in center comes out clean. Serve hot.

- Calories 167
- Fat 9
- Sodium 529
- Carbs 10
- Sugar 5
- Protein 12

Julia's Broccoli and Cauliflower with Cheese

Julia Lapp
New Holland, PA

Makes 6 servings
Prep. Time: 25 minutes
Cooking Time: 1½ hours
Ideal slow-cooker size: 4-qt.

5 cups chopped broccoli and cauliflower

¼ cup water

2 Tbsp. butter

2 Tbsp. almond flour

½ tsp. salt

1 cup whole milk

1 cup shredded cheddar cheese

1. Cook broccoli and cauliflower in saucepan in water, until just crisp-tender. Set aside.

2. Make white sauce by melting the butter in another pan over low heat. Blend in flour and salt. Add milk all at once. Cook quickly, stirring constantly until mixture thickens and bubbles. Add cheese. Stir until melted and smooth.

3. Combine vegetables and sauce in slow cooker. Mix well.

4. Cook on Low 1½ hours.

- Calories 174
- Fat 13
- Sodium 327
- Carbs 8
- Sugar 4
- Protein 8

Doris's Broccoli and Cauliflower with Cheese

Doris G. Herr
Manheim, PA

Makes 8 servings
Prep. Time: 5 minutes
Cooking Time: 1½–3 hours
Ideal slow-cooker size: 3-qt.

1 lb. frozen cauliflower, thawed and chopped

2 10-oz. pkgs. frozen broccoli, thawed and chopped

½ cup water

2 cups shredded cheddar cheese

1. Place cauliflower and broccoli in slow cooker.

2. Add water. Top with cheese.

3. Cook on Low 1½–3 hours, depending upon how crunchy or soft you want the vegetables.

- Calories 152
- Fat 10
- Sodium 225
- Carbs 8
- Sugar 2
- Protein 10

Cheesy Cauliflower

Joan Erwin
Sparks, NV

Makes 6 servings (¾ cup each)
Prep. Time: 5–10 minutes
Baking Time: 11 minutes

1 head cauliflower

1 Tbsp. water

1 cup mayonnaise

1 Tbsp. prepared mustard

½ cup chopped green or red onions

¼ cup shredded Monterey Jack cheese

¼ cup shredded sharp cheddar cheese

1. Place whole cauliflower head in microwavable glass baking dish. Add water. Cover. Microwave on High for 9 minutes, until crisp-cooked.

2. Meanwhile, combine mayonnaise, mustard, and onions in a small bowl. Spread over cooked cauliflower. Sprinkle with cheeses.

3. Cover and microwave on High for 1 minute, or until cheese is melted.

- Calories 307
- Fat 31
- Sodium 341
- Carbs 4
- Sugar 2
- Protein 4

Mashed Cauliflower

Ellie Oberholtzer
Ronks, PA

Makes 6–8 servings
Prep. Time: 10 minutes
Cooking Time: 15 minutes

1 large head cauliflower

1–2 Tbsp. butter

½ cup warm whole milk

½ tsp. salt

¼ tsp. pepper

1. Chop cauliflower coarsely.

2. Place in covered saucepan with a little water. Boil cauliflower until soft, 10–15 minutes. Drain.

3. Puree cauliflower in blender. Place in serving dish.

4. Add butter, milk, salt, and pepper. Stir well.

Tip: You can use a potato masher instead of the blender.

Variations:
1. *Roast the cauliflower instead of steaming it.*
2. *Add garlic cloves, cheese, or other seasonings your family likes in mashed potatoes.*

- Calories 35
- Fat 2
- Sodium 142
- Carbs 3
- Sugar 2
- Protein 1

Italian Vegetables

Susie Shenk Wenger
Lancaster, PA

Makes 6 servings
Prep. Time: 30 minutes
Cooking Time: 4–6 hours
Ideal slow-cooker size: 6-qt.

1 cup sliced fresh mushrooms

1 large sweet onion, chopped

½ cup chopped red bell pepper

3 cloves garlic, chopped

salt and pepper, to taste

1 Tbsp. butter

1 Tbsp. olive oil

1 large head broccoli, chopped

½ cup diced Parmesan cheese

1 tsp. dried basil

½ tsp. dried oregano

juice and zest of 1 lemon

1. Place mushrooms, onion, bell pepper, and garlic into crock; sprinkle lightly with salt and pepper. Dot with butter and drizzle with olive oil.

2. Sprinkle in broccoli and diced Parmesan. Sprinkle with basil and oregano, adding salt and pepper, to taste.

3. Cover and cook on Low for 4 hours.

4. Drizzle with lemon juice and zest before serving.

Serving suggestion: Serve over cauliflower rice.

- Calories 91
- Fat 6
- Sodium 134
- Carbs 6
- Sugar 15
- Protein 3.5

Golden Cauliflower

Carol Peachey
Lancaster, PA

Makes 6 servings
Prep. Time: 15 minutes
Cooking Time: 1½–5 hours
Ideal slow-cooker size: 4-qt.

2 10-oz. pkgs. frozen cauliflower, thawed

2 Tbsp. butter, melted

1 Tbsp. almond flour

1 cup evaporated milk

1 oz. (¼ cup) cheddar cheese

2 Tbsp. cottage cheese

2 tsp. Parmesan cheese

4 slices bacon, crisply browned and crumbled

1. Place cauliflower in slow cooker.

2. Melt butter on stove. Add almond flour and evaporated milk. Heat until thickened. Add cheeses.

3. Pour sauce over cauliflower. Top with bacon.

4. Cover. Cook on High 1½ hours and then reduce to Low for an additional 2 hours. Or cook only on Low 4–5 hours.

- Calories 175
- Fat 12
- Sodium 253
- Carbs 10
- Sugar 6
- Protein 9

Country Market Cauliflower

Susie Shenk Wenger
Lancaster, PA

Makes 6 servings
Prep. Time: 20 minutes
Cooking Time: 2–4 hours
Ideal slow-cooker size: 5- or 6-qt.

8 oz. fresh baby bella mushrooms, sliced

1 large Vidalia or candy sweet onion, chopped

½ cup red or yellow bell pepper

1 Tbsp. olive oil

1 Tbsp. butter

juice of 1 lemon

1 large head cauliflower, cut in pieces

3 cloves garlic, crushed

1 tsp. dried basil

salt and pepper, to taste

½ cup grated Parmesan cheese

1. Sauté mushrooms, onion, and bell pepper in a pan with olive oil, butter, and lemon juice.

2. Place cauliflower, garlic, basil, salt, and pepper in a greased 5- or 6-qt. slow cooker.

3. Stir in sautéed vegetable mixture.

4. Cook on Low, covered, for 2–4 hours, or until cauliflower is as tender as you like it.

5. Top with Parmesan cheese just before serving, while still hot.

- Calories 94
- Fat 6
- Sodium 139
- Carbs 6
- Sugar 2
- Protein 4

Bacon Cabbage Surprise

Jonathan Gehman
Harrisonburg, VA

Makes an adaptable number of servings!
Prep. Time: 10 minutes if cooking for 3–4 persons
Cooking Time: 15 minutes

bacon, 1–2 strips per person

onion, cut in thick slices, ¼ cup per person

garlic, minced, 1 small clove per person

cabbage, cut in thin strips, 1 cup per person

zucchini, shredded, ¼ cup per person

1. Cut bacon in ½-inch wide squares. Place in nonstick pan large enough to hold all ingredients. Sauté over medium heat until browned but not crispy. Drain off all but 2 Tbsp. drippings.

2. Turn heat to low. Add onion and garlic and cook until transparent.

3. Add zucchini and cabbage, stirring to coat with bacon drippings. Mix all ingredients together well.

4. The dish is done when the cabbage begins to wilt.

- Calories 129
- Fat 7
- Sodium 386
- Carbs 10
- Sugar 5
- Protein 8

Homestyle Cabbage

Sandra Haverstraw
Hummelstown, PA

Makes 6 servings
Prep. Time: 20–25 minutes
Baking Time: 20–30 minutes

1 medium head cabbage

2 Tbsp. butter

15 drops liquid stevia

1 medium onion, thinly sliced

1 medium green or yellow bell pepper, cut in thin rings

28-oz. can diced tomatoes, or stewed tomatoes

½ tsp. salt

⅛ tsp. pepper

1 cup shredded cheddar cheese

1. Cut cabbage into 6 wedges, removing core.
2. Place cabbage in small amount of water in pot.
3. Cover. Cook 10 minutes. Drain.
4. Place in greased 9×13-inch baking pan.
5. In a saucepan, melt butter.
6. Add stevia, onion, and green or yellow pepper rings.
7. Cook over medium heat until veggies are tender.
8. Add tomatoes, salt, and pepper. Stir.
9. Pour sauce over cabbage.
10. Bake at 350°F for 20–30 minutes.
11. Sprinkle with cheese during last 5 minutes of baking.

- Calories 159
- Fat 10
- Sodium 508
- Carbs 11
- Sugar 3
- Protein 6

Stir-Fry Cabbage

Esther Bowman
Gladys, VA

Makes 4–6 servings
Prep. Time: 10 minutes
Cooking Time: 15 minutes

2 Tbsp. butter

1 small onion, chopped

1 clove garlic, minced

4 cups shredded cabbage

½ cup shredded brussels sprouts

⅛ tsp. paprika

1 tsp. salt

dash pepper

2 tsp. soy sauce

1. Melt butter in large skillet or wok.
2. Briefly stir-fry onion and garlic, then add cabbage and brussels sprouts. Stir-fry over medium heat about 5 minutes or until vegetables are tender-crisp.
3. Add paprika, salt, pepper, and soy sauce and mix well. Serve at once.

- Calories 59
- Fat 4
- Sodium 452
- Carbs 5
- Sugar 2
- Protein 2

Cabbage Casserole

Edwina Stoltzfus
Narvon, PA

Makes 6 servings
Prep. Time: 40 minutes
Cooking Time: 4–5 hours
Ideal slow-cooker size: 4-qt.

1 large head cabbage, chopped

2 cups water

3 Tbsp. butter

1¾ tsp. konjac flour

¼ tsp. salt

¼ tsp. pepper

1⅓ cups milk

1⅓ cups shredded cheddar

1. Cook cabbage in saucepan in boiling water for 5 minutes. Drain. Place in slow cooker.

2. In a saucepan, melt butter. Stir in flour, salt, and pepper. Add milk, stirring constantly on low heat for 5 minutes. Remove from heat. Stir in cheese. Pour over cabbage.

3. Cover. Cook on Low 4–5 hours.

Note: You can replace cabbage with cauliflower.

- Calories 204
- Fat 18
- Sodium 266
- Carbs 4
- Sugar 2
- Protein 8

Scalloped Cabbage

Edwina Stoltzfus
Lebanon, PA

Makes 6–8 servings
Prep. Time: 25 minutes
Cooking Time: 3–5 hours
Ideal slow-cooker size: 4-qt.

1 Tbsp. butter

12 cups chopped cabbage

¼ cup chopped onion

¼ cup chopped fresh parsley

1 cup grated sharp cheese

1½ tsp. konjac flour

12-oz. can evaporated milk

½ cup diced, cooked bacon, *optional*

1. Use butter to grease slow cooker.

2. Combine cabbage, onion, parsley, and cheese in slow cooker.

3. In a mixing bowl, whisk together konjac flour and milk until lump-free.

4. Pour milk mixture over cabbage mixture.

5. Cover and cook on Low for 3–5 hours, until cabbage is soft and sauce is thick.

6. Sprinkle with bacon if you wish before serving.

Note: If you're adding bacon to the top, use bacon grease instead of butter to grease the crock. Add 1 tsp. of your favorite dried herb.

- Calories 178
- Fat 11
- Sodium 160
- Carbs 12
- Sugar 8
- Protein 9

Baked Cabbage

Karen Gingrich
New Holland, PA

Makes 6 servings (¾ cup each)
Prep. Time: 20 minutes
Cooking/Baking Time: 45 minutes

1 medium-sized head of cabbage

water

1 tsp. salt, *divided*

1½ cups whole milk

1¼ tsp. konjac flour

½ tsp. pepper

1 Tbsp. butter

½ cup grated sharp cheddar cheese

1. Cut cabbage in wedges ¾ inch thick. Cook, covered, in a saucepan in ½ inch of water, sprinkled with ½ tsp. salt, for 10 minutes. Drain and place cabbage in a greased 2-qt. baking casserole.

2. While cabbage is cooking, warm milk in a small saucepan until it forms a skin but does not boil.

3. Sprinkle cabbage with flour, ½ tsp. salt, and pepper.

4. Pour hot milk over, being careful not to wash off the flour and seasonings. Dot with margarine. Top with grated cheese.

5. Bake, uncovered, at 350°F for 35 minutes.

- Calories 101
- Fat 7
- Sodium 414
- Carbs 5
- Sugar 4
- Protein 5

Fast and Fabulous Brussels Sprouts

Phyllis Good
Lancaster, PA

Makes 4–6 servings
Prep. Time: 15 minutes
Cooking Time: 2–5 hours
Ideal slow-cooker size: 2- or 3-qt.

1 lb. brussels sprouts, bottoms trimmed off and halved

3 Tbsp. butter, melted

1½ Tbsp. Dijon mustard

¼ tsp. salt

¼ tsp. freshly ground black pepper

¼ cup water

½ tsp. dried tarragon, *optional*

1. Mix all ingredients in slow cooker.

2. Cover and cook on High for 2–2½ hours, or Low for 4–5 hours, until sprouts are just soft. (Some of the brussels sprouts at the sides will get brown and crispy, and this is delicious.)

3. Stir well to distribute sauce. Serve hot or warm.

- Calories 86
- Fat 6
- Sodium 187
- Carbs 7
- Sugar 2
- Protein 3

Brussels Sprouts with Pimentos

Donna Lantgen
Rapid City, SD

Makes 8 servings
Prep. Time: 10 minutes
Cooking Time: 6 hours
Ideal slow-cooker size: 3½- or 4-qt.

2 lbs. brussels sprouts

¼ tsp. dried oregano

½ tsp. dried basil

2-oz. jar pimentos, drained

¼ cup, or 1 small can, sliced black olives, drained

1 Tbsp. olive oil

½ cup water

1. Combine all ingredients in slow cooker.

2. Cook on Low 6 hours, or until sprouts are just tender.

- Calories 71
- Fat 2.5
- Sodium 61
- Carbs 11
- Sugar 3
- Protein 4

Very Special Spinach

Jeanette Oberholtzer
Manheim, PA

Makes 8 servings
Prep. Time: 10 minutes
Cooking Time: 5 hours
Ideal slow-cooker size: 4-qt.

3 10-oz. boxes frozen spinach, thawed and drained

2 cups cottage cheese

1½ cups grated cheddar cheese

3 eggs

¼ cup almond flour

1 tsp. salt

8 Tbsp. (1 stick) butter, melted

1. Mix together all ingredients.

2. Pour into slow cooker.

3. Cook on High 1 hour. Reduce heat to Low and cook 4 more hours.

- Calories 316
- Fat 25
- Sodium 677
- Carbs 8
- Sugar 2
- Protein 18

Creamed Spinach

Mary Reichert
O'Fallon, MO

Makes 4 servings
Prep. Time: 10 minutes
Cooking Time: 2–3 hours
Ideal slow-cooker size: 3-qt.

2 10-oz. boxes frozen spinach, thawed and drained

¼ cup dried onion

2 Tbsp. low-sodium beef bouillon granules

¼ tsp. onion powder

¼ tsp. parsley flakes

⅛ tsp. celery seed

⅛ tsp. paprika

⅛ tsp. black pepper

1 cup sour cream

8-oz. can water chestnuts, chopped, *optional*

1. In a mixing bowl, mix spinach, dried onion, beef bouillon granules, onion powder, parsley flakes, celery seed, paprika, black pepper, and sour cream. Add water chestnuts if using. Blend well.

2. Spray 3-qt. slow cooker with cooking spray. Add spinach mixture and top with cheese.

3. Cook on Low 2–3 hours, until bubbly.

- Calories 159
- Fat 10
- Sodium 258
- Carbs 13
- Sugar 4
- Protein 7

Absolutely Creamy Spinach

Vicki J. Hill
Memphis, TN

Makes 9 servings
Prep. Time: 5 minutes
Cooking/Baking Time: 8–30 minutes

4 10-oz. pkgs. frozen chopped spinach, thawed and squeezed dry

8-oz. pkg. cream cheese

8 Tbsp. (1 stick) butter

paprika, *optional*

1. Place spinach in lightly greased 2-qt. baking dish.

2. Soften cream cheese and butter in microwave for 1 minute. Beat until combined. Pour over spinach.

3. Sprinkle with paprika.

4. Heat uncovered in oven at 350°F for 20–30 minutes, or in the microwave, covered, for 8–10 minutes.

- Calories 215
- Fat 20
- Sodium 174
- Carbs 7
- Sugar
- Protein 26

Sautéed Tofu with Spinach

Donna Treloar
Muncie, IN

Makes 2 servings
Prep. Time: 5 minutes
Cooking Time: 5 minutes

6 oz. firm fresh tofu

2 Tbsp. extra-virgin olive oil

1 clove garlic, minced

8 oz. fresh spinach, washed

2 Tbsp. balsamic vinegar

1. Cut tofu in thin strips.

2. Heat oil in large saucepan.

3. Sauté tofu strips until brown on one side.

4. Stir in garlic and turn the tofu strips as you do so.

5. Toss in spinach and vinegar. Cover saucepan.

6. Cook for 1 minute or until spinach wilts.

7. Remove from heat and serve.

- Calories 228
- Fat 17
- Sodium 104
- Carbs 10
- Sugar 3
- Protein 11

Collard Greens

Judy Houser
Hershey, PA

Makes 2–4 servings
Prep. Time: 10 minutes
Cooking Time: 5 minutes

1 lb. kale or collard greens

2–3 cloves garlic, minced

2 tsp. olive oil

½–¾ tsp. salt

water

1. Wash the greens. Then remove stems and chop the leaves into ½-inch-wide strips.

2. Sauté garlic in oil for 30 seconds in a large skillet or saucepan. Do not let it brown.

3. Add the kale or collard greens and salt. Toss to mix.

4. Cover and cook over medium-low heat for 3–4 minutes.

5. Add water, 1 Tbsp. at a time, if necessary, to keep greens from sticking.

- Calories 71
- Fat 3
- Sodium 320
- Carbs 10
- Sugar 0
- Protein 3

Zucchini in Sour Cream

Lizzie Ann Yoder
Hartville, OH

Makes 6 servings
Prep. Time: 20 minutes
Cooking Time: 1–1½ hours
Ideal slow-cooker size: 3- or 4-qt.

4 cups unpeeled, sliced zucchini

1 cup sour cream

¼ cup whole milk

1 cup chopped onion

1 tsp. salt

1 cup grated sharp cheddar cheese

1. Cook zucchini in microwave on High 2–3 minutes. Turn into slow cooker sprayed with cooking spray.

2. Combine sour cream, milk, onions, and salt. Pour over zucchini and stir gently.

3. Cover. Cook on Low 1–1½ hours.

4. Sprinkle cheese over vegetables 30 minutes before serving.

- Calories 169
- Fat 13
- Sodium 464
- Carbs 7
- Sugar 5
- Protein 7

Fresh Zucchini and Tomatoes

Pauline Morrison
St. Marys, ON

Makes 6–8 servings
Prep. Time: 15 minutes
Cooking Time: 2½–3 hours
Ideal slow-cooker size: 3½-qt.

1½ lbs. zucchini, peeled if you wish, and cut into ¼-inch slices

19-oz. can stewed tomatoes, broken up and undrained

1½ cloves garlic, minced

½ tsp. salt

1½ Tbsp. butter

1. Place zucchini slices in slow cooker.

2. Add tomatoes, garlic, and salt. Mix well.

3. Dot surface with butter.

4. Cover and cook on High 2½–3 hours, or until zucchini are done to your liking.

- Calories 51
- Fat 2
- Sodium 237
- Carbs 6
- Sugar 3
- Protein 1

Something Special Zucchini

Mary C. Wirth
Lancaster, PA

Makes 4 servings
Prep. Time: 15 minutes
Baking Time: 50 minutes

2 medium zucchini, *divided*

1 large sweet, or Vidalia, onion, *divided*

2 medium tomatoes, *divided*

2 green peppers, *divided*

6 slices cheese of your choice

salt and pepper, *optional*

1. Slice zucchini diagonally into 1/8-inch-thick slices.

2. Slice onion and tomatoes into 1/8-inch-thick slices.

3. Seed and slice green peppers into strips.

4. Layer half the veggies into a lightly greased 2-qt. shallow baking dish.

5. Repeat the layers, using all remaining veggies.

6. Sprinkle with salt and pepper if you wish.

7. Cover tightly and bake at 375°F for 45 minutes.

8. Layer cheese on top.

9. Bake uncovered 2–5 more minutes, or until cheese has melted.

- Calories 219
- Fat 15
- Sodium 291
- Carbs 11
- Sugar 7
- Protein 12

Zucchini Casserole

Virginia R. Bender
Dover, DE

Makes 6 servings
Prep. Time: 30 minutes
Baking Time: 1 hour

4 cups grated fresh zucchini

1 medium onion, grated

1/4 tsp. konjac flour

4 eggs

1/2–3/4 cup grated cheddar cheese

black pepper, *optional*

salt, to taste, *optional*

1. Place grated zucchini and onion into lightly greased 2-qt. baking dish. Sprinkle with the konjac flour and mix together gently.

2. Beat eggs in a mixing bowl. Pour over all. Stir.

3. Sprinkle with grated cheese, and seasonings if you wish.

4. Bake uncovered at 350°F for 1 hour.

- Calories 104
- Fat 7
- Sodium 115
- Carbs 4
- Sugar 3
- Protein 7

Pizza-Style Zucchini

Marcella Roberts
Denver, PA

Makes 6 servings
Prep. Time: 20 minutes
Cooking Time: 2½ hours
Ideal slow-cooker size: 4-qt.

2 medium zucchini, unpeeled and cut in disks

2 medium yellow squash, unpeeled and cut in disks

½ cup tomato sauce

¾ tsp. Italian seasoning

5 drops liquid stevia

½ tsp. garlic powder

½ tsp. onion powder

1 large tomato, diced

1 cup grated mozzarella cheese

sliced black olives, *optional*

1. Layer zucchini and yellow squash in lightly greased slow cooker, alternating colors.

2. Mix together the tomato sauce, Italian seasoning, liquid stevia, garlic powder, and onion powder. Stir in the diced tomato. Pour over zucchini and yellow squash.

3. Sprinkle with mozzarella and black olives (if using).

4. Cover and cook on High for 2 hours, until bubbly. Remove lid and cook an additional 30 minutes on High to evaporate some of the liquid.

Tip: Add basil, oregano, and chopped garlic if you want to really amp up the pizza flavor.

- Calories 63
- Fat 3
- Sodium 215
- Carbs 4
- Sugar 2
- Protein 5

Caponata

Katrine Rose
Woodbridge, VA

Makes 10 servings
Prep. Time: 20 minutes
Cooking Time: 7–8 hours
Ideal slow-cooker size: 4-qt.

1 medium (1 lb.) eggplant, peeled and cut into ½-inch cubes

14½-oz. can diced tomatoes

1 medium onion, chopped

1 red bell pepper, cut into ½-inch pieces

¾ cup salsa

¼ cup olive oil

2 Tbsp. capers, drained

3 Tbsp. balsamic vinegar

3 cloves garlic, minced

1¼ tsp. dried oregano

⅓ cup packed, chopped fresh basil

1. Combine all ingredients except basil in slow cooker.

2. Cover. Cook on Low 7–8 hours, or until vegetables are tender.

3. Stir in basil.

- Calories 85
- Fat 6
- Sodium 245
- Carbs 8
- Sugar 4
- Protein 1

Batilgian, an Armenian Recipe

Donna Treloar
Muncie, IN

Makes 4–6 servings
Prep. Time: 15–20 minutes
Cooking Time: 3 hours
Ideal slow-cooker size: 5- or 6-qt.

1 large Spanish onion, diced

5 Tbsp. olive oil, *divided*

4 stalks celery, cut in 1-inch pieces

2 cups fresh green beans, trimmed, cut in 2-inch pieces

3 bay leaves

3 cloves garlic, pressed

2 Tbsp. finely chopped fresh basil or 2 tsp. dried basil

1 large eggplant, cubed

salt and pepper, to taste

28-oz. can tomatoes with juice

2 Tbsp. fresh lemon juice

2 Tbsp. capers, *optional*

1. In a large skillet, sauté onion in 3 Tbsp. oil.

2. Add celery. Cover and cook 5 minutes.

3. Add green beans, bay leaves, garlic, and basil. Cover and cook 7 minutes.

4. Transfer mixture to 5- or 6-qt. slow cooker. Add cubed eggplant on top of vegetables.

5. Sprinkle with salt and pepper. Drizzle 2 Tbsp. oil over all.

6. Top with tomatoes and their juice.

7. Cover. Cook on Low 3 hours, stirring gently once or twice.

8. Remove bay leaves. Add lemon juice, and capers if you wish, just before serving.

- Calories 170
- Fat 12
- Sodium 320
- Carbs 15
- Sugar 5
- Protein 2

Green Beans with Sesame Seeds

Anita Troyer
Fairview, MI

Makes 2 servings
Prep. Time: 20 minutes
Cooking Time: 10 minutes

8 oz. fresh green beans

¼ cup sesame seeds

20 drops liquid stevia

1 Tbsp. soy sauce

1 Tbsp. keto-friendly instant vegetable bouillon

1. Trim ends of beans.

2. Cook in boiling water for 4 minutes, or until they are tender to your liking.

3. Drop hot beans in cold water to stop the cooking and preserve their color. Drain well and cut in half or thirds.

4. Grind the sesame seeds in a mortar, leaving some seeds whole. If you do not have a mortar and pestle, roughly chop the seeds on a cutting board with a knife.

5. Stir in the stevia, then add soy sauce and bouillon. Mix well.

6. Add sauce to green beans. Serve at room temperature or reheat.

- Calories 133
- Fat 8
- Sodium 987
- Carbs 13
- Sugar 4
- Protein 5

Asian Green Beans

Norma Musser
Womelsdorf, PA

Makes 8 servings
Prep. Time: 20 minutes
Cooking Time: 10 minutes

1½ lbs. fresh green beans, ends trimmed

6 medium mushrooms, quartered

1 medium onion, halved and thinly sliced

2 Tbsp. butter

1½ tsp. Truvia Brown Sugar Blend

1 Tbsp. coconut oil, melted

1 Tbsp. soy sauce

2 cloves garlic, minced

½ tsp. crushed red pepper

1. Cook beans in covered saucepan with a little water until soft, about 7–10 minutes.

2. Meanwhile, in another pan, sauté mushrooms and onion in butter.

3. Turn heat to low. Add Truvia, oil, soy sauce, garlic, and red pepper. Stir and cook until heated through.

4. Drain beans. Combine beans with sauce. Serve hot.

- Calories 80
- Fat 5
- Sodium 130
- Carbs 8
- Sugar 4
- Protein 2

Mustard Green Beans

Renee Hankins
Narvon, PA

Makes 2 servings
Prep. Time: 10 minutes
Cooking Time: 10 minutes

½ lb. fresh green beans, trimmed

2 tsp. butter

2 tsp. coarsely ground mustard

1. In a covered saucepan, boil green beans in small amount of water until crisp-tender.

2. Drain. Remove green beans to serving dish and cover with pan lid.

3. In a saucepan, melt butter. Add mustard and stir well.

4. Pour hot green beans back into saucepan with the butter sauce. Mix well. Pour sauced green beans into serving dish and serve.

- Calories 73
- Fat 4
- Sodium 47
- Carbs 8
- Sugar 4
- Protein 2

Lemon Garlic Green Beans

Dorothy Lingerfelt
Stonyford, CA

Makes 4 servings
Prep. Time: 10 minutes
Cooking Time: 10–13 minutes

2 cloves garlic, minced

2 tsp. olive oil

1 lb. fresh green beans, trimmed and broken in pieces

1 Tbsp. lemon juice

1 Tbsp. lemon zest

¼ tsp. freshly ground pepper

⅛ tsp. salt

1. In a large skillet, cook garlic in oil over medium heat for 30 seconds.

2. Add green beans.

3. Cook and stir frequently for 10–13 minutes, until as tender-crisp as you like them.

4. Stir in lemon juice, lemon zest, pepper, and salt.

- Calories 58
- Fat 2.5
- Sodium 67
- Carbs 9
- Sugar 4
- Protein 2

Whole Green Beans in Garlic

Leona Yoder
Hartville, OH

Joyce M. Shackelford
Green Bay, WI

Doris Ranck
Gap, PA

Makes 4 servings
Prep. Time: 15–20 minutes
Cooking Time: 20–30 minutes

1 lb. green beans, ends trimmed

2 tsp. butter

⅛ tsp. finely chopped garlic

½ tsp. salt

¼ tsp. pepper

1 tsp. dried oregano, *optional*

⅓ cup shredded Parmesan cheese, *optional*

1. Cook beans in small amount of boiling water in covered saucepan until crisp-tender. Drain.

2. Melt butter in large skillet. Sauté beans and garlic in butter until heated through and done to your liking.

3. Season before serving with salt and pepper, and oregano, if you wish.

4. Place in serving dish. Just before serving, top with shredded Parmesan cheese, if you wish.

- Calories 65
- Fat 3
- Sodium 247
- Carbs 9
- Sugar 4
- Protein 2

Green Bean and Mushroom Sauté

Clara Yoder Byler
Hartville, OH

Makes 4 servings
Prep. Time: 10 minutes
Cooking Time: 20 minutes

1 lb. fresh, or frozen, green beans

¾–1 cup sliced fresh mushrooms

2 Tbsp. butter

2–3 tsp. onion powder or garlic powder

4 strips bacon, cooked and crumbled, *optional*

1. Cook green beans in water to cover, just until tender.

2. Meanwhile, in a skillet, sauté mushrooms in butter until tender.

3. Stir in onion or garlic powder.

4. Drain beans. Add to skillet and toss with mushrooms and seasonings.

5. Place in serving dish. Top with crumbled bacon, if you wish.

- Calories 152
- Fat 9
- Sodium 191
- Carbs 12
- Sugar 3
- Protein 6

Southern Green Beans

Pat Bishop
Bedminster, PA

Makes 4–6 servings
Prep. Time: 10 minutes
Cooking Time: 2–4 hours
Ideal slow-cooker size: 3- to 4-qt.

2 cups chicken bone broth

1 lb. fresh or frozen cut green beans

1 cup chopped onion

½ cup cooked, chopped bacon

1 Tbsp. white vinegar

1 Tbsp. liquid aminos

¼ tsp. pepper

1 clove garlic, minced

1. Toss all ingredients together in slow cooker.

2. Cover and cook on Low for 4 hours or on High for 2 hours.

- Calories 170
- Fat 9
- Sodium 663
- Carbs 12
- Sugar 5
- Protein 11

Dutch Green Beans

Edwina Stoltzfus
Narvon, PA

Makes 4–6 servings
Prep. Time: 20 minutes
Cooking Time: 4½ hours
Ideal slow-cooker size: 4- to 5-qt.

½ lb. bacon, or ham chunks

4 medium onions, sliced

2 qts. fresh or frozen green beans

4 cups canned stewed tomatoes, or diced fresh tomatoes

½–¾ tsp. salt

¼ tsp. pepper

1. Brown bacon until crisp in skillet. Drain, reserving 2 Tbsp. drippings. Crumble bacon into small pieces.

2. Sauté onions in bacon drippings.

3. Combine all ingredients in slow cooker.

4. Cover. Cook on Low 4½ hours.

- Calories 151
- Fat 3
- Sodium 760
- Carbs 22
- Sugar 8
- Protein 12

Green Beans with Bacon and Onions

Deborah Heatwole
Waynesboro, GA

Anne Nolt
Thompsontown, PA

Makes 6 servings
Prep. Time: 5 minutes
Cooking Time: 30 minutes

4 slices bacon

½ cup, or more, chopped onions

6 cups water

1 qt. fresh, or frozen, green beans

½ tsp. garlic salt

1. Sauté bacon in large skillet. Remove bacon and drain. Reserve drippings.

2. Add onions to drippings. Sauté until tender. Crumble bacon, add to skillet, and set aside.

3. Meanwhile, bring 6 cups of water to a boil in a large saucepan.

4. Add green beans. Return to boil, cook 8–15 minutes, or just until beans are tender. Drain.

5. Pour sautéed onions and crumbled bacon into beans in saucepan.

6. Sprinkle with garlic salt. Mix thoroughly and serve.

- Calories 153
- Fat 3
- Sodium 936
- Carbs 8
- Sugar 4
- Protein 25

Green Beans with Tomato, Bacon, and Onions

Hope Comerford
Clinton Township, MI

Makes 4 servings
Prep. Time: 10 minutes
Cooking Time: 4 hours
Ideal slow-cooker size: 2-qt.

2½–3 cups fresh green beans, ends snapped off, washed and halved

2 small tomatoes, chopped

1 small onion, chopped

3 Tbsp. cooked bacon pieces

1 tsp. onion powder

1 tsp. garlic powder

½ tsp. salt

⅛ tsp. red pepper

½ cup chicken bone broth

1. Add all ingredients to the crock and give it a stir.

2. Cover and cook on Low for 4 hours.

- Calories 49
- Fat 1
- Sodium 329
- Carbs 8
- Sugar 4
- Protein 4

Herbed Green Beans with Tomatoes

Doreen Miller
Albuquerque, NM

Makes 6–8 servings
Prep. Time: 45 minutes
Cooking Time: 25 minutes

1 clove garlic, minced

2 Tbsp. olive oil

⅓ cup thinly sliced green onion

1 Tbsp. minced fresh basil or 1 tsp. dried basil

1 Tbsp. minced fresh oregano or 1 tsp. dried oregano

½ tsp. salt

4 medium fresh tomatoes, peeled and chopped

4 cups fresh green beans, cut into 2-inch pieces

1 cup water

1. In a large frying pan, sauté garlic in olive oil for 1 minute. Do not allow to brown.

2. Add green onion, basil, and oregano. Cook a few minutes.

3. Add salt, tomatoes, green beans, and water. Cook uncovered until beans are as tender as you like them, 10–20 minutes.

- Calories 62
- Fat 4
- Sodium 128
- Carbs 7
- Sugar 4
- Protein 2

Spicy Green Beans

Miriam Kauffman
Harrisonburg, VA

Makes 8 servings (¾ cup each)
Prep. Time: 25 minutes
Cooking and Baking Time: 75 minutes

3 cups canned tomatoes

2 Tbsp. minced onions

2 Tbsp. diced celery

½–1 tsp. dried oregano, according to your taste preference

½–1 tsp. chili powder, according to your taste preference

15 drops liquid stevia

1 bay leaf

dash red pepper

¼ tsp. garlic salt

⅛ tsp. ground cloves

⅛ tsp. pepper

½ tsp. konjac flour

1 qt. canned green beans

½ cup grated Parmesan cheese

1. In a large saucepan, combine all ingredients except konjac flour, green beans, and cheese. Simmer, covered, for 15 minutes. Remove bay leaf.

2. Meanwhile, drain the beans. Place the beans in a large mixing bowl.

3. Whisk the konjac flour into the large saucepan until smooth. Cook until thickened. Pour thickened sauce over beans. Stir well.

4. Place mixture in a greased 3-qt. baking dish. Bake, covered, at 350°F for 45 minutes.

5. Top with grated Parmesan cheese. Bake, uncovered, an additional 15 minutes.

- Calories 54
- Fat 2
- Sodium 389
- Carbs 8
- Sugar 3
- Protein 3

Roasted Plum Tomatoes

Betti Russer
Lancaster, PA

Makes 4 servings
Prep. Time: 10 minutes
Baking Time: 30 minutes

8 plum tomatoes (about 1½ lbs.)

1 Tbsp. olive oil

¼ tsp. dried thyme

½ tsp. salt

¼ tsp. pepper

1. Preheat oven to 425°F.

2. Core tomatoes. Slice each one lengthwise. Place in a mixing bowl.

3. Toss tomatoes with olive oil and seasonings.

4. Arrange tomatoes in a single layer, with cut sides up, on a rimmed baking sheet.

5. Bake until softened, about 30 minutes.

- Calories 52
- Fat 4
- Sodium 246
- Carbs 5
- Sugar 3
- Protein 1

Baked Tomatoes

Lizzie Ann Yoder
Hartville, OH

Makes 4 servings
Prep. Time: 10 minutes
Cooking Time: 45–60 minutes
Ideal slow-cooker size: 2½- or 3-qt.

2 tomatoes, each cut in half

½ Tbsp. olive oil

½ tsp. parsley, chopped, or ¼ tsp. dried parsley flakes

½ tsp. dried oregano

½ tsp. dried basil

1. Spray slow-cooker crock with cooking spray. Place tomato halves in crock.

2. Drizzle oil over tomatoes. Sprinkle with remaining ingredients.

3. Cover. Cook on High 45–60 minutes.

- Calories 27
- Fat 2
- Sodium 3
- Carbs 2
- Sugar 2
- Protein 0.5

Stewed Tomatoes

Esther J. Mast
Lancaster, PA

Makes 5 servings (¾ cup each)
Prep. Time: 5 minutes
Cooking Time: 10 minutes

2 Tbsp. chopped onion

2 Tbsp. freshly chopped celery leaves

2 tsp. butter

2 cups canned diced tomatoes, undrained

2 Tbsp. Splenda Sugar Blend

¼ tsp. salt

⅛ tsp. cinnamon

½ tsp. konjac flour

1. In a large skillet or saucepan, sauté onion and celery leaves in butter until soft but not brown.

2. Add tomatoes, sugar blend, salt, and cinnamon and stir in well.

3. Sprinkle the konjac flour into the tomato mixture and whisk until smooth. Continue cooking and stirring until thickened.

- Calories 59
- Fat 1
- Sodium 262
- Carbs 10
- Sugar 6
- Protein 0.5

Hot Tomato Curry

Norma Musser
Womelsdorf, PA

Makes 2 servings
Prep. Time: 30 minutes
Cooking Time: 45 minutes

1 lb. fresh tomatoes

2 Tbsp. olive oil

¼ tsp. mustard seeds

¼ tsp. cumin seeds

2 bay leaves

⅓ cup finely chopped onion

½ tsp. ground ginger

2 cloves garlic

½ tsp. curry powder

½ tsp. turmeric

1 tsp. salt

¼ cup water

cooked cauliflower rice

½–¾ cup plain yogurt

2 hard-boiled eggs, chopped, *optional*

1. Peel tomatoes and dice. Set aside.

2. Heat oil in a skillet. Stir in mustard seeds, cumin seeds, bay leaves, and onion. Cook until golden brown.

3. Add ginger, garlic, curry powder, and turmeric. Cook for a few minutes until flavors blend.

4. Add tomatoes, salt, and water. Cover and simmer for 35 minutes. Remove from heat and let cool. Remove bay leaves.

5. Serve over cauliflower rice. Top individual servings with a dollop of plain yogurt.

6. If you wish, crumble hard-boiled eggs over top.

- Calories 278
- Fat 19
- Sodium 1010
- Carbs 17
- Sugar 11
- Protein 12

Steamed Mushrooms

Jean Binns Smith
Bellefonte, PA

Makes 4 servings
Prep. Time: 5 minutes
Cooking Time: 20 minutes

1 lb. small mushrooms, left whole or sliced

2 Tbsp. butter

¼ tsp. salt

⅛ tsp. paprika

½ cup whole milk

1. Place mushrooms in top of double boiler. Be sure to place them over, not in, hot water.

2. Dot mushrooms with butter.

3. Sprinkle with salt and paprika.

4. Pour milk around edge of double boiler pan holding the mushrooms.

5. Cover and steam 20 minutes, or until tender.

- Calories 107
- Fat 7
- Sodium 154
- Carbs 8
- Sugar 3
- Protein 5

Wild Mushrooms Italian

Connie Johnson
Loudon, NH
 SLOW COOKER

Makes 4–5 servings
Prep. Time: 20 minutes
Cooking Time: 6–8 hours
Ideal slow-cooker size: 5-qt.

2 large onions, chopped

3 large red bell peppers, chopped

3 large green bell peppers, chopped

2–3 Tbsp. olive oil

12-oz. pkg. oyster mushrooms, cleaned and chopped

4 cloves garlic, minced

3 fresh bay leaves

10 fresh basil leaves, chopped

1 Tbsp. salt

1½ tsp. pepper

28-oz. can Italian plum tomatoes, crushed, or chopped

1. Sauté onions and peppers in oil in skillet until soft. Stir in mushrooms and garlic. Sauté just until mushrooms begin to turn brown. Pour into slow cooker.

2. Add remaining ingredients. Stir well.

3. Cover. Cook on Low 6–8 hours. Remove bay leaves before serving.

- Calories 171
- Fat 9
- Sodium 410
- Carbs 22
- Sugar 10
- Protein 5

Roasted Asparagus

Barbara Hoover
Landisville, PA

Makes 3–4 servings
Prep. Time: 10 minutes
Baking Time: 10 minutes

1 lb. fresh asparagus

2½ Tbsp. olive oil

¼ tsp. salt

¼ tsp. black pepper

1-2 Tbsp. sesame seeds

1. Trim any tough, woody stems from asparagus. Place asparagus on a large, ungreased baking sheet.

2. Drizzle olive oil over asparagus. Sprinkle with salt and pepper. Toss asparagus to coat and arrange in a single layer on the baking sheet.

3. Roast at 400°F until tender, about 10 minutes. Turn the baking sheet front-to-back and end-to-end halfway through roasting.

4. Meanwhile, toast the sesame seeds in a large skillet over medium heat, stirring constantly until golden, 1–2 minutes. Sprinkle seeds over roasted asparagus. Serve immediately.

- Calories 109
- Fat 10
- Sodium 124
- Carbs 5
- Sugar 2
- Protein 3

Lemony Garlic Asparagus

Hope Comerford
Clinton Township, MI

SLOW COOKER

Makes 4 servings
Prep. Time: 5 minutes
Cooking Time: 1½–2 hours
Ideal slow-cooker size: 2- or 3-qt.

1 lb. asparagus, bottom inch (tough part) removed

1 Tbsp. olive oil

1½ Tbsp. lemon juice

3-4 cloves garlic, peeled and minced

¼ tsp. salt

⅛ tsp. pepper

1. Spray crock with nonstick spray.

2. Lay asparagus at bottom of crock and coat with the olive oil.

3. Pour the lemon juice over the top, then sprinkle with the garlic, salt, and pepper.

4. Cover and cook on Low for 1½–2 hours.

Serving suggestion: Garnish with diced pimento, garlic, and lemon zest.

- Calories 58
- Fat 4
- Sodium 123
- Carbs
- Sugar 2
- Protein 3

Parmesan Baked-or-Grilled Asparagus

Jean M. Butzer
Batavia, NY

Carol Findling
Carol Stream, IL

Colleen Heatwole
Burton, MI

Makes 4 servings
Prep. Time: 5 minutes
Baking Time: 15 minutes

1 lb. fresh asparagus

2 tsp. olive oil

¼ tsp. salt

¼ tsp. pepper

¼ cup grated Parmesan cheese

1. Preheat oven to 425°F.

2. Place asparagus (trimmed and washed) on a nonstick baking sheet. Drizzle with olive oil and sprinkle with salt and pepper. Toss to coat.

3. Bake 10 minutes. Toss again.

4. Sprinkle with cheese.

5. Return to oven and bake until the cheese melts, about 5 minutes longer.

- Calories 64
- Fat 4
- Sodium 213
- Carbs 5
- Sugar 2
- Protein 4

Asparagus with Sesame Butter

Doyle Rounds
Bridgewater, VA

Makes 6–8 servings
Prep. Time: 7 minutes
Cooking Time: about 10 minutes

2 lbs. fresh asparagus

1 cup boiling water

½ tsp. salt

¾ tsp. konjac flour

¼ cup vegetable broth

4 Tbsp. (½ stick) butter

3 Tbsp. sesame seeds, toasted

1. Place asparagus spears in a large skillet. Add boiling water and salt. Cook covered for 5–7 minutes, or until tender.

2. Remove asparagus and keep warm. Drain cooking liquid, reserving ½ cup in a small saucepan.

3. Whisk konjac flour and vegetable broth in a small bowl. Stir into asparagus cooking liquid. 4. Cook and stir over medium heat until thickened and bubbly. Cook and stir 1 minute more.

5. Stir in butter until melted.

6. Spoon over asparagus. Sprinkle with sesame seeds and serve immediately.

- Calories 92
- Fat 7
- Sodium 150
- Carbs 5
- Sugar 2
- Protein 3

Slow Cooker Beets

Hope Comerford
Clinton Township, MI

Makes 4–6 servings
Prep. Time: 10 minutes
Cooking Time: 3–4 hours
Ideal slow-cooker size: 3-qt.

4–6 large beets, scrubbed well and tops removed

3 Tbsp. olive oil

1 tsp. sea salt

¼ tsp. pepper

3 Tbsp. balsamic vinegar

1 Tbsp. lemon juice

1. Use foil to make a packet around each beet.

2. Divide the olive oil, salt, pepper, balsamic vinegar, and lemon juice evenly between each packet.

3. Place each beet packet into the slow cooker.

4. Cover and cook on Low for 3–4 hours, or until the beets are tender when poked with a knife.

5. Remove each beet packet from the crock and allow to cool and let the steam escape. Once cool enough to handle, use a paring knife to gently peel the skin off each beet. Cut into bite-sized pieces and serve with juice from the packet over the top.

- Calories 103
- Fat 7
- Sodium 426
- Carbs 10
- Sugar 7
- Protein 1

Bean Sprouts

Roseann Wilson
Albuquerque, NM

Makes 2 servings
Prep. Time: 5 minutes
Cooking Time: 8–10 minutes

1 clove garlic, minced

2 Tbsp. oil

1 lb. fresh bean sprouts

salt and pepper

1. Cook garlic in oil in a large skillet or saucepan until translucent.

2. Add bean sprouts. Stir fry 4–5 minutes.

3. Add salt and pepper, to taste.

- Calories 362
- Fat 15
- Sodium 265
- Carbs 51
- Sugar 12
- Protein 20

Garden Vegetable Medley

Ruth Fisher
Leicester, NY

Makes 4 servings (¾ cup each)
Prep. Time: 10 minutes
Cooking Time: 20 minutes

1 Tbsp. olive oil

4 cups zucchini, chopped into ½-inch pieces

1 cup chopped onion

1 red or green pepper, chopped

2 medium-sized tomatoes, chopped

¼ tsp. garlic powder

½ tsp. salt

4 slices of your favorite cheese

1. Heat oil in stir-fry pan over medium heat. Add zucchini and onion. Heat until tender, about 10 minutes.

2. Add peppers and tomatoes and stir-fry until just tender.

3. Stir in garlic powder and salt.

4. Lay cheese over top. Turn off heat and let stand until cheese is melted.

- Calories 195
- Fat 13
- Sodium 439
- Carbs 12
- Sugar
- Protein 9

Vegetable Medley

Joan S. Eye
Harrisonburg, VA

Makes 4 servings
Prep. Time: 20 minutes
Cooking Time: 4 minutes
Standing Time: 5 minutes

1½ cups raw broccoli, cut up

1½ cups raw zucchini, cut up

½ cup raw sweet red pepper, cut up

¼ cup raw onion, cut up

2 Tbsp. butter

2 tsp. chicken bone broth

1. Combine ingredients in a microwave-safe dish.

2. Cover and microwave on High for 4 minutes.

3. Let stand for 5 minutes before serving.

- Calories 107
- Fat 9
- Sodium 21
- Carbs 5
- Sugar 2.5
- Protein 2

Spring Veggie Bundles

Cheryl A. Lapp
Parkesburg, PA

Makes 8–10 servings
Prep. Time: 20 minutes
Cooking Time: 12 minutes

6 green onions

1 cup water

3 stalks celery

2 medium-sized bell peppers, ideally one red and one yellow

1 lb. thin asparagus

⅓ cups chicken bone broth

1. Trim off long green tops of onions and reserve.

2. Bring water to a boil in a skillet or good-sized saucepan. Add onion greens and boil 1 minute.

3. Drain onions. Submerge in ice water for a few minutes. Drain again. Pat dry.

4. Cut celery and peppers into long julienne strips. Divide into 8–10 bundles, along with asparagus.

5. Tie each with several of the green onion tops.

6. Place bundles in large skillet. Pour in chicken broth.

7. Cook uncovered, approximately 8–10 minutes, until tender.

8. Remove from skillet and place on serving platter. Pour remaining broth from pan over bundles.

- Calories 20
- Fat 0
- Sodium 65
- Carbs 3
- Sugar 1.5
- Protein 2

KETO TIP
You may find that your taste changes after being off sugar and carbs for a while. You'll start to notice the natural sweetness of certain vegetables and may enjoy foods you never thought you would!

Salads

Grand Tossed Salad

Kathy Hertzler
Lancaster, PA

Carol Stroh
Akron, NY

Makes 8 servings (¾ cup each)
Prep. Time: 45–60 minutes
Cooking Time: 10 minutes

½ cup sliced almonds

3 tsp. Truvia Brown Sugar Blend

medium-sized head of romaine lettuce

medium-sized head of red or green leaf lettuce

2 green onions, sliced

2 stalks celery, sliced

¼ cup olive oil

1 Tbsp. granulated Splenda

2 Tbsp. white wine vinegar

1 Tbsp. snipped parsley

¼ tsp. salt

Frank's RedHot Original Cayenne Pepper Sauce, to taste

1. Cook almonds and Truvia brown sugar blend over low heat, stirring constantly until sugar is melted and almonds are coated. Cool and break apart.

2. Toss together lettuces, green onions, celery, and sugared almonds.

3. Blend together oil, granulated Splenda, vinegar, parsley, salt, and Frank's RedHot sauce. Just before serving, pour over salad. Toss to mix.

- Calories 134
- Fat 12
- Sodium 88
- Carbs 6
- Sugar 4
- Protein 2

Bibb Lettuce with Pecans

Betty K. Drescher
Quakertown, PA

Makes 8 servings (¾ cup each)
Prep. Time: 10–15 minutes

4 heads Bibb lettuce

½ cup pecan halves, toasted

Dressing:
¼ cup vinegar

2 Tbsp. granulated Splenda

¼ cup olive oil

½ tsp. salt

½ small onion, chopped

1 tsp. dry mustard

2 Tbsp. water

1. Place lettuce and pecans in a salad bowl.

2. Combine dressing ingredients in blender. (You can make this ahead of time and refrigerate it.)

3. Toss dressing with salad ingredients just before serving.

- Calories 125
- Fat 12
- Sodium 12
- Carbs 4
- Sugar 3.5
- Protein 1

Chicken Salad with Bleu Cheese

Susan Smith
Monument, CO

Makes 6 servings (about 5 oz. per serving)
Prep. Time: 15 minutes

2½ cups cooked chicken breast, diced or julienned

6 cups shredded lettuce

¾ cup mayonnaise

2 Tbsp. tarragon vinegar

2½ Tbsp. chili sauce

2 Tbsp. chopped green pepper

1 oz. blue cheese, crumbled

whole lettuce leaves

1. Mix chicken with shredded lettuce.

2. Mix mayonnaise, vinegar, chili sauce, and green pepper. Add crumbled cheese.

3. Gently combine chicken and mayonnaise mixtures.

4. Place salad in a bowl lined with lettuce or in individual lettuce cups.

- Calories 4
- Fat 24
- Sodium 351
- Carbs 4
- Sugar 2
- Protein 20

Ed's Blue Cheese Salad

Andrea Zuercher
Lawrence, KS

Makes 4 servings
Prep. Time: 15 minutes

1 small bunch romaine lettuce

2 Tbsp. olive oil, or more or less to taste

salt and pepper, to taste

4 oz. blue cheese, crumbled

juice of ½ lemon, or more to taste

¼ cup grated Parmesan cheese, *optional*

1. Wash lettuce and tear into bite-sized pieces. Place in salad bowl.

2. Drizzle with olive oil. Toss.

3. Season leaves with salt and pepper, to taste.

4. Add blue cheese. Toss. Set aside until near serving time. (Refrigerate if more than 15 minutes.)

5. When ready to serve, add lemon juice, and Parmesan cheese if you wish, and toss again.

- Calories 188
- Fat 16
- Sodium 538
- Carbs 3
- Sugar 1
- Protein 8

Raspberry Walnut Salad

Jan Moore
Wellsville, KS

Lucy O'Connell
Northampton, MA

Makes 4 servings
Prep. Time: 10 minutes

6 cups mixed salad greens

¼ cup Raspberry Vinaigrette (recipe on pg. 277)

1 cup fresh raspberries

¼ cup feta cheese or blue cheese

¼ cup chopped walnuts

1. Mix greens and vinaigrette in a large bowl.

2. Divide mixture between 4 serving plates.

3. Top each plate of greens with raspberries, cheese, and walnuts.

4. Serve immediately.

- Calories 128
- Fat 15
- Sodium 355
- Carbs 7
- Sugar 4
- Protein 7

Strawberry Romaine Salad

Rose Hankins
Stevensville, MD

Makes 4 servings
Prep. Time: 15 minutes

8 cups romaine lettuce

1 pt. fresh strawberries

½ red onion

½ cup sunflower seeds, roasted

favorite keto-friendly salad dressing

1. Divide torn lettuce leaves among 4 individual salad bowls.

2. Slice 3–4 berries into each bowl.

3. Layer thin slices of onions over top.

4. Sprinkle with seeds.

5. Just before serving, drizzle with dressing.

- Calories 155
- Fat 10
- Sodium 11
- Carbs 15
- Sugar 6
- Protein 6

Summer Vegetable Cheese Salad

Jan Mast
Lancaster, PA

Makes 8 servings (¾ cup each)
Prep. Time: 15 minutes
Chilling Time: 1 hour

1¼ cups cheddar cheese, shredded

1¼ cups mozzarella cheese, shredded

½ cup Monterey Jack cheese, shredded

1 medium-sized cucumber, chopped

1 medium-sized tomato, seeded and chopped

1 onion, thinly sliced

1 cup green and red pepper, chopped

8 lettuce leaves

Dressing:
½ cup sour cream

¼ cup mayonnaise

1 Tbsp. lemon juice

1 clove garlic, minced

½ tsp. Dijon mustard

½ tsp. dried basil

½ tsp. paprika

10 drops liquid stevia

1. In a large mixing bowl, combine cheeses, cucumber, tomato, onion, and green and red peppers.

2. In a separate bowl, combine sour cream, mayonnaise, lemon juice, garlic, mustard, basil, paprika, and stevia.

3. Pour dressing over cheese and vegetables. Toss to coat.

4. Chill for 1 hour.

5. Serve in a lettuce-lined bowl.

- Calories 259
- Fat 22
- Sodium 367
- Carbs 4
- Sugar 2
- Protein 12

Caesar Salad

Colleen Heatwole
Burton, MI

Makes 8 servings (¾ cup each)
Prep. Time: 15–20 minutes

8-12 cups romaine lettuce, or spring mix, torn into bite-sized pieces
¼ cup olive oil
3 Tbsp. red wine vinegar
1 tsp. Worcestershire sauce
½ tsp. salt
¾ tsp. dry mustard
1 large clove garlic, minced
1½–2 Tbsp. fresh lemon juice
dash pepper
¼–½ cup grated Parmesan cheese

1. Place lettuce in a large bowl.

2. Combine next 6 ingredients in a blender or food processor.

3. Add fresh lemon juice and process until smooth.

4. Just before serving, toss with lettuce.

5. Sprinkle with pepper. Add Parmesan cheese and toss well.

- Calories 96
- Fat 8
- Sodium 229
- Carbs 3.
- Sugar 1
- Protein 2

Greek Salad

Ruth Feister
Narvon, PA

Makes 8 servings (¾ cup each)
Prep. Time: 20 minutes

1 head romaine lettuce, torn up
1 medium-sized cucumber sliced thin
2 medium-sized tomatoes, cut in pieces
½ red onion, finely chopped
parsley
4-oz. can sliced black olives, drained
2 oz. crumbled feta cheese
several artichoke hearts, quartered, *optional*

Dressing:
¼ cup chicken bone broth
2 Tbsp. red wine vinegar
2 tsp. lemon juice
5 drops liquid stevia
½ tsp. dried basil
½ tsp. dried oregano

1. Place lettuce, cucumber, tomatoes, onion, and parsley in a large serving bowl.

2. Combine dressing ingredients in a jar with a tightly fitting lid. Shake until mixed well.

3. Just before serving, drizzle with dressing and toss.

4. Top with olives, cheese, and artichoke hearts, if you wish.

- Calories 55
- Fat 3
- Sodium 191
- Carbs 5
- Sugar 2
- Protein 2

Spinach Salad

Ann Bender,
Fort Defiance, VA

Jackie Stefl
East Bethany, NY

Joyce M. Shackelford
Green Bay, WI

Laura R. Showalter
Dayton, VA

Makes 4 servings
Prep. Time: 10–15 minutes

8 oz. fresh spinach leaves, washed

½ cup chopped walnuts, or sliced almonds, or pecan halves, toasted

1 cup sliced fresh strawberries

your favorite keto-friendly berry vinaigrette, poppy seed, or oil and vinegar dressing

1. Toss all ingredients in a large salad bowl just before serving.

- Calories 72
- Fat 5
- Sodium 45
- Carbs 6
- Sugar 2
- Protein 3

Blueberry Spinach Salad

Judi Robb
Manhattan, KS

Makes 8 servings
Prep. Time: 15–20 minutes

⅓ cup olive oil

¼ cup raspberry vinegar

2 tsp. Dijon mustard

5 drops liquid stevia

10-oz. pkg. fresh spinach, torn

1 cup fresh, or frozen, blueberries

¼ cup chopped pecans, toasted

8 Tbsp. blue cheese, crumbled

1. In a jar with a tight-fitting lid, combine first 4 ingredients and shake well.

2. In a large salad bowl, toss spinach, blueberries, and pecans.

3. Add dressing and toss gently.

4. Top each salad with 1 Tbsp. blue cheese. Serve immediately.

- Calories 97
- Fat 8
- Sodium 219
- Carbs 6
- Sugar 3
- Protein 5

Spinach-Strawberry Salad

Pat Bechtel
Dillsburg, PA

Sarah M. Balmer
Manheim, PA

Makes 8 servings (¾ cup each)
Prep. Time: 20 minutes

12 oz. fresh spinach

1 qt. fresh strawberries, sliced

2 Tbsp. sesame seeds

1 Tbsp. poppy seeds

Dressing:
¼ cup olive oil

¼ cup granulated Splenda

1½ tsp. grated onion

¼ tsp. Worcestershire sauce

¼ tsp. paprika

¼ cup cider vinegar

1. Layer spinach, strawberries, sesame seeds, and poppy seeds in a large salad bowl.

2. Combine the dressing ingredients in a blender. Blend for 2 minutes.

3. Just before serving, pour the dressing over the spinach and toss lightly to coat the spinach and berries.

- Calories 130
- Fat 8
- Sodium 37
- Carbs 11
- Sugar 8
- Protein 2

Strawberry Spinach Salad with Turkey or Chicken

Genelle Taylor
Perrysburg, OH

Makes 4 main-dish servings
Prep. Time: 45–60 minutes

1 lb. asparagus spears

¼ cup keto-friendly poppy seed dressing

1 tsp. grated orange peel

1 Tbsp. juice of a freshly squeezed orange

8 cups torn fresh spinach, or assorted greens

2 cups sliced fresh strawberries and/or whole blueberries

¾ lb. cooked turkey or grilled chicken, cubed

¼ cup pecan halves

1. Snap off and discard woody bases from asparagus. Cut into 1-inch pieces.

2. In a 1-qt. microwavable covered dish, cook asparagus with 2 Tbsp. of water for 5–7 minutes, or until tender-crisp. Drain. Rinse with cold water; drain again.

3. In a medium bowl, stir together poppy seed dressing, orange peel, and orange juice. Set aside.

4. In a salad bowl, combine asparagus, spinach or other greens, berries, and turkey or chicken. Add dressing mixture and toss.

5. Top with pecans just before serving.

- Calories 246
- Fat 7
- Sodium 152
- Carbs 19
- Sugar 10
- Protein 31

Salad with Hot Bacon Dressing

Joanne E. Martin
Stevens, PA

Makes 32 cups salad greens and 2 cups dressing, for 2 Tbsp. dressing per serving
Prep. Time: 15 minutes
Cooking Time: 7 minutes

6-8 strips of bacon

¾ cup Splenda Sugar Blend

2 eggs, beaten

⅓ cup vinegar

⅔ cup water

32 cups salad greens

1 cup grated brussels sprouts

hard-boiled eggs, *optional*

1. In a skillet, brown bacon. Drain off drippings. Crumble and set aside.

2. In the same skillet, mix sugar blend, beaten eggs, vinegar, and water. Bring to boil, stirring up browned bacon drippings. Stir dressing until slightly thickened.

3. Stir in bacon.

4. Just before serving, toss warm salad dressing with mixture of salad greens, grated brussels sprouts, and hard-boiled eggs (if using).

- Calories 97
- Fat 2.5
- Sodium 118
- Carbs 13
- Sugar 10
- Protein 4

Spinach Salad Caprese

Jan Moore
Wellsville, KS

Makes 4 servings
Prep. Time: 10-20 minutes

6 cups fresh spinach

12 cherry tomatoes, halved

½ cup chopped fresh basil

4 oz. fresh mozzarella cheese, cubed

¼ cup olive oil

1. Gently combine all ingredients.

2. Toss to mix.

3. Serve immediately.

- Calories 213
- Fat 18
- Sodium 215
- Carbs
- Sugar 2
- Protein 9

Irish Pub Salad

Willard E. Roth
Elkhart, IN

Makes 4 servings
Prep. Time: 15–20 minutes

4 cups baby spinach, washed

½ cup sliced cucumbers

2 medium-sized tomatoes, sliced

2 hard-boiled eggs, sliced

4 oz. Irish cheddar cheese, cubed

Irish Pub Salad Dressing (see recipe on pg. 282)

1. Place washed spinach in salad bowl for serving.

2. Cover, in order, with cucumbers, tomatoes, eggs, and cheese.

3. Mix gently with salad dressing just before serving (or serve on the side).

- Calories 173
- Fat 12
- Sodium 243
- Carbs
- Sugar 2
- Protein 11

Tofu Salad

Sara Harter Fredette
Goshen, MA

Makes 6 servings (¾ cup each)
Prep. Time: 10 minutes
Cooking Time: 10 minutes
Chilling Time: 2–3 hours

1 pkg. extra-firm tofu, cubed

¼ cup shaved brussels sprouts

1 green onion, sliced

1 clove garlic, minced

⅓–½ cup sunflower seeds

1 Tbsp. soy sauce

2 Tbsp. lemon juice and rind

2 Tbsp. olive oil

¼ tsp. salt

⅛ tsp. pepper

1. In a saucepan, steam tofu in 1 inch of water for 10 minutes.

2. Drain, and cool. Crumble with fork.

3. Place crumbled tofu, brussels sprouts, green onion, garlic, and seeds in a large mixing bowl. Combine gently.

4. In a jar with a tight-fitting lid, combine all remaining ingredients.

5. Pour dressing over the tofu/veggies mixture. Combine well.

6. Cover and chill for 1–2 hours.

- Calories 137
- Fat 11
- Sodium 320
- Carbs 5
- Sugar 1
- Protein 6

Raspberry Vinaigrette

Colleen Heatwole
Burton, MI

Makes 1–1½ cups
Prep. Time: 5–10 minutes

1 cup raspberries, fresh or frozen and thawed

¼ cup raspberry vinegar

2 Tbsp. olive oil

1½ tsp. Truvia Brown Sugar Blend

¼ tsp. dry mustard

1. Blend all ingredients in food processor or blender.

2. Refrigerate.

- Calories 47
- Fat 3
- Sodium 2
- Carbs 3.5
- Sugar 2
- Protein 0

Rose's Balsamic Vinaigrette

Rose Hankins
Stevensville, MD

Makes 1 cup
Prep. Time: 5 minutes

¼ cup balsamic vinegar

¾ cup extra-virgin olive oil

2 Tbsp. lemon juice

1 Tbsp. Italian seasoning

1 tsp. garlic powder or salt

1. Mix ingredients together well.

2. Store in refrigerator.

- Calories 167
- Fat 17
- Sodium 5
- Carbs 5
- Sugar 1
- Protein 1

Mom's Vinaigrette Dressing

Mary C. Wirth
Lancaster, PA

Makes ⅓–½ cup
Prep. Time: 5–10 minutes

3 Tbsp. extra-virgin olive oil

1½–2 Tbsp. red wine vinegar

1 Tbsp. minced parsley

¾ tsp. garlic salt

3 drops liquid stevia

⅛ tsp. dried oregano, *optional*

1. Mix all ingredients together well.

2. Chill 2 hours or more if you wish, although it can be served immediately after mixing.

3. Serve over sliced tomatoes, cucumbers, or Vidalia onions.

- Calories 181
- Fat 20
- Sodium 363
- Carbs 05
- Sugar 0
- Protein 0

Herb Vinaigrette

Judy Koczo
Plano, IL

Makes ⅔ cup
Prep. Time: 5 minutes

6 Tbsp. cider vinegar

6 Tbsp. olive oil

2 Tbsp. finely chopped onion

1 tsp. salt

½ tsp. dried chives

½ tsp. dried tarragon

½ tsp. dried dill weed

1. Mix ingredients together thoroughly in a small bowl.

2. Pour over lettuce when ready to serve.

- Calories 124
- Fat 14
- Sodium 321
- Carbs 0.5
- Sugar 0
- Protein 0

Favorite Balsamic Dressing

Ann Bender
Fort Defiance, VA

Makes about ½ cup
Prep. Time: 5 minutes

¼ cup olive oil

2 Tbsp. balsamic vinegar

1 tsp. prepared mustard

1 clove garlic

30 drops liquid stevia

⅛ tsp. salt

⅛ tsp. pepper

1. Combine olive oil, vinegar, mustard, garlic, stevia, salt, and pepper in blender.

2. Blend until smooth.

3. Store in refrigerator.

- Calories 171
- Fat 18
- Sodium 101
- Carbs 2
- Sugar 2
- Protein 0

Flavorful Oil and Vinegar Dressing

Laura R. Showalter
Dayton, VA

Ruth Hofstetter
Versailles, MO

Makes ½ cup
Prep. Time: 3 minutes

¼ cup extra-virgin olive oil

30 drops liquid stevia

2 tsp.–2 Tbsp. vinegar, your choice of amount

1 tsp. parsley flakes or leaves

½ tsp. salt

½ tsp. pepper

1. Place all ingredients in jar with tight-fitting lid.

2. Cover and shake until ingredients are blended.

3. Pour over spinach salad. Toss. Serve immediately.

Tips:
1. *This is also good on cucumbers and onions, or fresh tomatoes.*
2. *It keeps covered in the fridge for several weeks.*

- Calories 161
- Fat 18
- Sodium 81
- Carbs 0
- Sugar 0
- Protein 0

Pesto Salad Dressing

Jennifer Kuh
Bay Village, OH

Makes 1 cup
Prep. Time: 5 minutes

½ cup pesto

3 Tbsp. Favorite Balsamic Dressing (see recipe on pg. 279)

2 tsp. prepared mustard

1. Mix all ingredients.

2. Store in refrigerator, tightly covered.

- Calories 122
- Fat 12
- Sodium 208
- Carbs 2
- Sugar 1
- Protein 1

Herb and Mustard Dressing

Susan Tjon
Austin, TX

Makes ¾ cup (2 Tbsp. per serving)
Prep. Time: 10 minutes

¼ cup water

3 Tbsp. balsamic, or cider, vinegar

1½ Tbsp. Dijon mustard

1½ Tbsp. extra-virgin olive oil

1 tsp. dried basil leaves

1 tsp. dried thyme leaves

1 tsp. dried rosemary

1 small clove garlic, minced

1. In a small jar with tight-fitting lid, combine all ingredients. Shake well.

2. Refrigerate until ready to use.

3. Shake before serving.

- Calories 51
- Fat 5
- Sodium 131
- Carbs 1
- Sugar 0
- Protein 0

Zesty French Dressing

Erma Rutt
Newmanstown, PA

Makes 16 servings (2 Tbsp. each)
Prep. Time: 5–10 minutes

1 small onion, chopped

⅔ cup olive oil

¼ cup granulated Splenda

⅓ cup vinegar

2 Tbsp. no-sugar-added ketchup

1½ tsp. Worcestershire sauce

1 tsp. salt

1 tsp. prepared mustard

1 tsp. paprika

½ tsp. garlic powder

½ tsp. celery seed

1. Combine all ingredients in blender.

2. Blend until smooth.

3. Store in refrigerator.

- Calories 104
- Fat 9
- Sodium 147
- Carbs 5
- Sugar 4.5
- Protein 0

French Dressing Mix

Marla Folkerts
Geneva, IL

Makes 1¼ cups
Prep. Time: 10 minutes

3–6 Tbsp. granulated stevia

1½ tsp. paprika

1 tsp. dry mustard

1½ tsp. salt

⅛ tsp. onion powder

¾ cup olive oil

¼ cup vinegar

1. Combine stevia, paprika, dry mustard, salt, and onion powder in small bowl.

2. Place in a glass container and store in a cool, dry place. Use within 6 months.

3. To make salad dressing, combine mix with olive oil and vinegar. Whisk well. Serve over lettuce.

- Calories 187
- Fat 20
- Sodium 369
- Carbs 2
- Sugar 1
- Protein 0

Ranch Dressing

Pat Unternahrer
Wayland, IA

Makes ¾ cup
Prep. Time: 5 minutes

⅔ cup cottage cheese

2 Tbsp. whole milk

1 Tbsp. tarragon vinegar

1 clove garlic, minced

1 Tbsp. sliced green onions

1. Blend cottage cheese, milk, vinegar, and garlic in blender or food processor.

2. Add green onions and blend just to combine.

3. Store in refrigerator.

- Calories 28
- Fat 1
- Sodium 87
- Carbs 1.5
- Sugar 1
- Protein 3

Irish Pub Salad Dressing

Willard E. Roth
Elkhart, IN

Makes ¾ cup
Prep. Time: 3 minutes

½ cup mayonnaise

2 Tbsp. white wine vinegar

1 Tbsp. whole-grain Dijon mustard

1 Tbsp. fresh tarragon

1 tsp. salt

1 tsp. freshly ground pepper

1. Whisk all ingredients together until smooth.

2. Pour over salad and toss.

- Calories 153
- Fat 17
- Sodium 593
- Carbs 1
- Sugar 0
- Protein 0

Cabbage Slaw with Vinegar Dressing

Betty Hostetler
Allensville, PA

Makes 12 servings (¾ cup each)
Prep. Time: 30–45 minutes
Chilling Time: 3–4 hours

8 cups grated cabbage

¼ cup grated brussels sprouts

¼ cup diced celery

¼ cup chopped red pepper

¼ cup chopped yellow pepper

⅛ cup chopped green pepper

1 Tbsp. celery seed

1½–2 tsp. liquid stevia

1 tsp. salt

½ cup white vinegar

¼ cup, plus 2 Tbsp., olive oil

1. Combine vegetables, celery seed, stevia, and salt in a large mixing bowl. Mix well.

2. In a small saucepan, bring vinegar to a boil. Add oil. Pour over vegetables. Mix well.

3. Refrigerate for 3–4 hours before serving.

- Calories 71
- Fat 6
- Sodium 175
- Carbs 4
- Sugar 2
- Protein 1

Pat's Southern-Style Coleslaw

Norma I. Gehman
Ephrata, PA

Makes 5–6 servings
Prep. Time: 20 minutes

½ small head of cabbage, shredded (4 cups)

¼ cup shredded brussels sprouts

¼ cup dill pickle relish

½ cup mayonnaise

salt and pepper, to taste

1. Mix shredded cabbage and brussels sprouts together in a good-sized bowl.

2. Blend dill pickle relish and mayonnaise together in a small bowl.

3. Blend dressing and seasonings into vegetables.

4. Serve immediately, or chill if you'll be serving it later.

- Calories 27
- Fat 1
- Sodium 203
- Carbs 5
- Sugar 1
- Protein 1

Vegetable Cabbage Slaw

Edna Good
Richland Center, WI

Makes 6–8 servings
Prep. Time: 30 minutes
Chilling Time: 2 hours

2 cups shredded cabbage

1 cup chopped celery

¼ cup shredded brussels sprouts

1 cucumber, thinly sliced

1 green bell pepper, chopped

1 small onion, chopped fine

4–6 radishes, thinly sliced, *optional*

½ tsp. liquid stevia

1 tsp. salt

½ tsp. dry mustard

¼ cup cream

3 Tbsp. vinegar or lemon juice

1. Combine cabbage, celery, brussels sprouts, cucumber, pepper, onion, and radishes (if using). Mix well.

2. Mix stevia, salt, mustard, cream, and vinegar or lemon juice in a small bowl.

3. Gently stir into vegetables. Chill at least 2 hours before serving.

- Calories 42
- Fat 3
- Sodium 261
- Carbs 4
- Sugar 2
- Protein 1

Greek Cabbage Salad

Colleen Heatwole
Burton, MI

Makes 10 servings (¾ cup each)
Prep. Time: 30 minutes
Chilling Time: 1 hour

6–8 cups thinly sliced cabbage

½ cup sliced black olives

½ cup thinly sliced red onions

½ cup feta cheese, diced or crumbled

Dressing:
1 cup apple cider vinegar

6 Tbsp. olive oil

1 tsp. dry mustard

½ tsp. celery seed

1. Combine first 4 salad ingredients in a large bowl.

2. Combine dressing ingredients in a blender, food processor, or beat well with a whisk.

3. Add salad dressing to cabbage mixture. Chill in refrigerator at least 1 hour before serving to combine flavors.

- Calories 114
- Fat 10
- Sodium 145
- Carbs 5
- Sugar 2
- Protein 2

Crunchy Cabbage Salad

Natalia Showalter
Mount Solon, VA

Makes 12 servings
Prep. Time: 30 minutes

¼ cup sliced almonds, or pecan pieces

2 Tbsp. sunflower seeds

1 Tbsp. sesame seeds

½ large head cabbage (about 6 cups)

4 green onions, sliced

½ green sweet bell pepper, sliced in quarter rings

½ red, or yellow, sweet bell pepper, sliced

Dressing:
2 Tbsp. olive oil

2 Tbsp. water

30 drops liquid stevia

1 Tbsp. vinegar

½ tsp. pepper

1 tsp. keto-friendly chicken bouillon granules

¼ tsp. garlic powder

¼ tsp. onion powder

¼ tsp. celery seed

1. Lightly toast nuts and seeds in a dry skillet. Stir frequently to prevent burning. Cool. Set aside.

2. Place cabbage flat side down on a cutting board. With a very sharp chef's knife, slice thin long strips of cabbage.

3. Combine sliced cabbage, green onions, and peppers in a good-sized bowl.

4. Combine dressing ingredients in jar with tight seal and shake well.

5. Pour over vegetables.

6. Add toasted nuts and seeds. Toss well to coat. Serve immediately.

- Calories 61
- Fat 5
- Sodium 62
- Carbs 4
- Sugar 0
- Protein 2

Greek Cabbage Slaw

B. Gautcher
Harrisonburg, VA

Makes 10 servings
Prep. Time: 20 minutes
Standing/Chilling Time: 12 hours

1 medium-sized head of cabbage head, shredded

1 medium-sized onion, grated

1½ tsp. liquid stevia

1 tsp. salt, *optional*

½ cup olive oil

½ cup vinegar

1. Put shredded cabbage in stainless steel or glass bowl.

2. Sprinkle onion on top.

3. Layer on stevia, salt if you wish, oil, and vinegar, in that order. Do not stir.

4. Put in cool place and let stand for at least 12 hours.

5. Stir before serving.

- Calories 114
- Fat 10
- Sodium 145
- Carbs 5
- Sugar 2
- Protein 2

Creamy Coleslaw

Tammy Yoder
Belleville, PA

Makes 6 servings (¾ cup each)
Prep. Time: 10 minutes
Chilling Time: 30 minutes

½ head of cabbage

½ cup mayonnaise

2 Tbsp. vinegar

2½ Tbsp. granulated Splenda

pinch salt

pinch pepper

1 Tbsp. celery seed, or to taste

¼ cup grated carrots

1. Shred cabbage. Place in a large mixing bowl.

2. Mix all remaining ingredients together in another bowl.

3. Stir dressing into shredded cabbage, mixing well.

4. Chill for 30 minutes before serving.

- Calories 160
- Fat 14
- Sodium 12
- Carbs
- Sugar 6
- Protein 1

Dreamy Creamy Coleslaw

Nancy Wagner Graves
Manhattan, KS

Makes 6–8 servings
Prep. Time: 5 minutes
Standing/Chilling Time: 60 minutes

1–1½ tsp. liquid stevia, depending upon your taste preference

1 tsp. salt

⅓ cup vinegar

1 cup whipping cream

1½ lbs. shredded green cabbage

1. In a large bowl, blend stevia, salt, vinegar, and whipping cream. Refrigerate for 30 minutes.

2. Meanwhile, shred cabbage.

3. After dressing ingredients have blended for 30 minutes, mix cabbage into dressing, blending well.

4. Cover and chill for 30 more minutes before serving.

- Calories 129
- Fat 11
- Sodium 264
- Carbs 7
- Sugar 4
- Protein 2

Mustard Coleslaw

Betty Moore
Avon Park, FL

Makes 24 servings
Prep. Time: 20 minutes

2 medium heads cabbage, shredded, or 2 1-lb. bags shredded cabbage

1 medium onion, diced

1 medium green bell pepper, diced

¼ cup shredded brussels sprouts

1 stalk celery, finely chopped

¾ cup prepared mustard

¾ cup cider vinegar

½ cup sour cream

½ cup no-sugar-added ketchup

¼ cup mayonnaise

1 Tbsp. salt

½ tsp. cayenne pepper

2½ tsp. liquid stevia

1. In a large bowl, combine cabbage, onion, pepper, brussels sprouts, and celery.

2. In a separate bowl, mix mustard, vinegar, sour cream, ketchup, mayonnaise, salt, and cayenne pepper. Blend well.

3. Stir in stevia and mix.

4. Pour desired amount of dressing over vegetables and toss to coat. Refrigerate any leftover dressing.

5. Refrigerate coleslaw until serving time.

6. Serve with slotted spoon.

- Calories 42
- Fat 3
- Sodium 389
- Carbs 4
- Sugar 2
- Protein 1

Broccoli Salad

Mary Seielstad
Sparks, NV

Makes 6 servings
Prep. Time: 15 minutes
Chilling Time: 8 hours, or overnight

Dressing:
½ cup mayonnaise

30 drops liquid stevia

2 tsp. red wine vinegar

Salad:
1 medium head broccoli, cut into florets (about 3 cups)

1 sweet red bell pepper, chopped

4 green onions, chopped

¼ cup chopped walnuts

1. Combine dressing ingredients in a jar with a tight-fitting lid. Shake to combine and chill overnight.

2. Combine salad ingredients. Pour dressing over salad and toss to mix.

- Calories 179
- Fat 17
- Sodium 134
- Carbs 5
- Sugar 2
- Protein 2

Dressed-Up Broccoli Salad

Elaine Vigoda
Rochester, NY

Makes 8 servings
Prep. Time: 20 minutes
Chilling Time: 1 hour or more

4 cups fresh broccoli florets, coarsely chopped

½ cup dried raspberries

½ cup finely chopped sweet, or red, onion

⅓ cup peanuts, dry roasted, unsalted

3 Tbsp. red wine, or rice wine, vinegar

30 drops liquid stevia

1 Tbsp. extra-virgin olive oil

3 Tbsp. water

¼ cup mayonnaise

1 Tbsp. prepared mustard

1. Combine broccoli, raspberries, onion, and peanuts in a large bowl.

2. In a separate bowl, combine dressing ingredients—vinegar, stevia, oil, water, mayonnaise, and mustard. Blend well.

3. Pour dressing over broccoli mix. Toss well.

4. Cover and chill at least 1 hour before serving.

- Calories 166
- Fat 14
- Sodium 81
- Carbs 10
- Sugar 5
- Protein 3

Cauliflower-Broccoli Salad

Melanie Thrower
McPherson, KS

Makes 4–5 servings
Prep. Time: 15 minutes

½ small head (about 1½ cups) cauliflower, chopped

½ bunch (about 1½ cups) broccoli, chopped

¼ cup raspberries

¼ cup shelled and lightly salted sunflower seeds

½ cup keto-friendly Italian dressing

1. Mix all ingredients together in a large bowl and serve.

- Calories 94
- Fat 7
- Sodium 154
- Carbs 7
- Sugar 3
- Protein 3

Trees & Seeds Salad

Nanci Keatley
Salem, OR

Makes 10 servings (¾ cup each)
Prep. Time: 10–20 minutes
Chilling Time: 30 minutes

4 cups cauliflower florets

3 cups cut-up broccoli

1 cup diced red onion

2 pts. cherry tomatoes, halved

8 slices bacon, cooked and diced

3 Tbsp. sesame seeds

¼ cup sunflower seeds

¼ cup slivered almonds

Dressing:

1 cup mayonnaise

4 Tbsp. granulated Splenda

3 Tbsp. cider vinegar

½ tsp. salt

½ tsp. pepper

1. In a large serving bowl, combine cauliflower, broccoli, onion, tomatoes, bacon, seeds, and nuts.

2. In a separate bowl, mix together mayonnaise, Splenda, vinegar, salt, and pepper. Pour over vegetables.

3. Refrigerate at least 30 minutes to blend flavors.

- Calories 159
- Fat 9
- Sodium 300
- Carbs 15
- Sugar 9
- Protein 6

Marinated Garden Tomatoes

Bonnie Goering
Bridgewater, VA

Makes 10 servings (¾ cup each)
Prep. Time: 10 minutes
Chilling Time: 1 hour or more

6 large firm tomatoes, cut in wedges

½ cup sliced onion

½ cup sliced green bell pepper

¼ cup olive oil

2 Tbsp. red wine vinegar

¼ tsp. garlic powder

½ tsp. salt

¼ tsp. pepper

1 Tbsp. granulated Splenda

2 Tbsp. minced fresh parsley, or 2 tsp. parsley flakes

1 Tbsp. snipped fresh thyme, or 1 tsp. dried thyme

1. Arrange tomatoes, onion, and pepper in a flat dish.

2. In a jar with a tight-fitting lid, mix together oil, vinegar, garlic powder, salt, pepper, and Splenda. Pour over vegetables.

3. In a small bowl, combine parsley and thyme and sprinkle on top.

4. Refrigerate for one hour or more before serving.

- Calories 73
- Fat 6
- Sodium 101
- Carbs 5
- Sugar 4
- Protein 1

Marinated Sliced Tomatoes

Dawn Alderfer
Oley, PA

Makes 6 servings
Prep. Time: 10 minutes
Chilling Time: 3–12 hours

6 medium tomatoes, sliced

⅔ cup olive oil

¼ cup vinegar

¼ cup minced fresh parsley

15 drops liquid stevia

2 tsp. fresh marjoram, or ¾ tsp. dried marjoram

1 tsp. salt

¼ tsp. pepper

1. Place tomatoes in a large bowl.

2. Combine oil, vinegar, parsley, stevia, marjoram, salt, and pepper in a container with a tight-fitting lid. Shake well.

3. Pour over tomatoes. Chill for several hours or overnight, spooning dressing over tomatoes at least twice.

4. To serve, use a slotted spoon to lift tomatoes out of marinade. Lay on a platter.

- Calories 245
- Fat 24
- Sodium 328
- Carbs 7
- Sugar 5
- Protein 1

Tomato Salad

Ruth Fisher
Leicester, NY

Makes 12 servings
Prep. Time: 25 minutes
Chilling Time: 3–4 hours

6 ripe tomatoes, diced

3 sweet bell peppers, sliced (try a red, a green, and a yellow for color)

1 red onion, sliced thin

1 cup pitted black olives

⅔ cup olive oil

¼ cup apple cider vinegar

¼ cup fresh parsley

¼ cup chopped green onions

¼ tsp. pepper

10 drops liquid stevia

¼ tsp. dried basil

1. Combine all vegetables in a large mixing bowl.

2. Mix remaining ingredients together in a separate bowl.

3. Pour dressing over vegetables. Mix thoroughly.

4. Cover and refrigerate 3–4 hours.

- Calories 139
- Fat 13
- Sodium 90
- Carbs 6
- Sugar 3
- Protein 1

Super Simple Tomato Salad

Doris Bachman
Putnam, IL

Makes 3 servings
Prep. Time: 15 minutes

2 tomatoes, peeled or unpeeled

1 green pepper

1 small onion

Tomato Salad Dressing (optional):
1 Tbsp. vinegar

2 Tbsp. lemon juice

15 drops liquid stevia

salt and pepper, to taste

1. Chop tomatoes, pepper, and onion. As you do, place in a mixing bowl.

2. Stir together gently.

3. If desired, assemble dressing by placing all dressing ingredients in jar with tightly fitting lid.

4. Cover and shake until well blended.

5. Pour dressing over vegetables.

- Calories 33
- Fat 0
- Sodium 166
- Carbs 7
- Sugar 4
- Protein 1

Bulgarian Salad

Gail Martin
Elkhart, IN

Makes 2 servings
Prep. Time: 8–10 minutes

1 tomato, diced
2 green onions, chopped
¼ cup chopped parsley
½ green bell pepper, chopped, *optional*
salt and pepper, *optional*
keto-friendly vinaigrette dressing
Bulgarian, or other, feta cheese

1. Mound tomato, green onions, and parsley on 2 salad plates. Add chopped green pepper if you wish.

2. Sprinkle with salt and pepper if you wish.

3. Drizzle with dressing.

4. Crumble feta over top.

- Calories 25
- Fat 0
- Sodium 250
- Carbs 5
- Sugar 3
- Protein 1

Quick Greek Salad

Melanie Mohler
Ephrata, PA

Makes 4 cups
Prep. Time: 10 minutes

3–4 tomatoes
1–2 cucumbers
4-oz. pkg. feta cheese, crumbled
drizzle olive oil
pepper

1. Chop tomatoes and cucumbers. Place in large bowl.

2. Toss with crumbled feta cheese.

3. Drizzle with olive oil.

4. Season with pepper.

5. Toss again and serve immediately.

- Calories 129
- Fat 10
- Sodium 266
- Carbs 6
- Sugar 5
- Protein 5

Refreshing Cucumber Salad

Kathy Alderfer
Broadway, VA

Makes 4 servings (¾ cup each)
Prep. Time: 15 minutes
Chilling Time: 1 hour

¼ cup mayonnaise

¼ cup sour cream

15 drops liquid stevia

1 Tbsp. vinegar

1 tsp. dill weed

salt and pepper, to taste

2 6-oz. cucumbers, thinly sliced (to make 3 cups)

1 cup grape tomatoes, halved

2–4 small green onions, sliced into rings, amount according to your preference

1. In a medium-sized mixing bowl, mix mayonnaise, sour cream, stevia, vinegar, dill, salt, and pepper. Blend thoroughly.

2. Add cucumbers, tomatoes, and green onions to creamy mixture and stir together.

3. Allow to marinate in refrigerator for at least 1 hour before serving.

- Calories 141
- Fat 13
- Sodium 217
- Carbs 6
- Sugar 3
- Protein 1

Cucumber Salad

Doris Beachy
Stevens, PA

Makes 6 servings
Prep. Time: 10 minutes
Chilling Time: 6 hours

2 large cucumbers

small onion

1 tsp. salt

2 cups vinegar

1 cup water

3 tsp. liquid stevia

1. Slice cucumbers and onion in thin slices into large bowl.

2. Stir in salt. Let stand 3–4 minutes.

3. In a separate bowl, mix vinegar, water, and stevia together until well blended.

4. Pour dressing over cucumbers. Cover with lid.

5. Refrigerate for 6 hours to allow dressing to penetrate the cucumbers.

- Calories 86
- Fat 0
- Sodium 342
- Carbs 17
- Sugar 14
- Protein 1

Old-Fashioned Cucumber Salad

Laraine Good
Bernville, PA

Makes 4 servings
Prep. Time: 10 minutes
Chilling Time: 30 minutes

2 large cucumbers, peeled and sliced

2 Tbsp. sliced onion

¼ cup heavy cream

1½ Tbsp. vinegar

dash salt

15 drops liquid stevia

¼ cup mayonnaise

1. Combine cucumbers and onion in a dish.

2. In another bowl, mix cream, vinegar, salt, stevia, and mayonnaise. Stir well. Pour over veggies.

3. Refrigerate 30 minutes before serving.

- Calories 161
- Fat 16
- Sodium 154
- Carbs 4
- Sugar 2
- Protein 1

Sour Cream Cucumber Salad

Mary Jones
Marengo, OH

Makes 6 servings (about 5 oz. per serving)
Prep. Time: 20–30 minutes

3 medium cucumbers, about 9 oz. each, unpeeled and sliced thinly

½ tsp. salt

½ cup finely chopped green onion

1 Tbsp. white vinegar

dash pepper, *optional*

¼ cup sour cream

1. Sprinkle cucumber with salt. Let stand 15 minutes. Drain liquid.

2. Add green onions, vinegar, and pepper, if using.

3. Just before serving, stir in sour cream.

- Calories 35
- Fat 2
- Sodium 166
- Carbs 5
- Sugar 2
- Protein 1

Marinated Cucumbers

Clarice Williams
Fairbank, IA

Makes 4 servings
Prep. Time: 15 minutes
Chilling Time: 2–24 hours

¼ cup water

15 drops liquid stevia

3 Tbsp. vinegar

2 tsp. olive oil

½ tsp. dried basil, crushed

⅛ tsp. pepper

several dashes bottled hot pepper sauce

2 medium cucumbers, thinly sliced (about 3 cups)

1 small onion, thinly sliced

½ cup sliced radishes

4 lettuce leaves, *optional*

1. In a medium mixing bowl, stir together water, stevia, vinegar, oil, basil, pepper, and hot pepper sauce.

2. Add cucumbers and onion. Toss to coat.

3. Cover and refrigerate 2–24 hours.

4. Just before serving, toss radishes with cucumbers and onion.

5. Serve on lettuce-lined plates, if you wish.

- Calories 62
- Fat 2
- Sodium 17
- Carbs 10
- Sugar 5
- Protein 1

Cucumber Salad with Cumin

Kim Patrick
Norwood, PA

Makes 6 servings
Prep. Time: 30 minutes

2 Tbsp. mayonnaise

juice of 1 lemon

zest of 1 lemon

1 tsp. cumin seeds, toasted

5–10 drops liquid stevia

¼ tsp. salt

2 peeled cucumbers, seeded and sliced

1. Whisk mayonnaise, lemon juice, lemon zest, cumin seeds, stevia, and salt together.

2. Toss over sliced cucumbers.

- Calories 49
- Fat 4
- Sodium 112
- Carbs 4
- Sugar 2
- Protein 1

Barb's Fresh Pickles

Carna Reitz
Remington, VA

Makes 1–2 cups
Prep. Time: 5–10 minutes
Chilling Time: 1–24 hours

½ cup white vinegar

½ cup water

1 tsp. liquid stevia

1 tsp. dill weed

1–2 cucumbers, sliced about ¼-inch thick

1. Mix first 3 ingredients in a medium-sized mixing bowl. Stir.

2. Mix in dill and cucumber slices.

3. Cover. Refrigerate for at least 1 hour for lightly flavored pickles, or up to 1 day for more pickled pickles.

Tip: When the pickle slices are all eaten, you can use the leftover liquid for up to 3 more batches of fresh pickles.

- Calories 6
- Fat 0
- Sodium
- Carbs 1
- Sugar 0
- Protein 0

Fresh Pickles

Arleta Petersheim
Haven, KS

Makes about 5 cups
Prep. Time: 15 minutes
Chilling Time: 8 hours, or overnight

6 small to medium-sized cucumbers

1 cup water

¼ cup vinegar

1 Tbsp. salt

1 tsp. liquid stevia

1. Wash, peel, and slice fresh cucumbers into ¼-inch-thick slices.

2. In a small bowl, mix other ingredients together. Pour over sliced cucumbers.

3. Cover. Refrigerate 8 hours, or overnight.

Tip: Add some onion slices to the brine for more flavor.

- Calories 5
- Fat 0
- Sodium 97
- Carbs 1
- Sugar 0.5
- Protein 0

New Dill Slices

Mary E. Wheatley
Mashpee, MA

Makes 4-5 cups
Prep. Time: 20-30 minutes
Standing Time: 1 hour
Chilling Time: 1-8 hours, or overnight

4-6 medium-sized pickling cucumbers (about 1 lb.)

1 Tbsp., plus 1 tsp., kosher salt, *divided*

cold water

3 Tbsp. cider vinegar

½ tsp. dill seed

1 clove garlic, thinly sliced

bay leaf and fresh dill sprigs, *optional*

1. Cut cucumbers into ⅛-inch-thick slices.

2. In a large bowl, toss cucumbers with 1 Tbsp. salt. Let stand 1 hour, tossing occasionally. Rinse and drain 3 times with cold water.

3. Meanwhile, in a saucepan, combine vinegar with dill seed, garlic, 1 tsp. salt, and 1 cup water, along with bay leaf, if used. Bring to boil. Boil 1 minute. Cool to room temperature.

4. With your hands, squeeze out excess moisture from pickle slices. Place in a small (glass) bowl. Add fresh dill sprigs, if you wish, and cooled brine.

5. Cover. Refrigerate for at least 1 hour before serving, or for 8 hours, or overnight.

- Calories 5
- Fat 0
- Sodium 97
- Carbs 1
- Sugar 0
- Protein 0

Green Bean Salad

Jean H. Robinson
Cinnaminson, NJ

Makes 8 servings (¾ cup each)
Prep. Time: 20 minutes
Cooking Time: 10 minutes
Chilling Time: 2 hours

4 cups water

1 Tbsp. salt

2 lbs. fresh green beans, cut into 2-inch pieces

1 stalk celery, chopped fine

½ cup chopped green onion

2 cups cherry tomatoes, halved

½ cup feta cheese

Dressing:
6 Tbsp. olive oil

2 Tbsp. rice vinegar

1 tsp. Dijon mustard

salt, to taste

pepper, to taste

1. Bring water and salt to a boil in a large stockpot. Place beans into boiling water and cook for 6 minutes. Remove from stove and drain. Plunge beans immediately into ice water. Drain.

2. In a large mixing bowl, combine beans, celery, onion, tomatoes, and cheese.

3. In a jar with a tight-fitting lid, combine oil, vinegar, mustard, salt, and pepper. Shake well.

4. Pour dressing over bean mixture. Toss.

5. Chill for at least 2 hours before serving.

- Calories 160
- Fat 12
- Sodium 894
- Carbs 10
- Sugar 5
- Protein 4

Colorful Bean Salad

Patricia Eckard
Singers Glen, VA

Betty B. Dennison
Grove City, PA

Makes 6 servings (¾ cup each)
Prep. Time: 30 minutes
Cooking Time: 5 minutes
Chilling Time: 2–8 hours, or overnight

2 15-oz. can green beans, drained

2 15-oz. can wax beans, drained

1 medium-sized red onion, chopped

4-oz. jar pimentos, drained

½ cup chopped celery

½ cup chopped red bell pepper

Dressing:
¾ cup apple cider vinegar

½ cup granulated Splenda

1. Mix all vegetables together in a large bowl.

2. Combine vinegar and granulated Splenda in a small saucepan. Bring to a boil. Boil for 3 minutes, stirring occasionally.

3. Pour over vegetables. Cover and refrigerate 2–8 hours, or overnight.

- Calories 112
- Fat 1
- Sodium 23
- Carbs 25
- Sugar 12
- Protein 6

Green Bean and Walnut Salad

Mary E. Wheatley
Mashpee, MA

Makes 4 servings (about 3¾ oz. per serving)
Prep. Time: 20 minutes
Cooking Time: 5–7 minutes

¾ lb. fresh green beans, trimmed

¼ cup walnut pieces

3 Tbsp. finely chopped fresh parsley

3 Tbsp. finely chopped onion

1 Tbsp. walnut or olive oil

1½ tsp. red wine vinegar

1 tsp. Dijon mustard

salt, to taste

freshly ground pepper, to taste

1. Steam beans in basket over boiling water for 4 minutes. Transfer to a medium serving bowl.

2. Toast walnuts in a small dry skillet, stirring frequently until fragrant, 3–5 minutes. Chop the toasted walnuts finely.

3. Stir parsley and onion into walnuts.

4. Whisk together oil, vinegar, and mustard. Add to green beans. Season with salt and pepper and top with walnut mixture.

5. Serve warm or at room temperature.

Tip: Pecans or almonds can be substituted for the walnuts.

- Calories 108
- Fat 8
- Sodium 15
- Carbs 8
- Sugar 3
- Protein 3

Grilled Vegetable Salad

Jana Beyer
Harrisonburg, VA

Makes 6-8 servings
Prep. Time: 20 minutes
Cooking Time: 10 minutes

1 red onion, sliced

1 eggplant, sliced

2 red bell peppers, cut into rings

1 medium zucchini, sliced

1 medium yellow squash, sliced

10-15 asparagus spears

¼ cup olive oil

salt, to taste

freshly ground pepper, to taste

4-6 cups torn mixed greens

¼ cup balsamic vinegar

¼ cup chopped fresh basil

1. Brush onion, eggplant, peppers, zucchini, squash, and asparagus with oil. Sprinkle with salt and pepper.

2. Grill onion, eggplant, and peppers 8–10 minutes over medium heat, until vegetables are softened and have grill marks.

3. Grill zucchini, squash, and asparagus for 5–6 minutes.

4. Set aside to cool to room temperature or put on the salads while hot.

5. Divide greens between 6–8 salad plates. Arrange grilled vegetables on top of greens.

6. Drizzle with balsamic vinegar. Sprinkle with basil. Serve immediately.

- Calories 95
- Fat 7
- Sodium 71
- Carbs 7
- Sugar 4
- Protein 2

24-Hour Salad

Elaine Martin
Palmerston, ON

Makes 12 servings
Prep. Time: 15 minutes
Chilling Time: 12–24 hours

1 head romaine lettuce

1½ cups cauliflower florets

1 red onion, sliced

½ cup grated Parmesan cheese

30 drops liquid stevia

1 cup mayonnaise

1. Tear lettuce into bite-sized pieces. Place in a bowl.

2. Layer cauliflower and onion on top.

3. Mix Parmesan cheese, stevia, and mayonnaise together.

4. Spread on top of vegetables. Cover. Refrigerate for 12 hours and up to 24 hours.

5. Toss before serving.

- Calories 148
- Fat 15
- Sodium 183
- Carbs 3
- Sugar 1
- Protein 2

Marinated Mushrooms

Lisa Harnish
Christiana, PA

Makes 12 servings (4–5 mushrooms per serving)
Prep. Time: 10 minutes
Cooking Time: 20 minutes

2 lbs. (50–60) medium-sized fresh mushrooms

2 cloves garlic

1 cup red wine vinegar

1 cup water

½ cup olive oil

1 bay leaf

1 tsp. salt

½ tsp. dried thyme leaves

12 whole black peppercorns

fresh parsley

1. Clean mushrooms and set aside.

2. Flatten garlic or use garlic press.

3. In Dutch oven, combine all ingredients except mushrooms and parsley.

4. Bring to a boil. Reduce heat and simmer 5 minutes.

5. Add mushrooms and simmer uncovered 10 minutes.

6. Remove from heat and let stand until cooled slightly.

7. Transfer mushrooms and marinade to a storage container. Cover and refrigerate until ready to serve.

8. To serve, remove mushrooms from marinade and place in serving dish. Garnish with fresh parsley.

- Calories 110
- Fat 9
- Sodium 176
- Carbs 5
- Sugar 1
- Protein 3

Tuna Salad

Frances Schrag
Newton, KS

Makes 4 servings (¾ cup each)
Prep. Time: 15 minutes

6-oz. packed-in-water can tuna, drained

3 hard-boiled eggs, diced

2 Tbsp. chopped onion

3 Tbsp. chopped pickle

½ cup chopped celery

⅛ tsp. salt

⅛ tsp. pepper

2 Tbsp. mayonnaise

1. Combine all ingredients in a good-sized mixing bowl.

Serving suggestion: Serve over lettuce.

- Calories 193
- Fat 13
- Sodium 402
- Carbs 1
- Sugar 1
- Protein 17

Super Simple Tuna Salad

Vera Martin
East Earl, PA

Makes 2–3 servings
Prep. Time: 15 minutes

6-oz. can tuna, drained and flaked

1 Tbsp. mayonnaise

1½ tsp. onion flakes

salt and pepper, to taste

lettuce leaves

green pepper, *optional*

radish, *optional*

1. Combine tuna, mayonnaise, onion flakes, salt, and pepper to taste in a medium-sized bowl.

2. When ready to serve, place lettuce leaves on a plate and put tuna mixture in center of lettuce.

3. If you wish, place pepper rings and radish roses around the tuna salad.

- Calories 146
- Fat 8
- Sodium 425
- Carbs 1
- Sugar 0.5
- Protein 17

Albacore Tuna Stuffed Tomato

Joe Barker
Carlsbad, NM

Makes 8 servings (2 tomato halves each)
Prep. Time: 1 hour

8 4-oz. Roma tomatoes
2 6-oz. packed-in-water cans albacore tuna, drained
1 Tbsp. mayonnaise
½ tsp. prepared mustard
1½ tsp. keto-friendly blue cheese dressing
2 tsp. thinly sliced green onion
1½ tsp. chopped chives
1½ tsp. chopped black olives
1½ tsp. chopped cucumber
1½ tsp. chopped red bell pepper
1½ tsp. chopped yellow bell pepper
celery leaves, for garnish
paprika, for garnish
6–8 mint leaves, for garnish

1. Cut tomatoes in half and remove seeds and veins. Keep for another use. Keep the tomato shells cool.

2. Mix remaining ingredients except garnish together in a bowl.

3. Stuff tomato halves with tuna mixture. Arrange on a bed of celery leaves.

4. Sprinkle paprika lightly over top.

5. Garnish each tomato with a mint leaf.

6. Keep cold until ready to serve.

- Calories 130
- Fat 9
- Sodium 207
- Carbs 3
- Sugar 2
- Protein 8

Avocado Egg Salad

Melanie Mohler
Ephrata, PA

Makes 4 servings
Prep. Time: 10 minutes

4 eggs, hard-boiled and chopped (reserve 2 yolks for another use)
1 large avocado, chopped
pepper, to taste
2 Tbsp. lemon juice
⅛ tsp. garlic powder, *optional*

1. In a serving bowl, combine eggs and avocado.

2. Sprinkle with pepper, lemon juice, and garlic powder. Stir gently.

3. Use as topping for crackers or as sandwich filling. Eat immediately or store in fridge.

- Calories 138
- Fat 11
- Sodium 65
- Carbs 4
- Sugar 1
- Protein 7

Desserts & Beverages

Lemon Pudding Cake

Jean Butzer
Batavia, NY

Makes 6 servings
Prep. Time: 30 minutes
Cooking Time: 2–3 hours
Ideal slow-cooker size: 3- or 4-qt.

3 eggs, separated

1 tsp. grated lemon peel

¼ cup lemon juice

1 Tbsp. butter

1½ cups heavy cream

15 packets stevia

¼ cup almond flour

⅛ tsp. salt

1. Beat egg whites until stiff peaks form. Set aside.

2. Beat egg yolks. Blend in lemon peel, lemon juice, butter, and heavy cream.

3. In a separate bowl, combine stevia, almond flour, and salt. Add to egg-lemon mixture, beating until smooth.

4. Fold into beaten egg whites.

5. Spoon into slow cooker.

6. Cover and cook on High 2–3 hours.

- Calories 286
- Fat 28
- Sodium 94
- Carbs 4
- Sugar 3
- Protein 6

Hot Fudge Cake

Maricarol Magil
Freehold, NJ

Makes 10 servings
Prep. Time: 25 minutes
Cooking Time: 2–3 hours
Ideal slow-cooker size: 4-qt.

1¼ cups Sukrin Gold, *divided*

1 cup almond flour

¼ cup plus 3 Tbsp. unsweetened cocoa powder, *divided*

2 tsp. baking powder

½ tsp. salt

½ cup heavy cream

2 Tbsp. melted butter

½ tsp. vanilla extract

1¾ cups boiling water

1. Mix together ¾ cup Sukrin Gold, almond flour, 3 Tbsp. cocoa, baking powder, and salt.

2. Stir in heavy cream, butter, and vanilla. Spread over the bottom of slow cooker.

3. Mix together ½ cup Sukrin Gold and ¼ cup cocoa. Sprinkle over mixture in slow cooker.

4. Pour in boiling water. Do not stir.

5. Cover and cook on High 2–3 hours, or until a toothpick inserted comes out clean.

- Calories 253
- Fat 13
- Sodium 178
- Carbs 29
- Sugar 25
- Protein 3

Peanut Butter and Hot Fudge Pudding Cake

Bernadette Veenstra
Rockford, MI

Makes 12 servings (3x3¼-inch rectangle each)
Prep. Time: 15 minutes
Baking Time: 30 minutes

1 cup almond flour

¾ cup Splenda Sugar Blend, *divided*

1½ tsp. Low-Carb Baking Powder (see recipe on right)

⅔ cup whole milk

2 Tbsp. coconut oil, melted

1 tsp. vanilla extract

7 Tbsp. no-sugar-added peanut butter

6 Tbsp. cocoa powder

2 cups hot water

1. In a large mixing bowl, mix together flour, ¼ cup sugar blend, and baking powder.

2. Add milk, oil, and vanilla. Stir until smooth.

3. Stir in peanut butter.

4. Place mixture in a greased 9x13-inch baking pan.

5. In a small bowl, combine ½ cup sugar blend and cocoa powder. Sprinkle on top.

6. Pour water over everything.

7. Bake at 400°F for 30 minutes.

- Calories 197
- Fat 12
- Sodium 65
- Carbs 18
- Sugar 14
- Protein 5

Low-Carb Baking Powder

Hope Comerford
Clinton Township, MI

Makes 3 Tbsp.
Prep. Time: 3 minutes

1 Tbsp. baking soda

2 Tbsp. cream of tartar

1. Mix all ingredients and store in an airtight container.

- Calories 1
- Fat 0
- Sodium 210
- Carbs 0
- Sugar 0
- Protein 0

Lotsa Chocolate Almond Cake

Hope Comerford
Clinton Township, MI

SLOW COOKER

Makes 10 servings
Prep. Time: 10 minutes
Cooking Time: 3 hours
Cooling Time: 30 minutes
Ideal slow-cooker size: 6-qt.

1½ cups almond flour

18 packets stevia

⅔ cup unsweetened cocoa powder

¼ cup keto-friendly chocolate protein powder

2 tsp. baking powder

¼ tsp. salt

½ cup coconut oil, melted

4 eggs

¾ cup unsweetened almond milk

1 tsp. vanilla extract

1 tsp. almond extract

¾ cup chopped 90% dark chocolate

1. Cover any hot spot of your crock with aluminum foil and spray crock with nonstick spray.

2. In a bowl, mix together the almond flour, stevia, cocoa powder, protein powder, baking powder, and salt.

3. In a different bowl, mix together the coconut oil, eggs, almond milk, and vanilla and almond extracts.

4. Pour wet ingredients into dry ingredients and mix until well-combined. Stir in chopped chocolate.

5. Pour cake mix into crock. Cover and cook on Low for 3 hours.

6. Turn the slow cooker off when the cooking time is over and let the cake cool in the crock for 30 minutes.

7. Place a plate or platter over the crock, then turn the crock upside down on the plate, so the cake releases onto the plate or platter.

- Calories 413
- Fat 31
- Sodium 192
- Carbs 25
- Sugar 9
- Protein 11

Fudgy Secret Brownies

Juanita Weaver
Johnsonville, IL

Makes 8 servings
Prep. Time: 10 minutes
Cooking Time: 1½–2 hours
Ideal slow-cooker size: 6-or 7-qt.

4 oz. unsweetened chocolate

¾ cup coconut oil

¾ cup frozen diced okra, partially thawed

3 large eggs

36 stevia packets

1 tsp. pure vanilla extract

¼ tsp. mineral salt

¾ cup coconut flour

½–¾ cup coarsely chopped walnuts or pecans,
optional

1. Melt chocolate and coconut oil in small saucepan

2. Put okra and eggs in blender. Blend until smooth.

3. Measure all other ingredients in mixing bowl.

4. Pour melted chocolate and okra over the dry ingredients and stir with fork just until mixed.

5. Pour into greased slow cooker.

6. Cover and cook on High for 1½–2 hours.

- Calories 421
- Fat 38
- Sodium 113
- Carbs 15
- Sugar 1
- Protein 8

Black and Blue Cobbler

Renee Shirk
Mount Joy, PA

Makes 6 servings
Prep. Time: 20 minutes
Cooking Time: 2–2½ hours
Ideal slow-cooker size: 5-qt.

1 cup almond flour

36 packets stevia, *divided*

1 tsp. Low-Carb Baking Powder (see recipe on pg. 305)

¼ tsp. salt

¼ tsp. cinnamon

¼ tsp. nutmeg

2 eggs, beaten

2 Tbsp. whole milk

2 Tbsp. coconut oil, melted

2 cups fresh, or frozen, blueberries

2 cups fresh, or frozen, blackberries

¾ cup water

1 tsp. grated orange peel

1. Combine almond flour, 18 packets stevia, baking powder, salt, cinnamon, and nutmeg.

2. Combine eggs, milk, and oil. Stir into dry ingredients until moistened.

3. Spread the batter evenly over bottom of greased slow cooker.

4. In a saucepan, combine berries, water, orange peel, and remaining 18 packets stevia. Bring to boil. Remove from heat and pour over batter. Cover.

5. Cook on High 2–2½ hours, or until toothpick inserted into batter comes out clean. Turn off cooker.

6. Uncover and let stand 30 minutes before serving.

- Calories 22
- Fat 16
- Sodium 174
- Carbs 21
- Sugar 8
- Protein 7

Berry Cobbler

Eileen Eash
Carlsbad, NM

June S. Groff
Denver, PA

Sharon Wantland
Menomonee Falls, WI

Makes 10 servings
Prep. Time: 30 minutes
Baking Time: 60–70 minutes

8 cups sliced fresh, or frozen, mixed berries (raspberries, blackberries, strawberries)
8 Tbsp. (1 stick) butter, softened
4½ Tbsp. granulated stevia
1 cup almond flour
¼ tsp. cinnamon mixed with ¼ tsp. granulated stevia

1. Place berries in ungreased 9×13-inch baking dish.

2. In a medium-sized mixing bowl, cream butter and stevia together, either with a spoon or an electric mixer.

3. Add flour and mix well. Sprinkle over berries.

4. Top with cinnamon-stevia mix.

5. Bake at 325°F for 60–70 minutes, or until top is golden brown.

6. Serve warm with milk or keto-friendly ice cream, if you wish.

- Calories 183
- Fat 15
- Sodium 6
- Carbs 12
- Sugar 6
- Protein 3

Fresh Berry Cobbler

Abbie Christie
Berkeley Heights, NJ

Makes 8 servings (4½x2¼-inch rectangle each)
Prep. Time: 10 minutes
Baking Time: 45–50 minutes

1 Tbsp. butter
3 Tbsp. coconut oil, melted
1 cup almond flour
1 cup whole milk
½ cup Splenda Sugar Blend
2 tsp. Low-Carb Baking Powder (recipe on pg. 305)
dash salt
3-4 cups fresh berries

1. Preheat oven to 350°F.

2. Melt butter in a greased 9x9-inch baking dish.

3. Add all other ingredients except fruit. Stir well.

4. Arrange fruit on top of dough.

5. Bake 40–55 minutes, or until lightly browned and fruit is tender.

6. Serve warm with keto-friendly ice cream or milk.

- Calories 210
- Fat 11
- Sodium 124
- Carbs 22
- Sugar 18
- Protein 4

Raspberry Almond Bars

Phyllis Good
Lancaster, PA SLOW COOKER

Makes 24 servings
Prep. Time: 20–30 minutes
Cooking Time: 2½–3 hours
Ideal slow-cooker size: oval 6-qt.

1½ cups almond flour

¼ cup flaxseed

12 packets stevia

8 Tbsp. (1 stick) butter, softened

½ tsp. almond extract

½ cup low-carb, no-sugar raspberry preserves

⅓ cup sliced almonds

1. Grease interior of slow cooker crock.

2. In a large bowl, combine flour, flaxseed, and stevia.

3. Cut in butter with a pastry cutter or two knives—or your fingers—until mixture forms coarse crumbs.

4. Stir in extract until well blended.

5. Set aside 1 cup crumbs.

6. Press remaining crumbs into bottom of crock.

7. Spread preserves over crust to within ½ inch of the edges (the preserves could burn if they touch the hot crock).

8. In a small bowl, combine reserved 1 cup crumbs with almonds. Sprinkle evenly over preserves, pressing down gently to hold the almonds in place.

9. Cover. Bake on High for 2½–3 hours, or until firm in center.

10. Uncover. Lift crock onto wire baking rack to cool.

11. When room temperature, cut bars into 20 squares and 4 triangles in the corners.

TIP: Watch for the raspberry preserves to ooze out around the edges as these bars bake!

- Calories 97
- Fat 8
- Sodium 123
- Carbs 4
- Sugar 0
- Protein 3

Lemon Almond Torte

Kathy Hertzler
Lancaster, PA

Makes 12 servings
Prep. Time: 15–20 minutes
Baking Time: 50 minutes
Cooling Time: 15 minutes

1 Tbsp. butter, softened

1 Tbsp. coconut oil, melted

1½ Tbsp. water

½ cup Splenda Sugar Blend

1½ cups finely ground almonds, *divided*

4 eggs

1 tsp. vanilla extract

1 tsp. lemon extract

1 tsp. almond extract

1 Tbsp. grated lemon rind

1 cup almond flour

1 tsp. Low-Carb Baking Powder (recipe on pg. 305)

¼ tsp. salt

¼ cup fresh lemon juice

Glaze:
¼ cup fresh lemon juice

1½–2 cups Swerve confectioners' sugar

10 whole almonds, *optional*

1. In a large electric mixing bowl, cream together butter, oil, water, Splenda, and 1 cup finely ground almonds until fluffy. Add a little water during this process if it becomes crumbly

2. Add eggs and beat well.

3. Add 3 extracts and lemon rind. Beat again to incorporate.

4. In a separate mixing bowl, stir together flour, baking powder, and salt. Add to creamed mixture alternately with lemon juice.

5. Spoon batter into a greased and almond-floured 8-inch springform pan.

6. Bake at 350°F for 50 minutes. Cool for 15 minutes. Release springform pan.

7. While cake is still warm, and with the pan sides removed, whisk together lemon juice and confectioners' sugar to make the glaze.

8. Spread glaze generously over top and sides of cake. Sprinkle remaining ground almonds over glaze while it is still wet. Garnish with whole almonds if you wish.

- Calories 271
- Fat 19
- Sodium 143
- Carbs 17
- Sugar 12
- Protein 8

Cheesecake

Sharon Shank
Bridgewater, VA

Makes 8 servings
Prep. Time: 15 minutes
Cooling Time: 2–3 hours

2 Tbsp. cold water

1 envelope unflavored gelatin

2 Tbsp. lemon juice

½ cup whole milk, heated almost to boiling

1 egg

½ tsp. liquid stevia

1 tsp. vanilla extract

2 cups cottage cheese

lemon zest, *optional*

1. Combine water, gelatin, and lemon juice in blender container. Process on low speed 1–2 minutes to soften gelatin.

2. Add hot milk, processing until gelatin is dissolved.

3. Add egg, stevia, vanilla, and cottage cheese to blender container. Process on high speed until smooth.

4. Pour into 9-inch pie plate or round flat dish.

5. Refrigerate 2–3 hours.

6. If you wish, top with grated lemon zest just before serving.

- Calories 87
- Fat 3
- Sodium 202
- Carbs 7
- Sugar 6
- Protein 7

Berries Jubilee

Hope Comerford
Clinton Township, MI

Makes 4 servings
Prep. Time: 15 minutes
Cooking Time: 3–4 hours
Ideal slow-cooker size: 2-to- 3-qt.

1 lb. fresh cherries, pitted

¼ cup erythritol

1 tsp. lemon juice

1 tsp. lemon zest

1 tsp. vanilla extract

⅓ cup rum

2 Tbsp. flaxseed

2 Tbsp. water

1. Spray crock with nonstick spray.

2. Place cherries in crock with erythritol, lemon juice, lemon zest, vanilla, and rum.

3. Mix together the flaxseed and water, then stir this into the contents of the crock.

4. Cook on Low for 3–4 hours.

- Calories 254
- Fat 3
- Sodium 6
- Carbs 52
- Sugar 11
- Protein 5

Slow Cooker Crème Brûlée

Phyllis Good
Lancaster, PA

Makes 4–6 servings
Prep. Time: 20 minutes
Cooking Time: 2–4 hours
Chilling Time: 5 hours
Ideal slow-cooker size: oval 6-qt.

5 egg yolks

2 cups heavy cream

¼ cup erythritol

1 Tbsp. high-quality vanilla extract

pinch salt

2 Tbsp. powdered erythritol

fresh berries, for garnish

1. Get a baking dish that fits in your slow cooker. Put it in the slow cooker and pour water around it until the water comes halfway up the sides of the dish. Push the dish down if you need to (as it would be when it's full of the crème brûlée), to see the water level. Remove the dish and set aside.

2. In a medium mixing bowl, beat egg yolks.

3. Slowly pour in cream and erythritol while mixing. Add vanilla and salt.

4. Pour mixture into the baking dish.

5. Carefully place dish into water in slow cooker, being careful not to get water in the cream mixture.

6. Cover cooker and cook on High for 2–4 hours, until set but still a little jiggly in the middle.

7. Very carefully remove hot dish from hot slow cooker and let it cool on the counter. Refrigerate for 2 hours.

8. Sprinkle the powdered erythritol evenly over the top. Broil for 3–10 minutes, until the sugar is bubbly and browning. Watch carefully! Or if you own a kitchen torch, use that instead to caramelize the sugar.

9. Return crème brûlée to refrigerator for at least 2 more hours. Serve cold with a few beautiful berries to garnish.

Tip: This is a perfect summer dessert if you don't have an ice-cream maker but still want to make something cold and creamy.

- Calories 323
- Fat 33
- Sodium 29
- Carbs 11
- Sugar 3
- Protein 5

Baked Custard

Barbara Smith
Bedford, PA

Makes 5-6 servings
Prep. Time: 10-15 minutes
Cooking Time: 2-3 hours
Ideal slow-cooker size: 4- to 5-qt.

2 cups whole milk

3 eggs, slightly beaten

2½ Tbsp., plus ¼ tsp., erythritol, *divided*

1 tsp. vanilla extract

¼ tsp. cinnamon

1. Heat milk in a small uncovered saucepan until a skin forms on top. Remove from heat and let cool slightly.

2. Meanwhile, in a large mixing bowl combine eggs, 2½ Tbsp. erythritol, and vanilla.

3. Slowly stir cooled milk into egg-erythritol mixture.

4. Pour into a greased 1-qt. baking dish that will fit into your slow cooker, or into a baking insert designed for your slow cooker.

5. Mix cinnamon and ½ tsp. reserved erythritol in a small bowl. Sprinkle over custard mixture.

6. Cover baking dish or insert with foil. Set container on a metal rack or trivet in slow cooker. Pour hot water around dish to a depth of 1 inch.

7. Cover cooker. Cook on High 2–3 hours, or until custard is set. (When blade of a knife inserted in center of custard comes out clean, custard is set.)

8. Serve warm from baking dish or insert.

Variations: Instead of the cinnamon, use ¼ tsp. nutmeg, or 1–2 Tbsp. grated coconut.

- Calories 88
- Fat 5
- Sodium 71
- Carbs 9
- Sugar 4
- Protein 6

Simple Egg Custard

Paula Winchester
Kansas City, MO

Makes 6 servings
Prep. Time: 25 minutes
Cooking Time: 2–4 hours
Ideal slow-cooker size: 6-qt.

1½ cups whole milk

1 cup half-and-half

3 eggs

3 Tbsp. erythritol

½ tsp. vanilla extract

pinch salt

1. In a mixing bowl, whisk ingredients well until smooth and totally combined.

2. Prepare slow cooker by finding a shallow oval baking dish that can fit inside. Place jar rings or lids or trivets on the floor of the crock so the baking dish is not touching the bottom or sides of the crock.

3. Pour custard liquid in baking dish. Set in crock.

4. Carefully pour water into the crock (not the baking dish!) to reach halfway up the side of the baking dish.

5. Cover slow cooker. Cook on High for 2–4 hours, or until custard is set in the middle.

6. Wearing oven gloves to protect your knuckles, remove baking dish from cooker. Allow to cool for at least 20 minutes before serving warm. May also serve chilled.

Tips: There are different ways to flavor the custard. Heat the milk and add 1 bay leaf. Allow to steep and cool. Remove bay leaf and proceed with Step 1. Alternatively, sprinkle top of custard with ½ tsp. nutmeg or cinnamon in Step 3.

Variations: May use 4–5 baking ramekins instead of 1 shallow baking dish.

Serving suggestion: Serve with fresh berries on top.

- Calories 123
- Fat 9
- Sodium 86
- Carbs 11
- Sugar 5
- Protein 6

Raspberry Custard

Phyllis Good
Lancaster, PA

Makes 6 servings
Prep. Time: 15 minutes
Cooking Time: 3–4 hours
Standing Time: 30–60 minutes
Ideal slow-cooker size: 4-qt.

5 eggs

¼ cup erythritol

½ tsp. salt

¾ cup almond flour

12-oz. can evaporated milk

1 tsp. vanilla extract

pinch cinnamon

2 Tbsp. butter

2 cups red raspberries, fresh or frozen, thawed and
    drained

1. Beat eggs, erythritol, and salt in mixing bowl until eggs no longer cling to whisk.

2. Add flour in three portions, whisking well after each addition until no lumps remain.

3. Whisk in evaporated milk, vanilla, and cinnamon.

4. Use butter to generously grease slow cooker.

5. Pour egg mixture into cooker. Sprinkle evenly with raspberries.

6. Cover and cook on Low for 3–4 hours, until set.

7. Remove lid and allow to cool for 30–60 minutes before serving. May chill before serving as well.

Variation: Of course you can use other berries in this custard, whatever you have in the freezer or find to pick.

- Calories 273
- Fat 19
- Sodium 285
- Carbs 22
- Sugar 8
- Protein 13

Pot de Crème

**Phyllis Good
Lancaster, PA**

Makes 4–6 servings
Prep. Time: 10 minutes
Cooking Time: 2–3 hours
Chilling Time: at least 2 hours
Standing Time: about 1 hour
Ideal slow-cooker size: 6-qt.

2 egg yolks

2 eggs

1 cup heavy cream

½ cup whole milk

½ cup plus 1 Tbsp. Sukrin Gold, *divided*

pinch salt

1 tsp. vanilla extract

¼ tsp. nutmeg

whipped cream, for garnish, *optional*

1. In a mixing bowl, beat egg yolks and eggs until light and frothy.

2. Add cream, milk, 1 Tbsp. Sukrin Gold, salt, vanilla, and nutmeg. Mix well.

3. Get a baking dish that fits in your slow cooker.

4. Pour mixture in baking dish and set it in slow cooker.

5. Carefully pour water around the baking dish until the water comes halfway up the sides.

6. Cover cooker. Cook on High for 2–3 hours, until pot de crème is set but still a little bit jiggly in the middle.

7. Wearing oven mitts to protect your knuckles, carefully remove hot dish from cooker. Set on wire rack to cool to room temperature.

8. Cover tightly and chill for at least 2 hours before serving. Garnish with whipped cream if you wish.

Note: Want an impressive, special dessert with very little effort? This is it! The texture is luscious, the flavor is delightful, and you can dress it up with fresh berries.

- Calories 192
- Fat 18
- Sodium 46
- Carbs 5
- Sugar 2
- Protein 5

Brussels Sprouts with Pimentos, page 246

Fresh Zucchini and Tomatoes, page 249

Pizza-Style Zucchini, page 251

Green Beans with Tomato, Bacon and Onions, page 257

Baked Tomatoes, Page 259

Lemony Garlic Asparagus, page 262

Black and Blue Cobbler, page 307

Lotsa Chocolate Almond Cake, page 306

Chocolate Pots de Crème

Judy Gascho
Woodburn, OR

Makes 6-7 servings
Prep. Time: 20 minutes
Cooking Time: 6 minutes
Chilling Time: 4 hours, or overnight
Setting: Manual
Pressure: High
Release: Natural then Manual

1½ cups heavy cream

½ cup whole milk

8 oz. unsweetened baking chocolate

5 large egg yolks

1½ Tbsp. granulated stevia

pinch salt

whipped cream and grated keto-friendly chocolate, for garnish, *optional*

1. In a small saucepan, bring the cream and milk to a simmer.

2. Melt chocolate at 50% power in 30-second increments in microwave, stirring after each increment.

3. In a large mixing bowl, whisk together egg yolks, stevia, and salt. Slowly whisk in hot cream and milk. Whisk in melted chocolate until blended.

4. Pour into 6–7 custard cups. Wrap each tightly with foil.

5. Add 1½ cups water to the inner pot of the Instant Pot and place the trivet in the bottom.

6. Place 3–4 wrapped cups on the trivet. Place a second trivet on top of the cups and place the remaining cups on the second trivet. (If you don't have a second trivet, place the remaining cups staggered on the top of the bottom layer of cups.)

7. Lock the lid in place and make sure vent is at sealing. Select high pressure in Manual mode and set the timer for 6 minutes. When cooking time is up, turn off the pressure cooker and let the pressure release for 15 minutes naturally, then do a quick pressure release to release any remaining pressure. When the valve drops, carefully remove lid.

8. Carefully remove the cups to a wire rack and remove foil immediately. Cool.

9. When cool, refrigerate cups covered with plastic wrap for at least 4 hours or overnight.

- Calories 451
- Fat 45
- Sodium 32
- Carbs 15
- Sugar 3
- Protein 10

Slow-Cooker Pumpkin Pie Pudding

Joette Droz
Kalona, IA

Makes 4–6 servings
Prep. Time: 5–7 minutes
Cooking Time: 6–7 hours
Ideal slow-cooker size: 3-qt.

15-oz. can solid pack pumpkin

12-oz. can evaporated milk

¼ cup plus 2 Tbsp. erythritol

½ cup keto-friendly baking mix

2 eggs, beaten

2 Tbsp. melted butter

1 Tbsp. pumpkin pie spice

2 tsp. vanilla extract

1. Mix together all ingredients. Pour into greased slow cooker.

2. Cover and cook on Low 6–7 hours, or until thermometer reads 160°F.

- Calories 218
- Fat 15
- Sodium 92
- Carbs 22
- Sugar 3
- Protein 9

Orange Panna Cotta

Marilyn Mowry
Irving, TX

Makes 4 servings
Prep. Time: 10 minutes
Cooking Time: 10 minutes
Chilling Time: 8 hours, or overnight

2 cups evaporated milk

1 envelope unflavored gelatin

1½ Tbsp. granulated stevia

1 tsp. vanilla extract

1 tsp. orange extract

1 tsp. grated orange peel

pinch salt

½ cup keto-friendly vanilla yogurt

cinnamon

1. Combine milk and gelatin in nonstick pan. Let stand until gelatin softens, about 5 minutes.

2. Cook over low heat, stirring constantly, until gelatin dissolves completely, about 5 minutes.

3. Whisk in stevia, both extracts, orange peel, and salt. Bring to a simmer, stirring frequently.

4. Divide evenly among 4 small ramekins or custard cups.

5. Cool slightly. Then cover and refrigerate overnight.

6. To serve, top each with 2 Tbsp. vanilla yogurt and a sprinkle of cinnamon.

- Calories 202
- Fat 10
- Sodium 145
- Carbs 14
- Sugar 13
- Protein 12

Mocha Chiffon Pie

Ann Bender
New Hope, VA

Makes 8 servings
Prep. Time: 15 minutes
Cooking Time: 5 minutes
Cooling Time: 2-3 hours

1 Tbsp. plain gelatin

¼ cup cold water

3 Tbsp. granulated stevia

2 Tbsp. unsweetened cocoa powder

1 tsp. dry instant coffee

⅛ tsp. salt

1½ cups evaporated milk

8 Tbsp. Extra Creamy Cool Whip

1. In a small bowl, dissolve gelatin in cold water.

2. Mix stevia, cocoa powder, dry coffee, and salt in saucepan.

3. Stir milk into saucepan. Heat to boiling, stirring frequently.

4. Add gelatin mixture and stir until dissolved.

5. Cool in fridge until mixture is slightly congealed.

6. Pour into 9-inch pie pan.

7. Cool in fridge until completely set.

8. Serve each pie wedge topped with 1 Tbsp. Cool Whip.

- Calories 90
- Fat 5
- Sodium 9
- Carbs 9
- Sugar 8
- Protein 4

Ice Cream-in-a-Bag

Annabelle Unternahrer
Shipshewana, IN

Makes 5 servings (½ cup each)
Prep. Time: 10 minutes
Shaking Time: 10-15 minutes

2 cups whole milk

⅓ cup granulated Splenda

1 tsp. vanilla extract

5 cups ice

¾ cup rock salt

¼ cup water

1. In a 1-qt. resealable bag, combine milk, Splenda, and vanilla. Seal bag.

2. In a 1-gallon resealable bag, combine ice, salt, and water. Then add bag with ice cream mix in it.

3. Close gallon bag very securely. Wrap with a heavy towel.

4. Shake 10–15 minutes, or until ice cream is frozen.

- Calories 125
- Fat 3
- Sodium 42
- Carbs 17
- Sugar 18
- Protein 3

Chocolate Mocha Sauce

Lorraine Arnold
Rhinebeck, NY

Jane S. Lippincott
Wynnewood, PA

Makes 16 servings (2 Tbsp. each)
Prep. Time: 5 minutes
Cooking Time: 15 minutes

¾ cup unsweetened cocoa powder

½ cup half-and-half

½ cup whole milk

1 Tbsp. butter

1 Tbsp. dry instant coffee

⅛ tsp. salt

½ cup Splenda Brown Sugar Blend

½ cup granulated Splenda

1 tsp. vanilla extract

1. Mix all ingredients except vanilla in a heavy saucepan. Bring to a boil over medium-high heat.

2. Turn heat down and simmer 5 minutes. When cool, stir in vanilla.

3. Serve with brownies or vanilla ice cream.

- Calories 35
- Fat 3
- Sodium 3
- Carbs 4
- Sugar 2
- Protein 1

Blueberry Sauce

Jeannine Dougherty
Tyler, TX

Makes 20 servings (2 Tbsp. each)
Prep. Time: 5 minutes
Cooking Time: 15–20 minutes

2 Tbsp. Splenda Sugar Blend

pinch salt

½ cup water

½ tsp. konjac flour

2 cups fresh or frozen blueberries

2 tsp. lemon juice

1. In a medium-sized saucepan, combine sugar blend and salt. Mix well.

2. Add water, konjac flour, and blueberries. Mix well.

3. Bring mixture to a boil, stirring constantly. Cook until thick and translucent.

4. Remove from heat and stir in lemon juice.

- Calories 15
- Fat 0
- Sodium 0
- Carbs 3
- Sugar 3
- Protein 0

Chocolate Chip Meringue Drops

Bonnie Whaling
Clearfield, PA

Makes 40 cookies (3 cookies per serving)
Prep. Time: 15–20 minutes
Baking Time: 1 hour
Standing Time: 2 hours

2 large egg whites

¼ cup powdered erythritol

1 tsp. vanilla extract

3 Tbsp. unsweetened cocoa powder

½ cup keto-friendly chocolate chips

1. Preheat oven to 250°F.

2. Line 2 baking sheets with parchment paper or aluminum foil. Set aside.

3. In a large mixer bowl, beat egg whites until they hold stiff peaks.

4. Beat in erythritol a bit at a time.

5. Beat in vanilla.

6. Reduce speed to low and beat in cocoa powder.

7. With a spatula, fold in chocolate chips.

8. Drop batter by rounded teaspoonfuls onto baking sheets, spacing cookies 1 inch apart.

9. Bake 1 hour.

10. Turn off oven and let cookies remain in oven 2 hours longer.

11. Remove from baking sheets and store in airtight container.

- Calories 13
- Fat 0.5
- Sodium 10
- Carbs 2
- Sugar 1
- Protein 1

Red, White, and Blue Parfait

Becky Gehman
Bergton, VA

Makes 4 servings
Prep. Time: 15 minutes

Creamy Filling:
1 cup keto-friendly vanilla yogurt

¼ cup cream cheese (Neufchâtel), softened

5 drops liquid stevia

1 pint fresh strawberries, sliced, *divided*

1½ cups fresh blueberries, *divided*

1. Make creamy filling by placing yogurt, cream cheese, and liquid stevia into bowl. Beat until fluffy.

2. Assemble parfaits by placing ⅓ cup strawberries in each of 6 parfait glasses.

3. Top each with 3 Tbsp. creamy filling.

4. Top that with ¼ cup blueberries in each glass.

5. Garnish each by dividing remaining topping.

6. Chill until ready to serve.

- Calories 106
- Fat 3.5
- Sodium 69
- Carbs 16
- Sugar 11
- Protein 5

Sugared Almonds and Pecans

Linda Hartzler
Minonk, IL

Makes 28 servings (¼ cup each)
Prep. Time: 15 minutes
Baking Time: 1 hour

1 egg white

1 Tbsp. water

1-2 tsp. cinnamon, according to your taste preference

1 tsp. vanilla extract

½ cup Splenda Sugar Blend

1 lb. almonds and/or pecans

1. In a large bowl, beat together egg white and water until fluffy.

2. Stir in cinnamon, vanilla, sugar blend, and nuts.

3. Spread in a single layer on a baking sheet with sides.

4. Bake at 200°F for 1 hour, stirring every 15 minutes.

5. Cool completely before storing.

- Calories 114
- Fat 9
- Sodium 5
- Carbs
- Sugar 4
- Protein 4

3-2-1 Lemonade

Tabitha Schmidt
Baltic, OH

Makes 16 servings (1 cup each)
Prep. Time: 15 minutes

3 lemons

2 cups granulated Splenda

water and ice to make a gallon

1. Thinly slice lemons, discarding tips.

2. Place in a one-gallon pitcher and add sweetener. Stir thoroughly until lemon slices are well-covered with Splenda. Let stand for 10 minutes.

3. Add ice and water to make one gallon.

4. Serve immediately or within hours, putting a lemon slice in each glass if desired.

- Calories 124
- Fat 0
- Sodium 8
- Carbs 26
- Sugar 25
- Protein 0

Mint Tea

Carol Eberly
Harrisonburg, VA

Makes 4 servings (1 cup each)
Prep. Time: 15–20 minutes
Steeping Time: 10 minutes

4 cups water

3 Lipton family-size iced tea bags (only Lipton!)

8–10 stalks fresh mint tea, or 2 Boston's Mint-in-Tea tea
  bags, or 8–10 stalks dried mint

1¼ cups granulated Splenda

1. Heat 4 cups water to boil in the microwave or on the stove.

2. Remove from heat and add family-size tea bags and mint tea, mint tea bags, or fresh mint.

3. Let steep at least 10 minutes.

4. Remove tea bags and mint.

5. Add sweetener. Stir until dissolved.

6. Add enough water to make a gallon.

7. Serve over ice in glasses.

- Calories 420
- Fat 0
- Sodium 65
- Carbs 88
- Sugar 88
- Protein 0

Indian Tea

Terry Stutzman Mast
Lodi, CA

Makes 4 servings (1 cup each)
Prep. Time: 5 minutes
Steeping Time: 5–10 minutes

4 cups water

3 black (regular or decaf) tea bags

3 whole cloves

1-inch piece of fresh ginger, chopped

3 pods cardamom, opened for seeds

1 stick cinnamon, chopped

6-oz. can evaporated milk

¼ cup granulated Splenda

1. Bring water to a boil in a covered saucepan. Turn off heat.

2. Place tea bags in to steep for 5 minutes. Keep covered.

3. In a tea ball or muslin bag (tied shut) place cloves, ginger, cardamom seeds, and chopped cinnamon. Place into steeping tea.

4. After 5 minutes, remove tea bags. (If you prefer a stronger tea, allow the tea bags to steep a few more minutes until tea is darker.)

5. Stir in evaporated milk.

6. Add sweetener, stirring until dissolved.

7. Remove tea ball or spice bag and serve.

- Calories 212
- Fat 3
- Sodium 65
- Carbs 39
- Sugar 35
- Protein 3

Seasonings & Sauces

Italian Seasoning Mix

Madelyn Wheeler
Zionsville, IN

Makes 13 servings (1 Tbsp. each)
Prep. Time: 10 minutes

6 tsp. marjoram

6 tsp. dried thyme leaves

6 tsp. dried rosemary

6 tsp. dried savory leaves

3 tsp. dried sage

6 tsp. dried oregano leaves

6 tsp. dried basil leaves

1. Combine all ingredients.

2. Store leftover mix for future use.

- Calories 10
- Fat 0
- Sodium 2
- Carbs 2
- Sugar 0
- Protein 0

Italian Dressing Mix

Hope Comerford
Clinton Township, MI

Makes 1 cup
Prep. Time: 5 minutes

2 Tbsp. oregano

1 Tbsp. garlic powder

1 Tbsp. onion powder

1 Tbsp. parsley

2 tsp. pink sea salt

1 tsp. basil

½ tsp. black pepper

1½ packets stevia

½ tsp. thyme

¼ tsp. celery seed

1. Mix all ingredients together and store in an airtight container.

- Calories 6
- Fat 0
- Sodium 281
- Carbs 1
- Sugar 0
- Protein 0

Taco Seasoning

Hope Comerford
Clinton Township, MI

Makes 9½ Tbsp.
Prep. Time: 10 minutes

4 Tbsp. chili powder

2 Tbsp. cumin

1 Tbsp. plus 1 tsp. garlic powder

1 Tbsp. plus 1 tsp. onion powder

2 tsp. salt

1 tsp. oregano

1 tsp. red pepper flakes

1. Mix all ingredients together and store in an airtight container.

Tip: Use about 2½ Tbsp. per pound of meat when seasoning meat for tacos.

- Calories 87
- Fat 2.5
- Sodium 1593
- Carbs 16
- Sugar 1
- Protein 4

Phyllis's Homemade Barbecue Sauce

Phyllis Barrier
Little Rock, AR

Makes 2 cups (16 servings, 2 Tbsp. each)
Prep. Time: 10 minutes
Cooking Time: varies according to microwave

2 8-oz. cans no-added-salt tomato sauce

¼ cup cider vinegar

1 Tbsp. Splenda Brown Sugar Blend

½ cup minced fresh onion

1 tsp. garlic powder

½ tsp. dry mustard

6 tsp. chili powder

⅛ tsp. Tabasco sauce

½ tsp. black pepper

6 tsp. Worcestershire sauce

1 tsp. paprika

1 tsp. liquid smoke

¼ tsp. salt

1. Mix all ingredients together and cook in microwave until minced onion is tender and sauce has thickened.

- Calories 38
- Fat 0
- Sodium 413
- Carbs 7
- Sugar 4
- Protein 1

Barbecued Chicken Basting Sauce

Paula King
Flanagan, IL

Makes 4–6 servings
Prep. Time: 5 minutes
Cooking Time: 5 minutes

¼ cup water

½ cup vinegar

8 Tbsp. (1 stick) butter

½ tsp. salt

dash paprika

dash pepper

1. Put all ingredients in a small saucepan. Heat on stove top or grill top until butter melts and all ingredients can be mixed together.

2. Keep warm while grilling chicken and baste chicken periodically.

- Calories 139
- Fat 15
- Sodium 63
- Carbs 0
- Sugar 0
- Protein 0

Tomato/Chili Poaching Sauce

Marlene Fonken
Upland, CA

Makes about 6 cups sauce (about 1 cup per serving)
Prep. Time: 5 minutes
Cooking Time: 15 minutes

1 Tbsp., plus 1 tsp., olive oil

1 cup thinly sliced onion

3 cups canned chopped tomatoes, no salt added, undrained

4-oz. can diced green chiles, undrained

1 cup chicken bone broth

⅛ tsp. pepper

1 tsp. taco seasoning (recipe on pg. 327)

1. In a saucepan, sauté onion in oil until tender.

2. Add tomatoes and green chiles to pan. Cook 5 minutes.

3. Add remaining ingredients. Cook at least 5 minutes more, or until hot.

- Calories 60
- Fat 3
- Sodium 180
- Carbs 7
- Sugar 3
- Protein 2

Metric Equivalent Measurements

If you're accustomed to using metric measurements, I don't want you to be inconvenienced by the imperial measurements I use in this book.

Use this handy chart, too, to figure out the size of the slow cooker you'll need for each recipe.

Weight (Dry Ingredients)

1 oz		30 g
4 oz	¼ lb	120 g
8 oz	½ lb	240 g
12 oz	¾ lb	360 g
16 oz	1 lb	480 g
32 oz	2 lb	960 g

Slow Cooker Sizes

1-quart	0.96 l
2-quart	1.92 l
3-quart	2.88 l
4-quart	3.84 l
5-quart	4.80 l
6-quart	5.76 l
7-quart	6.72 l
8-quart	7.68 l

Volume (Liquid Ingredients)

½ tsp.		2 ml
1 tsp.		5 ml
1 Tbsp.	½ fl oz	15 ml
2 Tbsp.	1 fl oz	30 ml
¼ cup	2 fl oz	60 ml
⅓ cup	3 fl oz	80 ml
½ cup	4 fl oz	120 ml
⅔ cup	5 fl oz	160 ml
¾ cup	6 fl oz	180 ml
1 cup	8 fl oz	240 ml
1 pt	16 fl oz	480 ml
1 qt	32 fl oz	960 ml

Length

¼ in	6 mm
½ in	13 mm
¾ in	19 mm
1 in	25 mm
6 in	15 cm
12 in	30 cm

Recipe and Ingredient Index

About the Author

Hope Comerford is a mom, wife, elementary music teacher, blogger, recipe developer, public speaker, ALM Zone fit leader, Young Living Essential Oils essential oil enthusiast/educator, and published author. In 2013, she was diagnosed with a severe gluten intolerance and since then has spent many hours creating easy, practical, and delicious gluten-free recipes that can be enjoyed by both those who are affected by gluten and those who are not.

Growing up, Hope spent many hours in the kitchen with her Meme (grandmother) and her love for cooking grew from there. While working on her master's degree when her daughter was young, Hope turned to her slow cookers for some salvation and sanity. It was from there she began truly experimenting with recipes and quickly learned she had the ability to get a little more creative in the kitchen and develop her own recipes.

In 2010, Hope started her blog, *A Busy Mom's Slow Cooker Adventures*, to simply share the recipes she was making with her family and friends. She never imagined people all over the world would begin visiting her page and sharing her recipes with others as well. In 2013, Hope self-published her first cookbook, *Slow Cooker Recipes 10 Ingredients or Less and Gluten-Free*, and then later wrote *The Gluten-Free Slow Cooker*.

Hope became the new brand ambassador and author of Fix-It and Forget-It in mid-2016. Since then, she has brought her excitement and creativeness to the Fix-It and Forget-It brand. Through Fix-It and Forget-It, she has written *Fix-It and Forget-It Lazy & Slow, Fix-It and Forget-It Healthy Slow Cooker Cookbook, Fix-It and Forget-It Cooking for Two, Fix-It and Forget-It Instant Pot Cookbook, Fix-It and Forget-It Freezer Meals, Fix-It and Forget-It Healthy 5-Ingredient Cookbook*, and *Fix-It and Forget-It Keto Comfort Foods*.

Hope lives in the city of Clinton Township, Michigan, near Metro Detroit. She's a native of Michigan and has lived there her whole life. She has been happily married to her husband and best friend, Justin, since 2008. Together they have two children, Ella and Gavin, who are her motivation, inspiration, and heart. In her spare time, Hope enjoys traveling, singing, cooking, reading books, spending time with friends and family, and relaxing.